India's State-Run Media

Moving deftly between philosophical systems and diverse intellectual traditions, this book presents a new perspective on broadcasting by bringing together two neglected areas of research in Indian media studies—the intertwined genealogies of sovereignty, public, religion, and nation in radio and television, and the spatiotemporal dynamics of broadcasting—into a single analytic inquiry. It argues that the spatiotemporalities of broadcasting and the inter-relationships among the public, religion, and nation can be traced to an organizing concept that shaped India's late colonial and postcolonial histories: sovereignty.

It traces the origins of 'broadcast public' through which the listenership for radio was constructed in the late colonial period, and the subsequent institutionalization of radio listeners and television viewers as audiences in postcolonial India. The book contends that studies of television have glossed over the meanings, experiences, and practices of the *religious* in televisual narratives and viewers' interpretations of television programmes. In much of the literature, 'religion' is characterized as an ideology, a 'false consciousness', and a form of domination to be exposed, and situated in opposition to the 'secular'—understood as an abstract, normative zone that is detached from the religious.

To this end, it develops theoretical insights from Michel Foucault and Paul Ricoeur's respective philosophical elaborations of 'the hermeneutics of the self/subject' as relational and dialogic, and connects their ideas with neo-Marxist writings on spatiotemporality. It draws on insights from media, cultural, postcolonial, and religious studies and examines the symbolic and cultural discourses, power relations, repertoire of meanings, mediations of human actions, social events, and so on, in broadcasting and television programmes in late colonial and postcolonial India.

Sanjay Asthana teaches at the School of Journalism and Strategic Media in Middle Tennessee State University. His areas of interest are media and cultural studies, postcolonial studies, visual communication, and international and global communication. He is the author of *Youth Media Imaginaries from Around the World* (2012), and has co-authored *Palestinian Youth Media and the Pedagogies of Estrangement* (2016).

India's State-Run Media

Broadcasting, Power, and Narrative

Sanjay Asthana

CAMBRIDGE
UNIVERSITY PRESS

For my Mother

Contents

List of Figures and Tables *ix*
Acknowledgements *xi*

Introduction 1

1. Broadcasting, Spatiotemporalities, and Power 24
2. Doordarshan, Literary Drama, and Narrative Identity 63
3. Televisual Representations of Socio-Spatial Conflicts, and the Religious–Secular Imaginaries 83
4. Patriotism and Its Avatars: Tracking the National–Global Dialectic in Music Videos and Television Commercials 107
5. Remembering Doordarshan: Figurations of Memories and Nostalgia on Blogs, YouTube, and in Oral Interviews 127

Epilogue 159
Bibliography 177
Index 205

Figures and Tables

Figures

1.1 Telegraph's spatial grid 32
1.2 Telegraph's spatial grid 33
1.3 Broadcasting's spatial grid: proposed map of India's radio broadcasting stations, 1937 33
1.4 Broadcasting's spatial grid, ATS-F coverage of India, receiving cluster locations, 1976 34
5.1 Doordarshan logo sequence 138

Table

1.1 Spatiotemporal Configurations of Broadcasting in India 36

Acknowledgements

The philosopher Paul Ricoeur considered narrative as constitutive of identity, selfhood, and temporality through which human and social lives take on a storied form. Although the English word 'narrative' is derived from its Latin lineage 'narro' (to tell), its roots originate in Sanskrit, 'gna' (to know). The etymology of the word 'narrative' carries thick traces of diverse intellectual and everyday traditions marking the play of our identities and the structure of our lives. I express my thanks to several individuals and institutions who in many ways have influenced my personal, social, and scholarly identity. This book emerged from conversations with my friends Anjum Zubairi, Shankerlal Srivastava, and C. V. S Sarma during my graduate school years at the University of Hyderabad. We would sit under the mango tree planted by Mahatma Gandhi in the 'Golden Threshold' building, gulp hot cups of *chai* and confabulate on matters mundane to serious issues about media, politics, and culture. I am beholden to my beloved late friends who also planted in me the idea of pursuing a philosophy degree, which I subsequently did.

I wish to thank my University of Hyderabad teachers, colleagues, and friends, especially P. L. V Rao, Pavan Kumar Manvi, the late C. V. S Sarma, Vinod Pavarala, B. P. Sanjay, Vasuki Belavadi, and Kanchan Malik at the Sarojini Naidu School of Arts and Communication; my MPhil. adviser, S. G. Kulkarni, Raghuram Raju, Tejaswini Niranjana, Satish Deshpande, and Probal Dasgupta, among others, at the Departments of Philosophy, Literature, Cultural Studies, Sociology, and Linguistics, respectively. At the University of Minnesota, sincere thanks to my PhD adviser, the late Hazel Dicken-Garcia, Michael Griffin, Albert Tims, and Dona Schwartz from the School of Journalism and Mass Communication; Richard Leppert, Keya Ganguly, Timothy Brennan, and John Mowitt at the Department of Cultural Studies and Comparative Literature; Vinay Gidwani and Ajay Skaria at the Departments of Geography, History, and the Institute for Global Studies; and Don Johnson and David Faust at the Ames Library of South Asia for their generous advice during my Minnesota days. My thanks to the Faculty Research and Creative Activity Committee at the Middle Tennessee State University for two summer stipends to pursue fieldwork in India.

My deep sense of gratitude for the interviewees who agreed to sit with me and talk for extended periods of time about their television memories. I am grateful to the staff of All India Radio and Doordarshan in Hyderabad and New Delhi for the archival materials. Several ideas sketched in the book were presented at conferences at the Universities of Amherst, Massachusetts, California, Berkeley, Wisconsin, Madison, Minnesota, Minneapolis, the 'Television in Transition' Conference at MIT, the annual conferences at the Association for Education in Journalism and Mass Communication, the International Association for Media and Communication Research, and the International Communication Association. My sincere appreciation and thanks to the amazing editorial team at the Cambridge University press, especially Lucy Rhymer, Qudsiya Ahmed, Sohini Ghosh, Aniruddha De, and Prerana Choudhury for the editorial and copyediting suggestions, and assistance in the preparation of the manuscript. A special thanks to Qudsiya for her initial interest in the manuscript, keen observations, and prescient insights into the publication process. My thanks to the two anonymous readers of the book for their perceptive critique, comments, and suggestions.

Chapters 1 to 4 have been adapted, reworked, and extended from my previously published work in the following journals and a book: Chapter 1, 'Broadcasting, Space, and Sovereignty in India', *Media, Culture and Society* 35, no. 4 (2013), by permission of SAGE Publications; Chapter 2, 'Television, Narrative Identity and Social Imaginaries: A Hermeneutic Approach', *Channeling Cultures: Television Studies from India*, edited by Biswarup Sen and Abhijit Roy, 2014, by permission of Oxford University Press; Chapter 3, 'Religion and Secularism as Embedded Imaginaries: A Study of Indian Television Narratives', *Critical Studies in Media Communication* 25, no. 3 (2008), by permission of Taylor & Francis Ltd.; and Chapter 4, 'Patriotism and its Avatars: Tracking the National–Global Dialectic in Indian Music Videos', *Journal of Communication Inquiry* 27, no. 4 (2003), by permission of SAGE Publications.

I appreciate the camaraderie of my friends Radhakrishnan, Surya Prakash, Sudhakerudu, Sundeep Muppidi, Himadeep Muppidi, Sai Prasad, and the late Gonzaga Da Gama in India and the United States. My thanks to Sudhakerudu for procuring documentaries from the Doordarshan office in New Delhi. I owe a debt of gratitude to my philosophy mate, Hara Prasad Padhy. He graciously offered his home in Paris whenever I visited the city for UNESCO presentations and workshops. Among other things, we would saunter the Parisian streets, chat with working-class youth from the *banlieue*s, cook Indian food, and talk ordinary language philosophy. Hara promised me that he would translate some sections of Fakir Mohan Senapati's brilliant Odia novel, *Chha Mana Atha Guntha* (Six Acres and a Third), and discuss these with me through a Wittgensteinian perspective. It was not to be as Hara passed away suddenly.

Sincere thanks to my cousins Naveen Saxena and Nirmal Saxena who have always been very supportive of my academic endeavors in India and the United States. Thanks also to my elder cousins and the extended family in Hyderabad, in particular, Narrottam Asthana, for his advice, and Amul Asthana, Jagjeevanlal Asthana, Purushottam Asthana, Surender Asthana, and Anil Asthana, for encouragement.

I cannot express my gratitude enough to my family for all their love and affection. My heartfelt thanks to my late father, Narendra Asthana, my mother, Krishna Kumari, sisters, Seema, Sarita, and Sangeeta, and brother, Ajay, and their spouses, Ramachandra Babu, Arvind Srivastava, Praveen Srivastava, and Preeti Asthana. I thank my brother-in-law Ramachandra Babu for his many kindnesses, moral support, and help. Most of all, to my caring spouse, Evangelina, for her patience, gentle advice, and support throughout, especially during the writing process, and to my sons, Jeremy and Justin, for their love, affection, and understanding. Last but not least, thanks to my kindhearted in-laws, Clemente and Gloria Guzman.

My parents' kin, and their inter-generational family networks were steeped in the heterolinguistic traditions of Hindi (in its multiple vernacular variations), Urdu, Punjabi, as well as Sanskrit, Persian, and Arabic languages. My mother, born in Lahore in the British-occupied India, and now Pakistan, was six years old when her parents, siblings, and her extended family had to undertake forced-migration to Delhi just before the impending Partition of India in 1947 when over a million lives were lost, displacing fifteen million people from their respective homes in India and the newly formed Pakistan. This book explores the heterolinguistic sensibility where religion, language, and our sociocultural worlds are not perceived in singular terms, rather, as an ethos of living well and living together in our perilous time.

Introduction

This book presents a new perspective on broadcasting by bringing together two neglected areas of research in studies of media in India—(*a*) the intertwined genealogies of sovereignty, public, religion, and nation in radio and television and (*b*) the spatiotemporal dynamics of broadcasting—into a single analytic inquiry. I argue that the spatiotemporalities of broadcasting and the interrelationships among the public, religion, and nation can be traced to an organizing concept that shaped India's late colonial and postcolonial histories: sovereignty. In what follows, I describe how sovereignty in its various incarnations functioned as an organizing concept for the associated ideas of public, religion, and nation; discuss the spatiotemporal underpinnings of broadcasting; elaborate the book's theoretical approach distinguishing it from other approaches; and sketch the chapter outlines.

In 1995, the Supreme Court of India, ruling in the case involving the Secretary, Ministry of Information and Broadcasting, versus the Cricket Association of Bengal, declared that 'the Air waves are public property'; the state-run television does not hold exclusive monopoly over broadcasting, and 'the broadcasting media should be under the control of the public as distinct from the government'. The Court's strictures precipitated a series of policy measures instituted by the Indian government through parliamentary and bureaucratic committees to create an autonomous corporation for the management of the state-run television network. The ruling also triggered spirited discussions among journalists, policy makers, non-governmental organizations (NGOs), and the scholarly community that centred around the category of 'the public': what was this public that the Court was putting in place, and how should one situate it in relation to the rapid transformations wrought by media privatization and economic liberalization?

While the arguments varied across ideological lines, all agreed that the Court's ruling marked a decisive moment for Indian broadcasting. Yet none broached the juridical reasoning that informed the judgment, that is, the particular ways in which law and legal codes were deployed, the citations as well as transfer of ideas and knowledge from earlier court decisions, broadcast laws from the US and Europe, mobilization of the rights discourse, and so on. Since the mid-1990s, India's courts have adjudicated a range of cases—financial regulations, non-banking companies, stock exchange law—by redefining the colonial notion of 'public interest' in the language of 'market governance' to produce a composite category, 'the public' as a subject of the state's authority as well as an 'instrument' of neoliberal economic order (Birla, 2015).

South Asian and postcolonial studies scholars have traced the genealogies of the public and religion in South Asia to the British colonial state's structuring of law—particularly, through the imposition of legal codes, juridical instruments, taxation, and so on—in order to bring them under the purview of state authority (Freitag, 1989; Hansen, 2008; Sturman, 2012; Gilmartin, 2015). The imbrications with sovereignty subsequently shaped the trajectories of the public and religion in colonial and postcolonial state policies and governance. Others have examined a range of political, legal, cultural, and religious texts and discourses from the colonial period to show how the public has been imagined by the colonial state as a 'deficient entity' that has to be contained and reformed (Rajagopal, 2009; Scott and Ingram, 2015). In the postcolonial period, the negative articulation of the public has persisted, and largely been rendered as an object of 'cultural regulation' (Mazzarella and Kaur, 2009).

In the context of broadcasting, however, while these specific forms of imagination of the public informed the construction of radio listeners and television viewers, a range of spatiotemporal discourses were mobilized to produce the 'broadcast public' of radio and television. Scholarly studies of broadcasting in India have not paid attention to the imbrications between sovereignty, public, religion, and nation, and ignored the spatiotemporal dynamics of broadcasting. The book traces the origins of broadcast public, that is, the particular congeries of class, caste, gender, linguistic, religious, rural, urban identities, and so on, through which radio listeners were constructed in late colonial period, and the subsequent institutionalization of radio listeners and television viewers as audiences in postcolonial India. To this end, I unpack the spatiotemporal and discursive framing of the public, the specific discourses that shaped its imagination, and more crucially, how these have informed the constitution of radio and television audiences in late colonial and postcolonial period.

The book is organized around the theoretical concepts of *power* and *narrative* developed through an engagement with Paul Ricoeur's and Michel Foucault's respective elaborations of 'the hermeneutics of the self/subject', and insights from South Asian, postcolonial, religious, media, and cultural studies (to be discussed in a later section). The book delineates two concepts, spatiotemporality and religious–secular, as embedded imaginaries; whereas the former is a reworked formulation, the latter is an original concept. In the following discussion, I explicate the two in terms of their analytic value, beginning first with a brief discussion of spatiotemporality, its usage, potential drawbacks, and my own reworking. I deploy this concept to examine the structural and institutional contexts of broadcasting and probe the spatial moorings and temporal dimensions of radio and television in relation to programme structures and formats, temporal arrangements of listening and viewing as well as the viewers' own understanding of televisual past, and the interplay of mediated and everyday temporality. Second, I outline the concept of religious–secular as embedded imaginaries, exploring its efficacy and utility in studying television narratives.

Social theorists have long insisted that space and time are not absolute, unitary entities. Rather, as relational concepts they constitute each other; intersect with, and are generative of, social practices; and therefore ought to be understood as the compound word 'spatiotemporality' (Harvey, 1989 and 1996; Massey, 1994). For the Marxist geographer David Harvey (1989: 232, emphasis in original),

> as space begins to shrink to a 'global village' of telecommunications and a 'spaceship earth' of economic and ecological interdependences—to use just two familiar images—and as time horizons to the point where the present is all there is, so we have to learn to cope with an overwhelming sense of *compression* of our spatial and temporal worlds. The experience of time-space compression is challenging, exciting, stressful, and sometimes deeply troubling.

Drawing on Henri Lefebvre's (1974) writings, among others, Harvey sketched the dialectic relations of time and space to study the postmodern condition, urbanization, and the historical trajectory of capitalism which reveal a complex spatiotemporal reconfiguration of geography, physical places, and landscapes.

Despite the detailed analysis of capitalism, Harvey's work places a preponderant emphasis on the spatial with inadequate attention to temporality to which I shall return below (Pickering and Murdoch, 2008; Castree, 2009). In their substantive critique of the spatial bias and the singular conceptualization of space–time in social theory, May and Thrift (2001: 3) argue for thinking in terms of 'multiplicity of space–times' which they anchor under the rubric 'TimeSpace'. Although these scholarly studies offer nuanced explications of space–time, I argue that the studies of spatiotemporality and TimeSpace exhibit two deficiencies. First, they posit broad generalizations about the media, broadcasting, and the internet, and do not pay enough attention to the multiple temporalities engendered by broadcasting, particularly radio and television.[1] Second, the studies offer inadequate understanding of the colonial-imperial-postcolonial spatiotemporalities that have underpinned the trajectory of capitalism in South Asia as well as in the Global South. For my purposes, the question of how emerging communication technologies and media—telegraph, radio, television—in late colonial and postcolonial India underpin the spatial and temporal relations, and intersect with sovereignty, public, religion, and nation, can be examined by reformulating the concept of spatiotemporality. To this end, the book considers space and time as contingent categories, but also favours a deeper engagement with temporality, particularly the phenomenological and hermeneutic dimensions of time enunciated in the writings of Paddy Scannell (1996a; 1996b; 1998) and Roger Silverstone (1993; 1994) (Chapters 1, 2, and 5).

Several scholarly studies have noted that the introduction of electric telegraph dissolved distance, and in conjunction with the railways, led to the standardization of time from the global to the local levels (Zerubavel, 1982; Bell, 2007; Wharf, 2008). Others have detailed the rise and consolidation of the newly formed private telegraph companies into cartels (Winseck and Pike, 2007), and the emergence of news agencies and global networks of trade and commerce (Muller and Tworek, 2015; Wenzlhuemer, 2013). According to Zerubavel (1982: 5), the standardization of time effected by the railways and telegraph precipitated the formation of 'national communication networks' which, I argue, constituted the spatiotemporal grid for the subsequent development of the broadcasting system in India.

In his seminal piece, the media and communication studies scholar, James Carey (1989: 203) explored the effects of the telegraph in industrial business, and cultural domains, as well as the crucial role of the telegraph restructuring news through the standardization of language and journalistic practice. Carey's thought-provoking account situated the telegraph as a key technology that 'freed communication from the constraints of geography', and more fundamentally, 'separated communication from transportation'. While Carey's (1989: 203) influential account offers deep insights into the unmooring of communication from transportation, it is also a partial view as its focus is on the role of the telegraph in the development of American communication without accounting for the telegraph's global historical itinerary, particularly in the colonies of Asia and Africa.[2] Since the publication of Carey's work, media and communication studies scholarship has focused on the telegraph and the emergence of global news agencies and networks (Rantanen, 2005). However, the history of the telegraph and its overlaps with other electronic media forms, radio and television, in the colonial and postcolonial world have remained unexplored.

The telegraph constituted a key information and communication technology for building imperial media in the colonial world. Aaron Worth's (2014) study portrays the powerful ways in which colonial networks constituted by the telegraph underpinned British literary imagination from 1857 to 1918.[3] A few critical accounts of the history of the telegraph in colonial India by South Asian studies scholars offers a corrective to media and communication studies which has largely remained centred on Euro-American contexts (Chowdhury, 2010; Headrick, 2010; Wenzlhuemer, 2013). These studies argued that the telegraph in the colonial world was put to use for military and security purposes as an instrument and a tool of empire, mobilized to manage, consolidate, and centralize power; in short, to dominate and control the colonial subjects rather than for the improvement and amelioration of their lives.[4] However, these studies do not engage with the spatiotemporalities of the telegraph that remained key to the development of broadcasting in late colonial and postcolonial India.

In Chapter 1, I discuss how telegraphic spatiotemporalities have underpinned the discourses of radio and television, and consider the developments in communication technologies—printing, telegraph, broadcasting, digital media, and the internet—as constituting a complex matrix of mediated forms and systems that continually interact with the sociopolitical, economic, and cultural interests. The book's approach, then, can be characterized as 'connective' or as a 'superimposition', wherein the 'introduction of a novel technology does not cancel out or replace existing systems. Rather, it modifies the prevailing ecology of communications, setting in motion a series of collisions between potentialities it offers and the requirements of various social interests' (Pickering and Murdoch, 2008: 3; see also Buonanno, 2008).

The book examines the particular ways in which the infrastructure and technologies of radio and television were mobilized by the colonial and postcolonial states to mark and map territories, geographic regions, cities, towns, and villages along with the temporal structuring and arrangement of broadcasting schedules, programme making practices, and so on. In addition, the colonial state's administrative modalities of governance such as 'dyarchy' and 'provincial autonomy' adumbrated in the Government of India Acts of 1919 and 1935 increasingly shaped the spatiotemporalities of radio broadcasting (Gupta, 1988; Pinkerton, 2008; Kalpagam, 2014; Legg, 2016). After India's Independence in 1947, the postcolonial state channelled the colonial spatial modalities of governance and instituted the process of modernization of the country.

While the spatiotemporal approach enables me to pursue a deeper examination of the structural and institutional dynamics of broadcasting, I analyse the discursive relations between spatiality, temporality, narrative, and television (Silverstone, 1994; Scannell, 1996a) in terms of the interplay between programme organization and schedules ('broadcast time'), viewers' everyday ('lived time'), and television programmes ('narrative time'). I engage with Indian theories of narrative inscribed in traditions of *katha* (Sanskrit, tale), *gatha* (Hindi, ballad), *qissa* (Urdu, tale), and *dastan* (Persian and Urdu, story form) to explore how these have shaped the televisual programmes, particularly in terms of mixing of story genres and plotlines which create multiple temporalities in literary drama and other fictional series on television (Hansen, 1981; Shackle and Snell, 1992; Khan, 2015; Orsini and Schofield, 2015).

Second, I contend that studies of television have glossed over the meanings, experiences, and practices of the *religious* in televisual narratives and viewers' interpretations of television programmes.[5] In much of the literature, 'religion' is characterized in terms of an ideology, as 'false consciousness', a form of domination to be exposed, and situated in opposition to the 'secular'—understood as an abstract, normative zone that is detached from the religious. Through a brief account of Indian secularism debates, I problematize the difficulties in maintaining a separation between religion and secularism, and posit that instead of treating them as binaries, it is useful to consider the religious and the secular as 'embedded imaginaries'.[6] While attentive to the state discourse of secularism as well as the right-wing articulations of a corrosive form of religion, the book will explore practices of religious coexistence and decentered pluralism in televisual narratives (Chapters 2 and 3). To this end, the religious and the secular are explored in their *ordinariness*, embodied in people's beliefs, habits, dispositions, and practices as well as inscribed in institutional doctrines and ideologies (Gaonkar, 2002; Asad, 2003; Das, 2010; Laughier, 2015).

The concept of secularism, a legacy of European modernity, which appealed to the imagination of nationalists in comprehending the vast social realities of India, particularly the interreligious and intercommunity relationships, embodies ideas of religious neutrality (*dharma nirpekshta*) and respect towards all religions (*sarvadharma sadbhava*).[7] During the mid-1930s, shortly before India attained formal independence, the British created legislative bodies based on Muslim and Hindu electorates as a blueprint for democratic governance. The division of people and communities along communal lines marked a crisis for the nationalist leaders at a time when internal tensions threatened to fracture the nationalist movement along communal and religious lines. Against this backdrop, the notion of secularism gained currency. It was sought to serve as a social cement for holding together the fragile unity among the nationalist and to provide a platform of stability for the Indian masses. From the late 1930s onwards, the nationalists assembled a range of political and conceptual instruments of governance in crafting a future independent Indian state. The concept of secularism got enshrined as a core principle.

The principle of secularism outlined in the Indian Constitution through Articles 25 (1), 26, and 27 guarantee individual and collective freedom of religion, and calls for a separation of state and religion. In a general sense, these Constitutional provisions provide a broad framework for the state-based concept of secularism expressed in terms of impartiality, neutrality, and tolerance toward all religions.[8] In actual practice, however, the secular credentials of the Indian state eroded for two main reasons. First, the state engaged in regulating religious institutions, thereby collapsing the separation of state and religion. Second, it failed to protect religious minorities on numerous occasions by indirectly (or in some cases directly) inciting communal violence. This indictment of the Indian state serves as a point of departure for recent debates on secularism.

The various theoretical explorations of Indian secularism may be conveniently divided into two broad perspectives.[9] The first perspective, outlined from left and liberal positions, argues for the continued relevance and unrealized potential of secularism in binding India together against divisive and communal forces, and has sought to uphold, with some modifications, the emancipatory ideals contained within the concept. Whereas the second perspective, outlined through communitarian positions, seeks to either abandon or radically refashion the concept due to its failure to apprehend Indian social realities. In an abbreviated manner, I summarize key writings on the topic to situate them in the context of my study and offer general remarks on why it is imperative to consider the religious and the secular as embedded imaginaries. Although these critiques agree on the crisis—and the subsequent failure—of the state-based conception of secularism, they tread theoretically different paths.

From a neo-Marxist perspective, Geeta Kapur (2000: 335) has argued that secularism is the bedrock of the postcolonial nation-state, and stresses its dialectic rearticulation because 'it is inscribed not only in the constitution but within the experience of tradition and in the ethics of modernity in India'. Drawing insights from liberal political theory, Rajeev Bhargava (1998: 31) outlined a normative notion of secularism through two interrelated versions: a minimalist political secularism 'that excludes religion from politics ... and advocates a principle of political neutrality', and ethical secularism which enables different religious communities to live with tolerance and democratic principles. Bhargava acknowledges that in India religious and non-religious practices overlap and intermesh which makes it difficult to separate them. However, an argument can be made 'for separation of some religious and non-religious institutions'. Akeel Bilgrami (1998: 346) considers Nehruvian secularism as a 'holding process', which had an 'Archimedean' existence standing outside the arena of substantive politics and commitments. Bilgrami advocates the notion of a 'negotiated' or 'emergent' secularism that takes its place in the domain of substantive politics through a creative dialogue between religious communities.

Critical traditionalists like Ashis Nandy (1997) call for getting rid of the concept because of its Western origins. This is an anti-modernist stance that throws the 'project of modernity' irrelevant tout court. The postcolonial theorist, Partha Chatterjee (1998) argues not so much for a refashioning of secularism, but favours a notion of religious tolerance obtained outside the secular-modernist discourse guided by democratic norms internal to religious groups. Thus, unlike Nandy, Chatterjee suggests that we need not debunk modernity; rather we must engage with its logics to refashion religious rights within the ambit of modern democratic politics. Both Nandy and Chatterjee, however, argue for religious tolerance in place of the state-based notion of secularism.

Sudipta Kaviraj's (1993) notions of 'fuzzy' and 'enumerated' communities explain the logic of the colonial state in producing 'social categories' of distinctive peoples, communities, and culture in attempts to govern them. As forms of the disciplinary apparatuses of colonial knowledge and power, the enumerative strategies first constitute the sheer diversity of communities as *population* in demographic terms along the lines of modernist practices. Earlier conceptions of communities, which Kaviraj called fuzzy, were fluid and existed along multiple axes of identifications and subjectivities. Chatterjee (1993: 224, emphasis in original) explains, 'an underlying current of thinking about the sociological bases of Indian politics continues to run along the channels excavated by colonial discourse', and 'the most obvious example of this is the notion of *majority and minority communities* defined in terms of *criteria such as religion*, *language*, *or tribe* and *applied* over a variety of *territorial units* ranging from a part of the district to a country itself'. Chatterjee's analysis reveals fundamental contradictions in the workings of secularism that Marxists have misconstrued and misidentified by characterizing communal and community conflicts either as an outcome of class interests or the governmental misuse of the principles of secularism enshrined in the constitution.

The rhetoric of the broadcasting, marked as it is with the developmental phraseology, rested on the premise of a *fundamental unity of India* constructed through the language of secularism in which religion had a peripheral importance. People, pre-constituted as secular subjects, were emptied of their religious identities. However, the analysis of television series and narratives revealed religion as a bedrock of people's daily lives, and the religious and the secular as embedded imaginaries shaping their social and cultural worlds. In the following section, I discuss the embeddedness of the religious and the secular in specific detail.

THEORETICAL ORIENTATION

This book has developed theoretical and methodological insights from Michel Foucault's (1988; 2006) concept of governmentality (which refers to the conduct of individuals and populations through techniques of domination and power); Paul Ricoeur's (1965, 1981, 1996) formulation of narrative identity (which refers to the ability of an individual to narrate his/her world, and thereby produce forms of practices that resist domination and power); neo-Marxist writings on spatiotemporality; and specific conceptual resources from media, cultural, postcolonial, and religious studies in examining the symbolic and cultural discourses, power relations, repertoire of meanings, mediations of human actions, social events, and so on, in broadcasting and television programmes. While I do not posit a homology between Foucault and Ricoeur's philosophical projects, I draw upon a set of common concerns and motifs in their work that centre on their respective elaborations of 'the hermeneutics of the self/

subject' as relational and dialogic. Although Foucault is generally understood as an anti-hermeneutic thinker, his late work points to some affinities with hermeneutics.[10]

While Foucault's work provides compelling analyses of the constitution of self through techniques of disciplining and self-regulation, what is missing is an account of social action that can explain the self's capacity to act upon and narrate her/his world in constructing alternatives—political or other—to power and domination (McNay, 1999; Barnett et al., 2008). If Foucault has been primarily interested in undertaking a critical interrogation of the 'what' of the subject, Ricoeur is concerned with the 'who' of the self (Nijman, 2007). For Ricoeur, hermeneutics, in addition to concerning itself with the interpretation of texts, narratives, literary works, institutions, and technological and cultural artifacts, is about human action itself. Ricoeur's notion of the self is not the Cartesian or psychoanalytic self, but a public self that is culturally mediated and historically situated in a continuously changing world.

A main drawback of Ricoeur's hermeneutic approach, however, is a weak conceptualization of power. It is here that Foucault's (1988) work connects questions of power through his conceptualization of the triangle of 'sovereignty-discipline-governmentality', where sovereignty represents the language of rights, discipline works through the bodily and mental techniques of the individual, and governmentality refers to the various techniques and strategies of managing populations. Hence, to understand the ways in which state power is implicated in broadcasting, we need to examine two overlapping modalities of power that prefigured the late colonial and postcolonial state practices: sovereignty and governmentality. To this end, the book argues that the operations of sovereignty and governmentality in late colonial and postcolonial India can be apprehended in terms of multiple configurations of authority, contract, generosity, welfare, force, and violence manifesting in state practices, governmental apparatuses, law, and by local landholding elites (Prakash, 2000; Chatterjee, 2004; Legg, 2007, 2016; Hansen 2008; Kalpagam, 2014).

Bhrigupati Singh (2014) studied the state's operations of power and authority in the late colonial and postcolonial period in India in terms of a combination of force and contract, where force represents coercion, terror, and violence, and contract denotes generosity and welfare.[11] Singh's approach opens up the analytic space to examine the state and broadcasting in India. However, unlike Singh, who does not pursue Foucault's insights on governmentality, this book posits that state power is exercised through a combination of sovereignty and governmentality. While Foucault's theoretical elaborations of power has remained Eurocentric in the sense that it does not account for the colonial contexts within which the sovereignty, discipline, and governmentality intersect, several scholars—some identified above—have extended his insights to explore the specific manifestations of power underpinning the colonial–imperial–postcolonial complex. Since Foucault considered that sovereignty and governmentality are complementary and not substitutive and oppositional, some have suggested that both can be brought together within a single rubric to pursue analyses of power (Dillon, 1995; Legg, 2007).

Following Ricoeur, the book envisions a mode of analysis that considers the utility of a 'double hermeneutic'; that is, 'the hermeneutic of suspicion' as well as 'the hermeneutic of restoration'.[12] Ricoeur's (1965) double hermeneutic, first sketched briefly in his *Freud and Philosophy*, posits that the hermeneutics of suspicion is involved in the exegesis of meaning by unmasking the ideological content of symbolic and cultural discourses; the hermeneutics of restoration goes beyond the ideological to decipher surplus meanings (Scott-Baumann, 2009; Kearney, 2011; Felski, 2015). Ricoeur's hermeneutic approach, therefore, moves beyond the semiotic, psychoanalytic, and poststructuralist approaches that consider the human subject as passive and constructed by discourses, relegating the speaking subject to the margins. Furthermore, unlike the semiotic and poststructuralist-oriented approaches, Ricoeur's hermeneutic account enables deeper insights into the interconnections between narrative and temporality.

Drawing key ideas from Ricoeur's work, yet departing from it, this book engages with Indian theories of narrative, distinguishing their several key characteristics and temporal dimensions. Overall, Ricoeur's double hermeneutic is essential to engaging with the polysemy of language, and forms a comprehensive framework for examining literary and cultural texts, data, and human and social action including an 'almost infinite variety of narrative expressions (oral, written, graphic, gestural) and narrative classes (myths, folklore, legends, novels, epics, tragedies, drama, film, comic strips, etc)' (Valdes, 1991: 27). Since the 1960s onwards, the philosophic work of Freud, Marx, and Nietzsche has served as a point of departure for theories and methods in literary, cultural, communication, and media studies where the task of 'critique' became the singular and exclusive pursuit of uncovering ideological, repressed, and hegemonic forms of power. In contrast, Ricoeur's writings in the same period have pursued an egalitarian and open-ended approach by considering the pluricity and multivocality of literary and cultural texts, and human and social action. Ricoeur's formulation of a hermeneutic of restoration, therefore, sought to bridge the aporias of interpretation, where the restorative hermeneutic is not a mere supplement to a hermeneutic of suspicion, but rather both dialectically linked and integral to each other. To this end, Bernstein (2013: 135) noted that 'the genuine hermeneutics of restorative meaning must pass through the fire of merciless suspicion. This is what Ricoeur wants to show'.

Unlike the Marxist and poststructuralist approaches which consider religion as 'false consciousness', a 'neurosis', and an anachronism, Ricoeur's restorative hermeneutics offers substantive conceptual resources to pursue an 'immanent' critique of religion and religious traditions.[13] While Ricoeur agreed that religion is capable of generating 'terror' and violence, promoting orthodoxies and dogmas, he did not extend its wholesale denunciation, and instead viewed the religious as a 'transcendental', a 'post-critical faith' in a dialectical struggle with the secular (Kearney, 2009; Marcelo, 2010). Similarly, recent scholarship in South Asian, postcolonial, and religious studies noted that the religious cannot be relegated as an ideological object, and should be comprehended in its expansiveness and diversity (Chakrabarty, 2000; Nandy, 2001; Spivak, 2004; Bilimoria, 2008; Das, 2010; Singh, 2014). Despite their differing emphases on religion, they all agree on the co-imbrication of the religious and the secular. Referring to the utility of Ricoeur's philosophical hermeneutics, Bilimoria (2008: 72) noted:

> To be sure, Mohanty would agree with Ricoeur in arguing that the way to handle the issue of tradition [religion] is not to reduce it univocally to a set of antiquated and anachronistic beliefs, nor to blindly regurgitate its apparently receding spirituality, or to suppress it with an iron-hand, but rather to enter it, empathetically, interact with it and in this dialectic allow a fresh understanding to emerge.[14]

A crucial aspect of Ricoeur's philosophic hermeneutics has been an engagement with theology that centers on a hermeneutic understanding of 'theos' as religious and sacred.[15] Apart from bringing theos and philosophy dialogue, Ricoeur has attempted to tackle head-on some of the conceptual conundrums around the religious and the secular. This is evident in Ricoeur's (1995) receptive reading of Kant's work, *Religion within the Limits of Reason Alone*, as a philosophical hermeneutic of religion dealing with thematic of evil, belief, grace, and hope. According to Ricoeur, Kant's work could be seen as an attempt at situating the religious within the parameters of his critical philosophy. For Ricoeur, therefore, religion is not to be viewed as a sue generis phenomenon, and that religious belief and faith should be examined in terms of the interplay of 'symbols, myths, narrative, metaphors, and models' (Wallace, 1995: 17).

In a similar vein but from a deconstructionist reading of Kant's *Religion within the Boundaries of Mere Reason*, Spivak (2004) argued that although it is a Judeo-Christian understanding of religion as 'the religion of reason' and detranscendentalized into secularism, Kant's ideas offer resources in articulating a revisioned notion of secularism as a form of critique against religious orthodoxies, while at the same time open to 'dialogue' with the religious that she identifies as 'the transcendental'—a term that has a broader provenance than the name 'religion'. Hence, for Spivak, secularism and the transcendental are bound together and subject to reason and critique.

The two readings of Kant, a hermeneutic one by Ricoeur and a deconstuctionist one by Spivak, offer interlinked yet contrasting approaches on the reconfiguration of the religious and the secular.[16] A common element in both readings is the programmatic manner in which the religious is rethought as 'post-critical faith' (Ricoeur) and 'the transcendental' (Spivak), allying themselves with reason in contesting the global forms of 'terror', domination, and violence instigated in the name of religion; in the immediate context of India, they offer egalitarian and democratic resources in addressing sociopolitical challenges to right-wing movements such as Hindu majoritarianism and Muslim extremism, religious bigotry and fundamentalism, proselytization, caste-based oppression and violence against Dalits, and the baleful effects of gender ideologies and practices.

Although Ricoeur's explorations of religion offer conceptual insights into understanding religion and secularism as embedded imaginaries, a main drawback of his work as well as most other writings on religion relate to two issues: first, the category of religion itself has a Western lineage, a Judeo-Christian understanding of religion where religions are 'distinguished by differing belief-systems and differing conceptions of the sacred' (Seth, 2004: 50). Second, as philosophers and social theorists have noted, modern juridico-political concepts such as state, civil society, secularism, and so on, have their roots in religion, and, hence, ought to be considered as 'theologico-political' (Asad, 1993; King, 1999; Derrida, 2001).

The above issues preclude an adequate understanding and interpretation of 'religion' in the context of Hinduism and Islam in India.[17] Thus, as Nandy (2001: 126) indicated, 'Deities in everyday Hinduism ... are not entities outside of everyday life, nor do they preside over life from outside; they constitute a significant part of it ... Gods are above and beyond humans but they are paradoxically not outside human fraternity'. Indeed, even for the liberal political theorist, Rajeev Bhargava (2017), the separation of the religious and the secular in the Indian context is problematic, and that the secular (rational) and religious (sacred) ought to remain committed to a basic understanding of reason and belief.[18] In addition to the category 'religion', how do we understand the 'theologico-political' concepts that have shaped India's colonial and postcolonial histories? Chakrabarty (2002b: 865) provided a conceptual approach in 'engaging the universals'—whether rights, citizenship, imagination, sovereignty—central to European thought by insisting that we need to rethink the historicism of European thought in terms of 'heterotemporality', since

> these universals ... as thought concepts, come packaged as though they have transcended the particular histories in which they were born. But being pieces of prose and language, they carry intimations of histories of belonging, which are not everybody's history. When we translate them—practically, theoretically—into our languages and practice, we make them speak to other histories of belonging, and that is how difference and heterogeneity enter these words.

After India's Independence in 1947, while the interweaving of sovereignty, public, religion, and nation informed state projects of 'national integration' and 'national development' instituted to mitigate the baleful effects of colonial rule, and to chart political, social, economic, and scientific progress for the newly independent country, the postcolonial state incorporated colonial notion of sovereignty and governmentality into its administrative techniques of governance. In examining the issues outlined above, I have drawn upon a range of sources: broadcast policies, legislative documents, governmental and expert committee reports; interviews with radio and television officials; television programmes; interviews with viewers; commentaries and reflections on radio and television from online forums, blogs, YouTube, and apps; journalistic writings; newspaper and magazine articles and reports; figures and data on radio and television from All India Radio and the state-run television network, Doordarshan (Hindi for 'distant vision'), and trade publications.

A main concern of the book is to explore broadcasting not as a closed-off 'ideological apparatus', but rather to pursue an integrated analysis which pays attention to the particular ways in which the dynamics of structure and agency operate in radio and television. To this end, the book will examine the ideological characteristics of the medium; the discursive construction of

CAMBRIDGE
UNIVERSITY PRESS

University Printing House, Cambridge CB2 8BS, United Kingdom

One Liberty Plaza, 20th Floor, New York, NY 10006, USA

477 Williamstown Road, Port Melbourne, vic 3207, Australia

314 to 321, 3rd Floor, Plot No.3, Splendor Forum, Jasola District Centre, New Delhi 110025, India

79 Anson Road, #06–04/06, Singapore 079906

Cambridge University Press is part of the University of Cambridge.

It furthers the University's mission by disseminating knowledge in the pursuit of education, learning and research at the highest international levels of excellence.

www.cambridge.org
Information on this title: www.cambridge.org/9781108481700

First published 2019

Printed in India by Nutech Print Services, New Delhi 110020

A catalogue record for this publication is available from the British Library

ISBN 978-1-108-48170-0 Hardback

sovereignty, nation, public, and religion in the discourse of radio and television; and how the aesthetic, cultural, mythic, and symbolic resources of television point to the presence of multiple meanings in the televisual narratives as well as in viewers' interpretations. The mixing of story genres across languages have shaped popular literature, historical, and entertainment narratives in colonial India (Orsini, 2009). More importantly, the linguistic fluidity questions the attempts to create sharp boundaries between Hindi and Urdu languages, other vernacular formations, as well as in people's ordinary speech (Das, 2010; Ahmad, 2000). The book argues that these traditions of story genres that have influenced televisual literary drama and fictional programme series aired on Doordarshan in the mid-1980s have remained unexplored.

While I extend Ricoeur's double hermeneutic and Foucault's 'hermeneutics of the self', and their respective concepts of power and governmentality, narrative and temporality, I draw upon South Asian, postcolonial, media, and television studies as well. The overall approach is to situate the analysis in what David Thorburn (1987: 165) indicated as the characteristic feature of aesthetic analysis:

> An attentiveness to tone, to plot and character, to visual strategies, to the workings of narrative and symbolic texts—are essential to the task of describing and judging such systems ... To understand our television system, I want to insist, even in its historical and ideological dimensions, we must be sensitive in part to literary matters; we must be able to read these texts in something of the way the audience experiences them: as stories or dramas, as aesthetic artifacts, whose meaning will fully be available only if we employ, along with other interpretive methods, the strategies of reading traditionally used by critics of literature and film.

Furthermore, according to Thorburn (1987: 168), most television programmes can be characterized as producing a 'consensus narrative', which articulates a society's central myths, beliefs, and values organized in terms of 'shared stories, plots, character types, cultural symbols, and narrative conventions', that cannot be reduced to the ideological. Indeed, Thorburn's arguments for aesthetic methods of interpretation is an important corrective to the dominance of ideological studies of television, one that enables a better grasp of narrative forms and mixing of story genres on Indian television. However, some recent scholarly work in television has pursued this line of analyses, ignoring the power dynamics and ideological features that underpin television (Thompson, 2003; Peacock and Jacobs, 2013).

In contrast, the book will examine the complex interplay of power and ideologies while at the same time exploring the aesthetic and narrative dimensions of the medium. As indicated earlier, most ideological analyses of television, drawing on Marxist, Freudian, Lacanian, and Semiotics frameworks, have offered a wholesale denunciation of the medium, disregarding the surplus meanings generated by the expansive programme universe of television. More crucially, however, these studies treat television as a 'bad object', and its audience either distracted or ensnared by the televisual 'ideological apparatus'. Instead, this book adapts a stance akin to Milli Buananno (2008: 41) who adumbrates that

> it is precisely because television allows us to switch between looking and listening, between involvement and detachment, and because it offers us both demanding and relaxing forms of cultural entertainment and social participation, that it can claim to possess the true and authentically distinctive qualities of an open medium. It is flexible; and it is resistant both to theoretical imposition and to the empirical experience of fixed, innate and unchanging characteristics.

CHAPTER OUTLINES

While the chapters are thematically linked they are also stand-alone and can be read individually. Overall, the chapters are organized under the rubrics of power and narrative, distinguishing their hermeneutic provenance, outlining religion and secularism as 'embedded imaginaries', and space and time as 'spatiotemporal' concepts for the study. The theoretical orientation posits that critique ought to broaden the horizon of interpretation so as to understand multiple and plurivocal meanings in texts, traditions, media systems, social practices, and people's life-worlds.

In Chapter 1, 'Broadcasting, Spatiotemporalities, and Power', I examine the spatiotemporal dynamics of broadcasting, and the intertwined genealogies of sovereignty, public, religion, and nation through an examination of radio and television policies, experiments, and programmes: the village broadcasting initiatives in the 1930s, music and language debates in the 1940s, radio rural forums of the 1950s, television experiments and projects in 1970s–80s, expansion of state-run television in the 1980s, formulation of broadcast policies and legislations, and so on. To this end, the chapter takes up a set of interrelated questions: How did sovereignty operate in broadcasting, and what forms did it take? What were the particular ways in which sovereignty was imbricated with public, religion, and nation? How was the public imagined in radio and television experiments and programmes, and how did this conception of the public relate to the notion of audience?

The second chapter, 'Doordarshan, Literary Drama, and Narrative Identity', explores television's narrative forms, the repertoire of cinematic codes, techniques, and styles, and the overlapping between myth, realism, and melodrama. I discuss the television serials, *Mailā Anchal* (1987–88, dir. Ashok Talwar), *Rāg Darbārī* (1986–87, dir. Krishna Raghav), and *Godān* (2004, dir. Gulzar) transmitted on the state-run television network, Doordarshan. These serials, adapted from literary works, deal with questions of late colonial and postcolonial identity in the countryside in terms of the dialectic tensions between the forces of tradition and modernity, local politics, nationalism, development, encroaching capitalism, public life, and more specifically, on the human condition. They frame the various issues through complex 'mythic-realist' narrative forms. For instance, the literary adaptations look at the effects of the process of development—through local (rural) politics, state institutions, and bureaucracies—in the lives of ordinary Indians, mostly peasants and the working class.

Chapter 3, 'Televisual Representations of Socio-Spatial Conflicts, and the Religious–Secular Imaginaries', explores two fictionalized television drama series, *Choli Daman* (1989, dir. by M. S. Sathyu) and *Gul Gulshan Gulfam* (1990–91, dir. by Ved Rahi); and news-based documentaries, *Kashmir File* (1995, prod. by Arun Kaul) and *Punjab 1983* (1991, prod. by Nalini Singh). In the mid-1980s, especially around the time when 'separatist' and subnational movements in Punjab and Kashmir were threatening the project of national integration, a slew of programmes were produced on the themes of national and religious harmony. At first glance, the television programmes on Kashmir and Punjab seem to crudely present state-based ideological notions of secularism and national integration, but a closer look reveals an entanglement of the religious and secular practices. Although most political and religious conflicts have their beginnings in this entanglement, various responses to these conflicts have generally taken two approaches: they either assume the resurgence of religious identities as a result of an encroaching secularism, or consider secularism and religion as two opposing and incompatible value systems.

In the fourth chapter, 'Patriotism and Its Avatars: Tracking the National–Global Dialectic in Music Videos and Television Commercials', I study the hegemonic articulations of the national and the global, and the constitution of 'new' forms of patriotism in the music videos, 'Vande Mataram' (Hail

Motherland!), 'Apna Desh' (Our Country), and 'Kho Jaane Do' (Let Me Get Lost). In addition, I briefly examine two Bajaj Scooter commercials aired during the late 1980s and the early 1990s. The music videos (around 4–5 minutes each), marketed and released in 1997, and the 50th Independence Day celebrations in India were a regular fixture on all major television channels (state-run, private, local cable, and transnational networks) for the major part of 1997, the year of the celebrations, and thereafter. These videos mobilized aspects of nationalism, globalization, and consumerism in generating ideas around patriotism. The chapter makes an argument for pursuing the visual as one site where the relationships between the national and the global in the articulation of patriotism can be tracked.

Drawing insights from scholarship in media memory studies, Chapter 5, 'Remembering Doordarshan: Figurations of Memories and Nostalgia on Blogs, YouTube, and in Oral Interviews', examines the particular ways in which the state-run television, Doordarshan is remembered in people's personal reflections, and print and digital media forms such as newspapers, apps, blogs, and YouTube in recuperating childhood memories, and in the productive imagination of nostalgia. While the acts of reminiscing and remembering are themselves 'mnemonic modes' activated through a variety of 'graphic artifacts' such as personal diaries, journals, weblogs, and audio-visual accounts, what is interesting to study is how television itself as a 'mnemonic device' and 'evocative object' shapes people's/viewers' memories, and the ways in which different spatiotemporalities intersect. How do people reminisce about the arrival of the medium in their homes, the shaping of their viewing practices, intergenerational reflections and recollections of a wide repertoire of programmes, newsreaders, characters, commercials, imaginations of nation, family, class, caste, religion, and so on (Bourdon, 2003; Turkle, 2007; Keightley, 2011).

In the final chapter, 'Epilogue', I explore and contextualize key insights from the various chapters with respect to the spatiotemporal dynamics and the imbrications of sovereignty, public, religion, and nation in broadcasting and television, and relate it to contemporary developments in television in India. I offer commentary on the Eurocentric/Western conceptions of history, modernity, and religion, especially since the presence of the universal categories in contemporary India continue to obfuscate, rather than illuminate and clarify historical, social, and cultural processes. The epilogue will explore recent scholarship in television studies in India as well as the West, pointing to their possibilities and problems in reconceptualizing media and communication studies (MCS) in India. To this end, it outlines programmatic arguments for their utility in conjunction with hermeneutics and philology as interpretive approaches for MCS in India.

Despite the increasing number of studies on Indian media in general and television in particular, the intertwined genealogies of sovereignty, public, religion, and nation that have framed the histories of radio and television have remained unexplored. While a few studies offered a potted overview of the formative history of broadcasting from the 1930s to the 1970s, several scholarly works examined ideologies of gender, nation, class, citizenship, Hindu nationalism, and soon, on pro-development, mythological, and other series that aired on Indian television in the mid-1980s, and recent writings have looked at the representations of nationalist imagination and globalization on state-run as well as private television in post–1990s (Awasthy, 1965; Luthra, 1986; Chatterjee, 1991; Mitra, 1994; Gupta, 1998; Mankekar, 1999; Rajagopal, 2001; Butcher, 2003; Kumar, 2006). While the studies offer critical overviews of the history of television in India, and have examined several key media developments and policy discourses, they have ignored the spatiotemporalities of broadcasting, and the intertwined genealogies of sovereignty, public, religion that have underpinned the discourse of radio and television in late colonial and postcolonial India. In addition to filling a crucial gap in scholarly literature, my book offers several fresh new insights on state-run media, radio and television, in late colonial and postcolonial India.

NOTES

1. Some examples of the generalizations can be gleaned from the following arguments. John Urry (1995: 21), referring to postmodern TV, talks about watching television change the temporal and spatial organization and fragmentation of social life. Harvey (1989: 232) notes, 'Innovations dedicated to the removal of spatial barriers ... the railroad and telegraph, the automobile, radio and telephone, the jet aircraft and television, and the recent telecommunications revolutions are cases in point.' Likewise, May and Thrift (2001: 4, 8) consider the significance of broadcasting temporalities, particularly how 'VCR has altered the perception of shared broadcast community', and the role of communication networks such as railroads, telegraph, and telephone in people's experience of time. There is not much by way of analysis of communication and media beyond the broad claims, especially with regards to temporality. There is no reference to the rich body of phenomenological studies of broadcasting and temporality by Scannell and Silverstone, among others.
2. The idea of a global itinerary of communication and media technologies ought to be pursued as an interdisciplinary endeavour, tracing the uneven topographies of power across multiple contexts. The global histories, thus, should not be thought

of as linear peregrinations of ideas, ideologies, and artifacts; rather, as Chris Bayly (2004: 2) noted, 'all local, national, or regional histories must, in important ways, therefore be global histories'. Carey (1989: 212) does mention the role of colonial rule but does not specify much. He indicates that the domain of empire remains a crucial site of investigation. 'Although colonies could be held together with printing correspondence, and sail, the hold, as the American experience shows, was always tenuous over great distance ... It was the cable and telegraph, backed of course by sea power, that turned colonialism into imperialism: a system in which the center of an empire could dictate rather than merely respond to the margin.' Here, Carey is drawing on Innis' work on empire and communication.

3. Worth (2014) examined the fiction of Kipling, Haggard, Corelli, among others, who framed their narratives around the telegraph, the telephone, the phonogram, and so on. Referencing the 2005, Hindi–Urdu commercial film, *Mangal Pandey: The Rising*, which is based on the events of 1857, Worth refers to scenes from the film where the natives torch the telegraph office in their struggle against the British 'Company' magic of the telegraph wires.
4. For instance, the classical liberal theorist John Stuart Mill (1858: 74), in his famous *Memorandum of the Improvements in the Administration of India*, an extensive propaganda piece written for the East India Company, argued that 'even more important as a means of communication than railways, is the electric telegraph; the use of which, at the commencement of the late disturbances [referring to the 1857 Indian Mutiny], may be said with scarcely any exaggeration to have saved our empire. Having already, in a wonderfully short space of time, connected the seats of the different Governments by lines of telegraph upwards of three thousand miles in length, the Government of India is now engaged in establishing additional lines of about the same extent, through which the most important places will be brought into communication with each other by alternative routes'.
5. An exception here is Mankekar (1999) who offered a substantive discussion of monolithic and dominant construction of religion, particularly Hinduism, by state-run television and right-wing political groups. Even though Mankekar offers a detailed explication of religion, her arguments and the subsequent analysis consider the religious and the secular as separate entities.
6. Lata Mani (2009: 2) uses the compound word, 'SacredSecular' to overcome the binary of thought that constitutes them as separate entities. According to Mani, we need to pursue a sort of 'contemplative critique' of religious extremism and secular dogmas that are at loggerheads creating an impasse and conflict. To this end, Mani suggests that we engage in 'transcoding' between the sacred and secular knowledges and practices because 'there is much in common to the emancipatory streams within both knowledge traditions'.
7. These terms are taken from T. N. Madan's (1997: 343) 'Secularism in Its Place' in *Politics in India*, edited by Sudipta Kaviraj (Delhi, Calcutta, Chennai, Mumbai: Oxford University Press). In the Urdu language it is denoted by the phrase *ghair-mazhabi*—implying its non-religious character.

8. The Constitutional provisions regarding secularism came out of key debates among members of the Constituent Assembly in 1946–49. The debates produced differing inflections and meanings of secularism, minority–majority relations, electoral representations, and social justice among other pressing concerns of a newly emerging nation-state from colonial rule and partition violence. See Rochana Bajpai (2000). Two understandings of secularism in India have been common: *dharma nirpekshata*, referring to separation of religion from politics, and *sarva dharma sambhava* based on the principle of equal respect for all religions. While India's first Prime Minister, Jawaharlal Nehru adhered to *dharma nirpekshata*, the idea of *sarva dharma sambhava* is derived from Mahatma Gandhi's vision that rejects any separation of religion and politics. See Brenda Crossman and Ratna Kapur (1999).
9. For an excellent overview of the debates and the 'crisis' of secularism in India, see Dingwaney Needham and Sundar Rajan (2007).
10. Johan Michel (2014: 103) says, 'It is not a mere chance that a secondary literature is beginning to emerge that pays closer attention to the distances and proximities between the ethical project of the hermeneutics of the self, in Ricoeur, and the history of a hermeneutics of the subject, in Foucault, or shows how "the ontology of understanding" in Ricoeur fills in a lacuna in the Foucauldian theory of subjectification.' Charles Hallisey (2010) has recently pointed out that Ricoeur and Foucault's respective conceptualizations of the self/other relations and ethics share a greater affinity than has been acknowledged. See also Goetz (2004) and Vilchis (2013). Ricoeur (1998: 79, emphasis in original) himself noted his affinity to Foucault's later work when he noted, 'How could we forget the Stoic concern, the mastery of desires and passions, to which Foucault himself returns in his later texts, which I greatly admire, *The Use of Pleasure* and *Care of the Self*.'
11. Singh (2014) has drawn on the French mythologist, Georges Dumezil's conceptualization of sovereign power as 'force', and 'contract' is derived from the Vedic deities, Mitra and Varuna and the Roman figures, Romulus and Numa, each representing a particular manifestation of power, as violence and welfare. Singh's study of the state's presence in the life of the Sahariya community of bonded labourers in the Shabad district of Rajasthan, India reveals fresh insights into the workings of power and authority.
12. Despite its utility in analysing literary and cultural texts, Ricoeur's hermeneutic approach had been either overlooked and/or ignored by scholarship in cultural, communication, media, and postcolonial studies. Andrew (1993), Sobchack (2009), Fornäs (2012), and Felski (2015) argued that theories and methods influenced by Marxist, Freudian, Lacanian, and Semiotics were favoured over the rich interpretive repertoire offered by Ricoeurian hermeneutics. Vivian Sobchack (2009: 3) refers to the dominance of the methods in the academia thus: 'I remember the kind of hegemonic policing that went on in the field when neo-marxism and psychoanalysis were dominant theoretical paradigms. I obviously felt this personally … because I was trying to do something else, something I hoped was more positive than negative critique.' See also Scannell (1998), Mathieu (2015), and Phelan (2016)

on the significance of employing Ricoeur's hermeneutics of 'trust' to media and communication studies. From a postcolonial religious studies perspective, see Bilimoria (2004).

13. According to Roland Boer (2014: 108), the leading Marxist scholar, Fredric Jameson's '*The Political Unconscious* is a reworking of Paul Ricoeur's theologically inspired hermeneutics of suspicion and recovery. Working his way through Ricoeur's early *Freud and Philosophy*, Jameson seeks to turn this double hermeneutics into a distinctly Marxist one, that is, in terms of ideological and utopian hermeneutics'. Boer further notes that in Jameson's theoretical corpus religion remains salient despite the fact that Jameson had tried to sidestep it. Boer points out to the influence of Northrop Frye's medieval Biblical allegory in Jameson's four level Marxist interpretive model—the literal, allegorical, moral, and analogical. See also Cornel West (1982) for the influence of religious *weltanschauungen* in Jameson's work.
14. Purushottama Bilimoria (2008: 9) noted that the field of 'philosophy of religion concerns itself with certain questions arising from the traditional tussle between the judgment of reason and the commitment to faith, augmented by disputes over whether it is language and conceptual analysis or some direct intuitive experience that provides access to the truth claims underpinning specific scriptural utterances, as articulated in philosophical (or "natural") theology'.
15. According to Kearney (2009: 172), 'the so-called "religious turn" in contemporary French philosophy was deeply informed by three main thinkers schooled deeply in the phenomenological tradition—Emmanuel Levinas, Jacques Derrida, and Paul Ricoeur'. Furthermore, Kearney notes that 'in his pioneering essay, "Religion, Atheism Faith", Ricoeur developed several points about a post-critical faith. He speaks of the "religious meanings of atheism," suggesting that an atheistic purging of the negative and life-denying components of religion needs to be taken on board if a genuine form of faith is to emerge in our secular culture'.
16. In their respective readings, Kant's work is titled slightly differently in English. The following two crucial passages from their respective works signal the overlaps and affinities. Ricoeur (1995: 75) states, 'Religion, owing to its historical, "positive" character, constitutes something specifically outside philosophy, an otherness that philosophy can take into account only by lying at its margins, at its boundaries, and, if I may put it this way, at the inner edge of the line that divides the ahistorical transcendental realm and the historical religious realm.' According to Spivak (2004: 107), 'Kant was deeply aware of the limits of reason, he asked himself if it was possible to forge a species of what we might as well call secularism, which would incorporate intuitions of the transcendental. Let us see how he solved his problem, and what we, who must undo him, can learn from him.'
17. For Bilimoria (2008: 13), 'Philosophy of religion has always remained aloof, inward looking, and immersed in its own Judeo-Christian roots (with occasional acknowledgment of Arabic scholastic falāsifah, but where Ibn Sina becomes unrecognizably Hellenized as Aviccena, and Ibn Rushd as Averroes), or occluded by the terms defined mostly since medieval (European) scholasticism, and for the

most part remained totally closed to possible responses and analyses that other traditions and cultures might have on the same "big questions" it sets out to solve or resolve.'

18. By way of an example, Bhargava (2017) posits that Hindu rituals such as Śrāddha, a ceremony performed in honour of a dead ancestor and embedded in people's beliefs, carry spiritual and performative meanings coexisting with the secular and the rationalist ideals and practices.

1 | Broadcasting, Spatiotemporalities, and Power

In recent years, postcolonial media scholars have begun to focus their attention on the dialectic relations between state and media policies (McDowell, 1997; Chakravartty, 2004; Kumar, 2006; Jeffrey, 2006). While such scholarship has persuasively analysed the construction of nationalism and examined the debates surrounding autonomy and deregulation in Indian media policies in the context of economic liberalization, a significant absence from this body of work is an engagement with *how* the concept of sovereignty is being reworked in the moment of globalization. In addition, two issues manifest within communication research and postcolonial media studies that pertain to an understanding of the state as a container and a fixed entity, and the absence of adequate theorization of broadcasting and space. According to Raka Shome (2004: 40), 'Communication research, for the most part, has yet to address in a systematic way the role space plays in the (re)production of social power.' A few studies—collected in a book, *MediaSpace*—have taken up questions of space in terms of different media modalities: radio, television, computers, and video-gaming. Clive Barrett (2004) offers persuasive theoretical reflection on space and public life via the specific writings of John Dewey, Harold Innis, and Raymond Williams. Despite these contributions, broadcasting and space in the postcolonial contexts remains unexamined. More importantly, however, such studies have not produced a theoretical account of how broadcasting and media policies are connected with state spatialities as well as temporalities.

This chapter makes two interrelated claims. First, a 'spatiotemporal' discourse can be discerned in broadcasting and media policies that has framed nationalism, globalization, sovereignty, and citizenship, and India's nation state has historically elaborated two overlapping modalities of power: national sovereignty from 1947 to 1990, and governmentality since 1991.[1] Second, taking a cue from Manu Goswami's (2004: 4) insights, I suggest that to understand the spatiotemporal discourses and the modalities of power, we need to move beyond 'methodological' nationalism: that is, explanations that treat the state as a container and a fixed entity, where social relations are organized within territorially bounded national spaces. Indeed, the spatiotemporal discourse of the state can be grasped through a *trans*national framework that considers national and international as part of the wider global field of relations. To this end, the chapter examines particular imaginations of nationalism and globalization, and demonstrates how the spatiotemporal constructions of sovereignty and citizenship—both in terms of abstract principles and performative practices—have been/are produced in broadcasting and media policies. This chapter proposes to rethink the history of Indian broadcasting and media policies by foregrounding the question of spatiotemporality and argues that such an approach opens up fresh new insights on broadcasting and media policies not only in the Indian case, but also in postcolonial and other contexts as well.

In the first section, I outline theoretical underpinnings of my arguments by drawing upon a number of studies that have developed key ideas pertaining to state, power, policies, and spatiotemporalities in the work of Antonio Gramsci, Michel Foucault, and Henri Lefebvre. The next section examines spatiotemporal contexts of nationalism, globalization, citizenship, and sovereignty in Indian broadcasting, and in the third section, I analyse a range of discourses through which sovereignty, territoriality, and citizenship have been produced in media policies. Finally, in the last section, the conclusions are situated against the background of the findings.

STATE, POWER, AND POLICIES: TOWARDS A SPATIAL PERSPECTIVE

Monroe Price (2002: 13) offered a substantive normative framework to account for a range of state strategies in coping with sovereignty and authority. Price pointed out that

> states have undergone frenzied testing of new and modified techniques aimed at regulating, if not mastering, the market for speech in response to the forces that seem to undercut their autonomy ... there is a shift away from the regularly inward forms of state control to outward-looking, regional, or multinational approaches.

Price's broad-based 'mixed' model approach sheds light on how states reassert their power through a combination of strategies: regulation/deregulation of communication media, and policy transfer mechanisms.

Sandra Braman (1995: 4), commenting on the complex relationships between state and media policies, urged that communication researchers pay greater attention to the epistemological issues in media policies because the 'failure to understand the state leads to an inability to analyze policy [and] understanding information and communication policy as power is particularly important in today's environment'. Following Braman's arguments, Stephen McDowell (1997) considered India's software policy in terms of a concept of network state. However, this chapter posits that Gramsci's concept of hegemony, along with Foucault's notion of governmentality and combined with Lefebvre's theory of state spatiality, sheds analytic insights into the power dynamics of postcolonial state, construction of sovereignty and citizenship in broadcasting while enabling a detailed analysis of the intertwined relations between nationalism and globalization.[2]

Pointing out that cultural and media studies have typically ignored policy dimensions in understanding the relations between culture and power that has a bearing on theories of the state, Tony Bennett (1992: 23) argued that culture, power, and policy are central to the 'field of government'. Taking a cue from Bennett and other scholars like Ian Hunter, Terry Flew (1997: 90) pointed out that Foucault's notion of governmentality is an important counterpoint to various state theories beset with problems of reductionism and functionalism. Flew maintains that 'Foucault proposed a move from sovereignty to materiality of power relations [and] from state theory toward what can be termed as a general theory of government, where the conduct of the state shifts from a primarily juridical to an increasingly administrative and technical basis'. Flew also suggested that 'theories of governmentality' are particularly attuned to policy discourses that seek to link individuals, ideologies, institutions, and social programmes via a range of ethical, moral, and reform techniques.

Applying the concept of governmentality[3] to state spaces, James Ferguson and Akhil Gupta (2002: 981–82) argued that because states are 'powerful sites of symbolic and cultural production', they ought to be considered as 'spatializing' apparatuses, and that 'discussions of the imagination of states have not attended adequately to the ways in which states are spatialized'. They usefully extend Foucault's ideas via the notions of 'vertical encompassment' and 'transnational governmentality' to study the spatial properties of the Indian and South African states in terms of large-scale development policies.

The work of Partha Chatterjee (1998) and Gyan Prakash (2000) usefully deployed the notion of governmentality, thus moving away from overarching state theories, to probe the formation of culture and power in colonial and postcolonial contexts. Postcolonial scholars pointed out that Foucault paid little attention to the effects of colonialism in developing theoretical formulations about modernity, power, and governmentality. Nonetheless, the concept of governmentality has been productively reworked to examine colonial rule in India. In his study of Indian nation and nationalism, Chatterjee (1998) offered a brilliant critique of Benedict Anderson's ideas on nation and nationalism as 'modular' forms common to Europe, Asia, Africa, and Latin America. However, Chatterjee's thesis that the Indian bourgeois nationalists divided social practices and institutions into two broad and distinct domains, the material and the spiritual, had been critiqued by Manu Goswami (2004: 24) as well as Gyan Prakash (2000: 170) for positing the spiritual domain as being a pure, autonomous repository of cultural difference. According to Chatterjee (1998), the material domain represents the West (which the nationalists called 'outside'), and the spiritual domain represents the East (termed 'inner'). Goswami noted that the two domains were increasingly shaped by geographic and spatial imperatives of colonialism and capitalism, and Prakash (2000: 179) argued that the 'material' and 'spiritual' division frequently overlapped, and, in fact, 'subjugation drove anti-colonial nationalism in a more ambitious direction as it simultaneously drew upon and transgressed inner/outer dichotomy, distinguishing community from the state while seeking to realize the former in the latter'. In the following analysis, drawing upon Goswami and Prakash's critiques, I shall demonstrate some of the contradictory spatiotemporal modalities and contexts through which anti-colonial nationalism borrowed the procedures of colonial governmentality, and how Nehru's nation-building project incorporated Gandhian ideas and idioms as they sought to articulate conceptions of nation, sovereignty, and citizenship in the sphere of broadcasting and media policies.

Satish Deshpande's (1998: 183) discussion of Indian nationalism via Foucault's notion of 'heterotopias' is persuasive and offers substantial analytic insights into how particular spatial strategies brought together the 'physical-material and mental-imaginative aspects of social space' in the hegemonic construction of nationalism. A significant feature of Deshpande's study is its ability to examine the overlapping spatial practices of nationalism that allows him conceptual clarity in showing how distinct forms of nationalism—Nehru's *economic geography* and Sarvarkar's *sacred geography*—get embedded in nation-state practices. Deshpande noted that during the 1950s–60s, the nation was thought of as a space of production and imagined in terms of various economic associations, and the names of regions and towns where large-scale public sector corporations were established became the principal heterotopias fashioned by the Nehruvian regime. An important absence from Deshpande's study, however, is the role of global relations in shaping India's nationalist discourse. An engagement with Henri Lefebvre's writings on state spatiality would have provided the way forward and shed more light not only on the spatial transformations of nationalism, but also illuminated the role of transnational forces that inflected the Nehruvian heterotopias.

Manu Goswami (2004) and Subir Sinha (2008) argued that nationalism has been historically produced in terms of global restructuring of interstate relations and as transnational development regimes. Indeed, for Sinha (2008: 59, emphasis in original), 'the periodization of the history of development as part of a *national* history is inadequate, and that it needs to be located on another register, that of transnational regimes'. In contrast to Deshpande's approach and other Foucault-centred studies, Goswami extended Lefebvre's theory of state spatialities to examine historical–geographic developments of Indian nationalism from 1885 to 1930. These developments, Goswami pointed out, were marked by global restructuring of capitalist relations where the 'self-understanding and trajectory of colonial India was inseparably tied to *colonial spatial practices* and capitalist expansion' (2004: 244, emphasis added).

For Goswami, Lefebvre's work offered both a critique of the Cartesian conceptualization of a bounded and pre-given container notion of territoriality as well as the discursive approaches to space in favour of materialist understanding of space embedded in social relations. Sinha (2008) examined several community development programmes in postcolonial India, not only as a result of a global restructuring of interstate relations (pace Goswami), but in terms of a wider set of ideas that flowed among several individuals and institutions that he characterized under 'transnational development regimes' (2008: 59). Both Goswami and Sinha present key arguments on the historical–geographic aspects of nationalism in colonial and postcolonial contexts. Thus, on the one hand, their analysis is attentive to the transnational and spatial contexts of nationalism and on the other, it leads to a deeper understanding of sovereignty and territoriality.

Drawing insights from the preceding discussion, and more specifically Lefebvre's (1974: 38) notion of 'representations of space', this chapter considers sovereignty, citizenship, nationalism, and globalization as spatiotemporal concepts. In Lefebvre's theory of space, outlined through a tripartite model, space is socially produced and characterized in terms of 'spatial practice' (perceived space), 'representations of space' (conceived space), and 'representational space' (lived space). Since the focus of this study is the production of space in broadcasting and media policies, I draw upon the concept of 'representations of space', a dominant form of space tied to relations of production, characterized as the 'space of scientists, planners, urbanists, technocratic subdividers and social engineers', through which power and hegemony are materialized.

For the purposes of this chapter, I define sovereignty as the power of the state—and other national and global entities—to reorganize and control space either through policies, legislation, law, or other extralegal activities. A persuasive account (Held, 1995: 20) of globalization refers to it as 'the stretching and deepening of social relations and institutions across space and time', and nationalism is understood as involved in the political and economic 'production of space' that is marked by territorial and geographic associations. Goswami and Sinha's work offers concrete analytic strategies to study the spatial discourse in broadcasting, particularly in terms of how nationalism and globalization have been and are involved in the reshaping of sovereignty and citizenship. In the following section, I contextualize the ideological construction of space and time in late colonial India that has implications for postcolonial developments. To this end, I briefly discuss a few influential accounts on colonial knowledge that have a bearing on my subsequent arguments about the spatiotemporal dynamics of broadcasting.

BROADCASTING AND SPATIOTEMPORALITY, AND POWER

Bernard Cohn (1996) argued that beginning in the 1770s, the colonial production of knowledge involved large-scale translations of Indian administrative, legal, and religious texts and treatises, and the concomitant deployment of investigative, historiographic, survey, and enumerative modalities through procedures of observation, measurement, classification, and ordering information and data about India. The colonial production of knowledge, Cohn (1996: 5) notes, was 'transformed into usable forms such as published reports, statistical returns, histories, gazetteers, legal codes, and encyclopedias' deployed by the East India Company to legitimize its rule and authority. According to Mathew Edney (1997), the utilitarian and imperial projects such as the Great Trigonometric Survey initiated in 1799–1800 that mobilized technical, geographic, topographic, and cadastral surveys to map and envision spatial contours of 'India' shaped the colonial ideologies of the Company rule until the Indian Mutiny of 1857 shook the foundation of the colonial enterprise.

For Goswami (2004: 7), British colonial India, 1858–1920, witnesses a 'profound restructuring of social space and time' that began with the transfer of power from the East India Company to the British Crown in 1858, as colonial domination gradually transformed itself from the mercantilist to the territorial phase. Goswami (2004: 8) deployed the term 'colonial state space' to describe 'the complex ensemble of practices, ideologies, and state projects that underpinned the restructuring of the institutional and spatiotemporal matrices of colonial power and everyday life'. Furthermore, Goswami (2004: 57) noted that 'the development of massive transportation structures—railways, bridges, irrigation projects, ports, canals, telegraph networks, postal services—marked the shift from the mercantilist policies of the East India Company to a new colonial political economy of space in post-1857 era'.

Goswami's study covered the period from 1858 to 1920, and her analysis of the then 'new' and emerging communication network of the telegraph is rather perfunctory, subsumed within other colonial state works such as railways, postal services, and irrigation projects. In fact, Goswami's discussion of the telegraph is limited to just three references and a page of analysis, describing how the global-imperial communication network facilitated the increasing circulation of capital and commodities across the British imperial space economy, the general effects of information, printing, and the telegraph on Indian society remained unexplored (Goswami, 2004: 45, 53). For instance, the telegraph's role in unsettling the existing communicative contexts and modes as it 'freed communication from the constraints of geography' and consequently 'separated communication from transportation' (Carey, 1989: 203). Thus, how the emergence of the telegraph in late colonial period impacted printing traditions and information networks is crucial to understating the spatiotemporal history of communication in colonial South Asia (for a similar critique of Goswami, see Sinha, 2012).[4]

Bayly's (1996) study of the intersections between precolonial and colonial information networks and printing traditions in India enables a better understanding of the communicative forms and systems. While generally agreeing with Foucault-oriented studies on the role of knowledge as crucial to colonial domination and conquest, Bayly (1996: 7), however, diverges from these studies arguing that the production of 'colonial knowledge and discourse was derived to a considerable extent from indigenous knowledge, albeit torn out of context and distorted by fear of prejudice'.[5] For Bayly (1996: 4), then, a deeper investigation into the knowledge/power complex requires that we study the relationship and interchange, wherein 'knowledge implies socially organized and taxanomized information'.[6] To this end, Bayly draws on theories of social communication of Harold Innis and Karl Deutsch, and adapts Manuel Castells' concept of 'information order' as the central framing device to examine the 'dialogic' and unequal interaction between the British information and surveillance networks, such as print and telegraph, and the South Asian elite scribal traditions constituted by languages and the emerging print cultures: *akhbarat* (newsletters, newspapers), *dawk* runners (native postal carriers), Hindu and Muslim religious and legal texts, and so on.

Bayly's historical study is compelling as it foregrounds the multiple, interpenetrating communicative and information modalities of knowledge. Indeed, this is in line with his earlier argument about the neglect of information and communication contexts; that is, the persistence of a 'deplorable gap between studies of economic structures, on the one hand, and of orientalism and ideology on the other' (Bayly, 1993: 97). This book has addressed this gap by situating the analysis of broadcasting and communication networks in relation to the wider social processes in late colonial and postcolonial India. Bayly's work is germane to my approach, particularly the analysis of how the spatial and temporal dynamics were shaped by colonial and imperial categories as well as nationalist consciousness. For instance, ideas about India's physical and geographical boundaries drew on the colonial forms of knowledge alongside ideas grafted from ancient Hindu texts such as the Puranas that circulate in the discourse of broadcasting.

Overall, the studies briefly discussed above point out that in the spatiotemporal production of India, the British categorized the administrative technologies and graphic representational practices of measurement, surveying, mapping into a classificatory grid of knowledge that was mobilized to control territories, govern and exercise authority. We can explore the configurations of power through what Foucault characterized as 'the triangle of power': sovereignty–discipline–governmentality that are clearly visible in the spheres of revenue collection, property rights, taxation, juridical practices, censuses, policing, establishment and introduction of institutions, and communication networks such as telegraph and broadcasting. The discourse of the telegraph, which significantly shaped the subsequent introduction of broadcasting in late colonial and postcolonial India, is at once evident in the spatiotemporal traces of the telegraph in broadcasting 'designs', reports, policies, experiments, and soon.

Roland Wenzlhuemer's (2013) structural analysis of the electric telegraph in the 1870s India pointed to its exclusive concentration in major urban cities and seaports: Bombay, Calcutta, Madras, and Karachi. The British telegraph network, Wenzlhuemer (2013: 225) argued, 'had not been designed to spread evenly across the colony. From its beginning, it concentrated mainly on important administrative and business centers and connected these with each other'. Wenzlhuemer's analysis of the spread of telegraph cables and routes, and communication traffic in the 1870s through the visual rendering of the telegraphic system (Figures 1.1 and 1.2) points to a remarkable similarity with broadcasting's evolving spatial grid in the 1930s and 1970s (Figures 1.3 and 1.4). While the figures empirically demonstrate the spatial similarities between telegraph and broadcasting, the spatiotemporal antecedents of telegraph in broadcasting can be traced to the imperatives and logics of colonial knowledge that prefigured broadcasting designs, plans, experiments, policies, legislations, and so on, for over seventy years.[7] Scholarly studies of broadcasting have not examined the persistence of colonial knowledge and telegraph ideologies that underpinned the spatiotemporality of broadcasting—radio and television—in late colonial and postcolonial India.

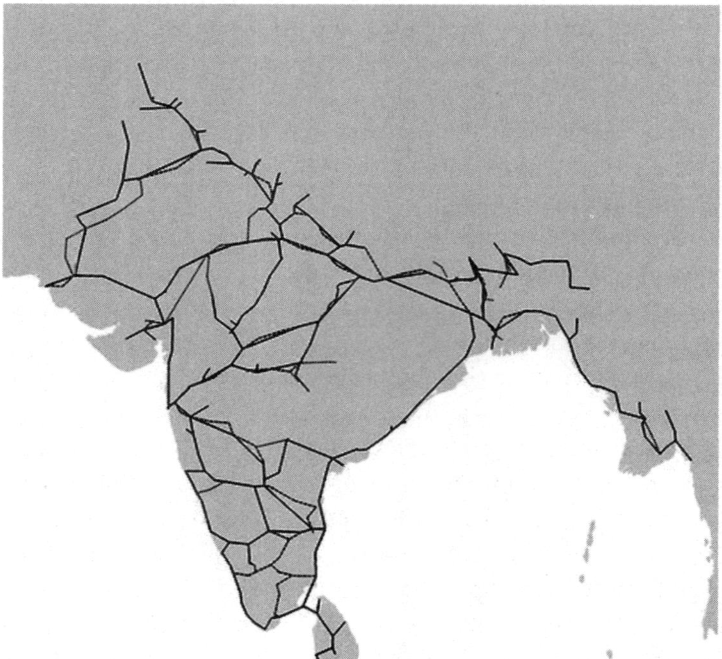

Figure 1.1 Telegraph's spatial grid

Source: Wenzlhuemer (2017: 221–223).

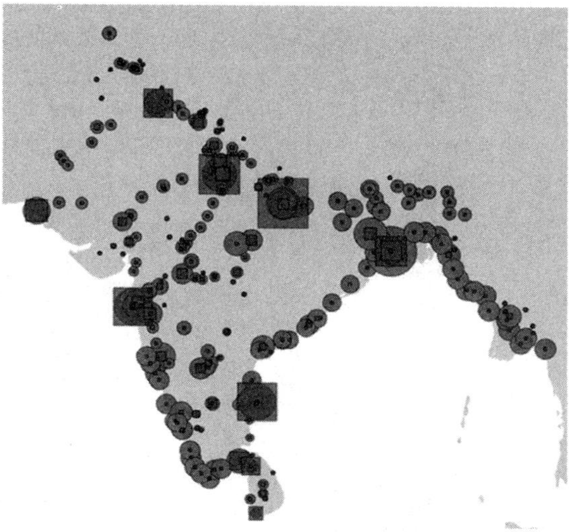

Figure 1.2 Telegraph's spatial grid

Source: Wenzlhuemer (2017: 221–223).

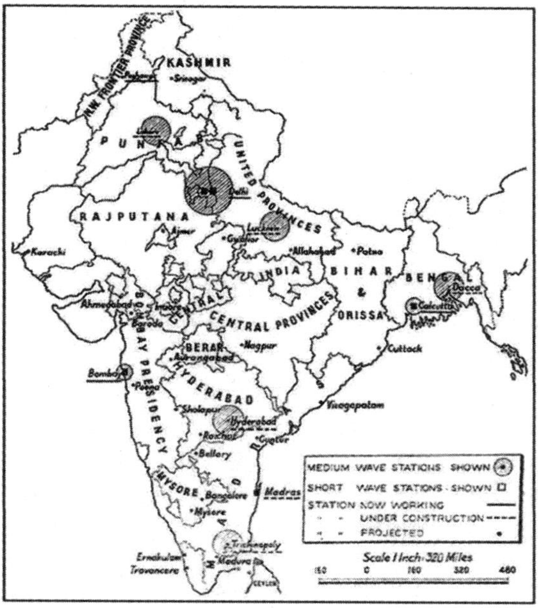

Figure 1.3 Broadcasting's spatial grid: proposed map of India's radio broadcasting stations, 1937

Source: Pinkerton (2008: 13).

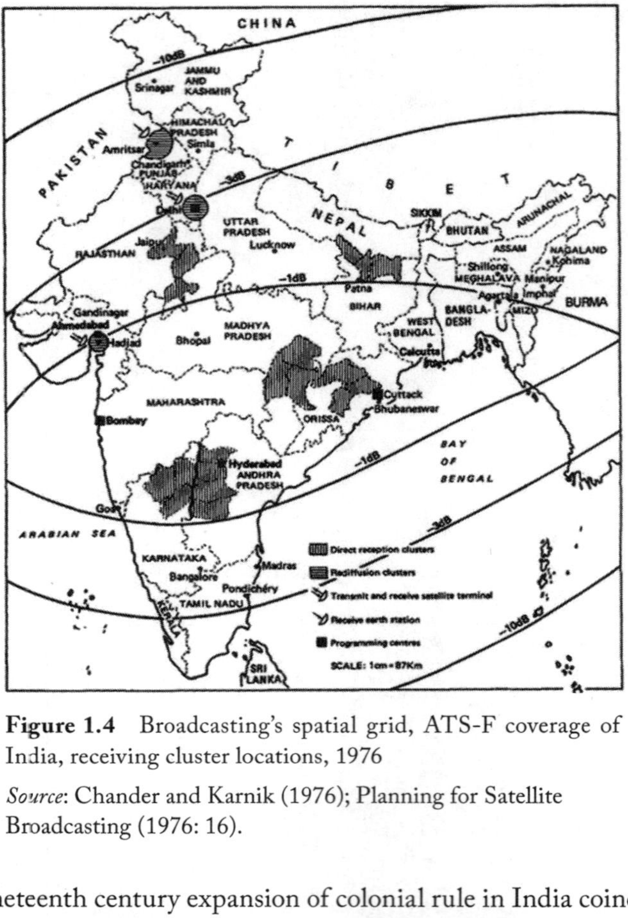

Figure 1.4 Broadcasting's spatial grid, ATS-F coverage of India, receiving cluster locations, 1976

Source: Chander and Karnik (1976); Planning for Satellite Broadcasting (1976: 16).

The nineteenth century expansion of colonial rule in India coincided with the establishment of the principles of liberalism in Britain. Liberal theorists have reframed the concept of sovereignty to include citizens' rights and freedom. However, these principles contradicted colonialism in India. In order to justify colonial rule, theorists like John Stuart Mill produced intellectual arguments for the postponement of these rights to Indians on the grounds that they have not yet reached the stage of political and civilizational maturity. As an organizing discourse of colonial sovereignty, then, liberal imperialism shaped administrative and bureaucratic procedures that the British applied in terms of various 'state projects' in India—geographic, cartographic, statistical surveys, enumerative practices, and so on—in the name of colonial modernization. Indeed, the configurations of colonial forms of sovereignty in India operated through several overlapping layers of power involving local landholding elite, provincial rulers, and religious authorities, who were granted permission by the colonial state to impose taxation, and adjudicate local courts and *panchayats* (village councils), but the ultimate power vested with the British colonial state (Hansen, 2008: 172).

The colonial construct of sovereignty—and with it, the procedures of governmentality—significantly shaped the spatialities of broadcasting. An example of liberal imperialism articulated in the *Plymouth Report* published by the Colonial Office in 1937 situated broadcasting as part of the 'machinery of civilization and administration' of native populations. Although the colonial and postcolonial spatialities of broadcasting exhibited distinct modalities of power, they share several common ideologies. For instance, colonial broadcasting's centralized control, programme formats, and construction of audiences through essentialized cultural categories were imbricated with postcolonial state's upper caste–class Hindu ideologies in subsequent developments in broadcasting (Lelyveld, 1990: 43). While agreeing with the overall arguments of Lelyveld, I (pace Sinha and Goswami) contend that several significant continuities and changes, informed by national and transnational contexts, shaped the development of broadcasting in colonial and postcolonial India.

Thus, on the one hand, the postcolonial state translated nationalist ideas embodied in the *swadeshi–swaraj* dialectic,[8] and on the other, reproduced the colonial state's administrative habits and procedures to realize progress and development in the name of nation building. In the following pages, highlighting the continuities and changes in the construction of the public, citizenship, sovereignty, and so on, I discuss the spatial and temporal discourse of broadcasting in several radio and television experiments—community listening schemes, public loudspeakers, low-power transmitters, linguistic–geographical surveys, programme formats and schedules, music and language debates, rural radio forums (henceforth, RRF), the Satellite Instructional Television Experiment (henceforth, SITE), Kheda Project, the subsequent privatization of television, and so on. To understand the transnational dynamics, to examine the dialectic relations between the national and the global, and to examine the construction of sovereignty and citizenship in broadcasting and media policies, I outline a heuristic framework (see Table 1.1 below) with particular emphasis on the intermeshing between and across the two modalities of power: sovereignty and governmentality.

The development and growth of broadcasting from the colonial to the postcolonial period has been increasingly shaped by transnational exchange of ideas and resources among several individuals and institutions—private capital,

British bureaucrats, engineers, army officers, American and British missionaries, the British Broadcasting Corporation (BBC), the colonial and the postcolonial state (Zivin, 1998; Das, 2006). In sketching the spatiotemporal modalities of radio, these bureaucrats drew upon colonial categories of knowledge about village communities inscribed in the colonial state's geographical and linguistic surveys. Strickland (1934) and Hardinge (1934) drew upon the liberal imperialist ideas espoused by the Indian Village Welfare Association (IVWA) of London on how to situate broadcasting as an instrument of administration in villages of India. While Strickland (1934) proposed a scheme for establishing several low-power 'district transmitters' and 'communal receivers' in rural areas, Hardinge (1934: 620) argued that 'the rural population of India is in urgent need of enlightenment', and 'broadcasting is the ideal method of producing both the stimulus and knowledge to move the villager to carry out those simple changes in his habits'. Hardinge (1934: 619) pointed out that the 'peasant needs short daily talks of a homely nature upon rudiments of hygiene, sanitation, child welfare, improved agricultural methods and marketing, and similar helpful subjects leavened with entertainment'.

Table 1.1 Spatiotemporal Configurations of Broadcasting in India

Time Period	*Spatial and Power Configurations*	*Broadcasting and Media Policies*
Late Colonial 1920–46	Absolutist concept of space Imperial *Trans*-nationalization Sovereignty and Colonial Governmentality	Radio shaped by colonial-spatial modalities; village 'uplift', public loudspeakers, community receivers, linguistic-geographic distribution of radio transmitters, music and language debates
Postcolonial I 1947–91	Absolutist concept of space *Inter*nationalization 'National' Sovereignty and Postcolonial Governmentality Sovereignty as a single-point perspective	Broadcasting and nation building: Radio rural forums, language and music debates, nationalization of programming, SITE and Kheda television initiatives, Verghese, Joshi committees, Special Expansion Plan for Television, INSAT
Postcolonial II Since 1991	Relativist concept of space Neo-liberal *Trans*nationalization 'National' Sovereignty and Postcolonial Governmentality Sovereignty disaggregated and unbundled	Privatization of television, local and transnational networks: Approach paper on culture, Haksar, Paswan, and Sengupta reports, Prasar Bharati Act

During the 1930s, India's villages figured prominently on the agenda of the colonial administrators who wanted to 'produce better villages through radio' (Zivin, 1998) and the anti-colonial nationalists led by Gandhi who considered villages and peasants as crucial to their struggle (Brayne, 1929; see also Sackley, 2011). Through paternalistic village broadcasting experiments, British bureaucrats, and later the colonial state, sought to curb the increasing popularity of anti-colonial nationalism in the countryside. In several radio experiments, the colonial state could only conceptualize the Indian 'public' as an amorphous collective of imperial subjects, rather than rights-bearing citizens. Framing their ideas of a bounded village space, and envisioning a collective radio audience, the colonial bureaucrats constructed the Indian 'public' through the design of loudspeakers, acoustic spread of community receivers, and the territorial gaze of transmitters. Ostensibly designed for village 'uplift' and for the peasants, the loudspeakers and community receivers 'locked' the rural audience into a one-way modality of communication.

By installing community receivers in the courtyards and rooftops of local elites—*lambardar*s, *Khans*, *zamindar*s, and village headmen—colonial bureaucrats incorporated local idioms of rule and power to prevent possible peasant unrest. Initially, the colonial state had authorized the police to install, maintain, and operate radio broadcast equipment, but colonial bureaucrats suggested that local village leaders and landowners would serve the British interests better that the police (Zivin, 1998). Thus, by embedding the spatialities of colonial radio in conjunction with the local 'power-geometries' (Massey, 1994: 39) in the villages and the countryside, colonial bureaucrats constructed a negative notion of the public, one that is to be controlled through broadcasting.

The 1930s colonial 'rural broadcasting model' in the North-West Frontier Province (NWFP), Peshawar, and Punjab can be seen as the progenitor for subsequent rural broadcasting initiatives in 1954–55 and 1975–77. Several key themes and arguments enunciated in the early 1930s found their way into RRF and SITE that centred on 'community listening', 'community receivers', district-level transmitters and production centres, construction of rural audiences, and so on.[9] In the early 1930s several colonial officials, army officers, retired British bureaucrats, missionaries, radio enthusiasts in Britain and India—Brayne, Hardinge, Strickland—as well as private individuals and interests referred to as the 'Guardians of village India' envisioned rural broadcasting for the improvement of socioeconomic conditions of villagers (Zivin, 1998: 718). Several 'village uplift' schemes were proposed with radio as the disseminator of information for the rural subjects. Zivin (1998: 724) noted that 'the guardians dedicated their energies to harnessing the radio to producing "better villages", as Brayne titled one of his handbooks'. More significantly, however, they were pursuing the ideologies of utilitarians, colonial liberalism, and missionaries inscribed within the rubric of 'moral and social improvements'.[10] Thus, for Hardinge (1934: 619), 'wireless, a miracle of the West, can be even greater service to the East, where scattered village communities live isolated, drab lives, and illiteracy predominates'.

Hardinge's (1934: 621) scheme of a three-tier structure for broadcasting comprised several high-power 'regional' stations in the vernacular languages and in English, numerous low-power transmitters in each province administered by provincial governments to serve rural areas, and a centralized high-power broadcasting stations catering to 'upper class' Indians featuring English programming and rebroadcasts of European and British programmes. Although the broadcasting structure proposed by Hardinge did not come to fruition, the ideas and sketches developed into concrete plans and designs in later iterations of rural broadcasting models in late colonial and postcolonial India. Another aspect of the early discussions of rural broadcasting in the 1930s relates to the international comparisons drawn between India and the Soviet Union, especially their vast geographic spaces and similar socio-economic conditions of the peasants. Strickland (1934), speaking on the topic, 'Broadcasting in the Indian Village' in London, outlined such a comparison which rattled the British colonial officials in Delhi. For them, radio was to be used as a tool of propaganda and was not imagined for India's rural development.

Despite the arguments and proposals for local, village broadcasting, the rural broadcasting model was subsequently situated within the constitutional principles of 'dyarchy' (dual government) adumbrated in the Government of India (GOI) Act 1919 wherein the overall power was vested with the central government, but several governmental duties and functions 'outsourced' to provincial governments (Gupta, 2002; Legg, 2016).[11]

The erstwhile Indian Broadcasting Service started in 1924 by private entrepreneurs staggered to remain afloat, and was eventually taken over by the British government and renamed as All India Radio (AIR) in 1935. In 1936, the Reith sent an engineer, H. L. Kirke (1936) to develop a broadcasting map of India. After an extensive tour and analysis of Indian conditions, Kirke proposed a decentralized system of broadcasting with numerous low-power transmitters around Delhi and other cities. While Kirke's surveys and maps drew on colonial knowledge practices, 'his technical surveys were remarkably sensitive to Indian conditions. This included an analysis of atmospheric conditions and their seasonal variations, geology (the magnetic properties of different soils), topography (mountains and plateaus) as well as population distribution and densities' (Lelyveld, 1990: 46). Kirke's surveys were attentive to the linguistic variations and led him to argue for a decentralized broadcasting system with several low-power transmitters with programming in the hands of local and provincial governments. However, his successor C. W. Goyder (1936–46), ignored Kirke's recommendations in favour of a centralized system wherein radio programmes would originate in Delhi and relayed to several regional centres. The idea of 'zones of broadcasting circles' was developed that employed colonial geographic and linguistic surveys, and soil and topographic studies of various towns and cities fit for radio transmission (Fielden, 1940: 41; see also Lelyveld, 1990). Thus, this particular spatial discourse of broadcasting envisaged through broadcasting circles and zones, and as a centralized system, gradually consolidated during the late colonial period and shaped several postcolonial experiments in radio and television. The Kirke report and the Goyder's plan, nonetheless, suggested distinct yet overlapping spatiotemporal modalities, especially in terms of low-power and short-wave transmitters, connecting the capital, Delhi with regional broadcasting networks.

In 1940, Lionel Fielden, the first controller of broadcasting produced a detailed report titled *Report on the Progress of Broadcasting* (henceforth *Report*), the first definitive official document on radio in late colonial India, through a selective ideological appropriation of the NWFP rural broadcasting experiment, Kirke's report, Goyder's plan, linguistic and census surveys, and the GOI Acts of 1919 and 1935, respectively, outlined a centralized broadcasting structure (see Lelyveld, 1993). The *Report* begins with a brief overview of broadcasting initiatives in India, with chapters of installations of terrestrial transmitters, broadcast stations, mapping the geographic reach of radio broadcasts and demarcation of coverage areas in terms of Service 'A', 'B', and 'C', and hours of programming; specifications on programme formats, rural broadcasting, categories, schedules, and so on, thus defining the temporal arrangements of broadcasting; creating categories of audiences in terms of rural, urban, class, caste, linguistic, gender, and religious variables and profiles; radio journals in vernacular languages and English; technical and engineering discussion of measurement of time, rays, field strengths, and relationship with posts and telegraph department, and so on.

While the *Report* did not explicitly invoke the BBC model and the overseas Empire Radio Service, it borrowed elements of the Reithian discourse of broadcasting with regards to the centralization of authority and power, and the imperial ideology of colonial broadcasting as an 'instrument of advanced administration' (Hill, 2010: 29), and for the 'moral and material improvement' of colonial subjects (Mill, 1858: 2). As Andrew Hill (2010: 34), among others, noted, the idea and practices of 'communal listening' was perfected by colonial administrators and missionaries in Africa and South Asia. Indeed, the ideological basis for this line of argument can be traced to how colonial broadcasting was imagined in the colonies, especially Africa and India, in the 1920s by colonial officials like Bowyer, who considered colonial broadcasting 'not as an instrument of entertainment ... but as an instrument of advanced administration ... for the enlightenment and education of native populations and their instructions in public health, agriculture, etc.' (quoted in Hill, 2010: 34).

The colonial administrative strategies in conjunction with orientalist presuppositions about India constituted the spatial and temporal arrangements of broadcast programming. For instance, the broadcast formats and schedules drawn up by the *Report* segmented programming into several categories, divided and subdivided across socio-economic and cultural variables such as rural, urban, language, religion, class, caste, gender, and so on. In fact, the notion of 'rural broadcasting' put in place through the early experiments, plans, programme formats, schedules, and the envisioning of the special category, 'the village programming' (Fielden, 1940: 51–53), draws on the idea of the 'village', a key ideological and spatiotemporal component located in Henry Sumner Maine's writings, channelled by colonial officials and missionaries (Thakur, 2014a). With regards to the News Services, the *Report* (Fielden, 1940: 28), for instance, argued in favour of centralizing the news broadcasts in conjunction with 'the Posts and Telegraph Department for the supply of special lines as those used by the BBC in England'. Similarly, the *Report* reproduced BBC's model of programme formats and schedules by constructing distinctive categories for urban ('educated') and rural ('illiterate' and 'backward') regions and audiences.

While Lelyveld (1990: 43) suggested that the structures of broadcast programmes and schedules such as rural programming developed during the first decade of radio (1927–37) in late colonial India have persisted into the postcolonial period, I argue that while the typology of the programmes remained in place, the rural broadcast formats in the postcolonial period expanded under the developmental state through planning and technocratic imperatives. What remained in place, however, were the colonial spatiotemporal constructions of the 'rural' and the 'village' which continue to frame the postcolonial iterations of rural broadcasting. The lineages of the 1920–30s colonial-imperial imagination of the rural and the village were reconfigured in the post–1950s period under the guise of the international–global discourses, thereby engendering complex topographies of power within which the rural and the village came to be embedded. For instance, several of these discourses underpinned the rural programming in radio and television in postcolonial India where the rural and the village were reconstituted as 'a category of development knowledge' (Sinha, 2008: 59) wherein a network of transnational knowledge experts at the behest of the United States foreign policy—integrated within the modernization paradigm—designed campaigns of 'rural reconstruction' and 'community development'.[12] For Sackley (2011: 482),

> While the focus on the village form began with the movement for rural reconstruction during the 1920s and 1930s, it assumed a new geopolitical urgency during the Cold War. Interwar projects to 'uplift' villagers had involved a loose transnational constellation of elite actors, from missionaries and colonial administrators to nationalist politicians and social reformers. In the era of decolonization and Cold War rivalry, village transformation became inextricably tied to projects of state formation, global hegemony, and imperial preservation.

The spatiotemporal organization of rural broadcasting in late colonial India, 1938–44, involved segmented broadcast structures, organized around broadcast 'zones' and 'circles' that comprised of clusters of villages around Delhi hooked up through transmitters, broadcast stations, and receiving radio sets. The 'audience' were groups of villagers assembled at a central location, usually in the guest areas and public spaces, *baithak*s and *choupal*s, which are part of the residences of local leaders and feudal notables such as *zamindar*s (landlords) *lambardar*s (hereditary landlords, with powers to collect revenue, exercising policing authority in the villages), and school teachers. Indeed, the template for this 'communal' or 'community' listening was drawn from the 1930s NWFP village broadcasting. For instance, AIR's Basic Plan of 1944, developed by Goyder, utilized linguistic surveys and censuses to produce geographic distribution of populations by languages in rural and urban provinces of India, mapping a spatial grid form radio broadcasting with over 125 broadcasting stations of which 90 stations were for rural audiences (Lelyveld, 1990). This particular spatiotemporal model persisted and consolidated in the postcolonial period, especially in RRF and SITE (Dhawan, 1974; Sanjay, 1989).

Furthermore, the spatial and temporal configurations of broadcasting adumbrated in the *Report* were structured in terms of the administrative modalities of governance and authority inscribed in the notions of 'dyarchy' and 'provincial autonomy' in the GOI Acts of 1919 and 1935 respectively. The GOI Acts were designed to rescale colonial sovereignty from the all-India, national to the regional/provincial levels, a governmental strategy to break up the rising tide of anti-colonial nationalist movement led by Gandhi which has been ascending since the early 1930s.[13] Thus, broadcasting in India was shaped by the economic and political imperatives of the British administration, particularly the global economic situation wrought by the 1929 depression in England, the rising popularity of Gandhi's anti-colonial nationalist 'Civil Disobedience' Movement in India, the mobilization of peasants in the countryside, and the provincial elections of 1937.[14] Partha Sarathi Gupta (2002) and Alasdair Pinkerton (2008) argued that the British sought to deal with anti-colonial nationalism's challenge to its authority by promoting the policy of 'provincial autonomy'. In 1937, under British constitutional reforms, local elections brought the Congress Party to power in several provinces of India. In the sphere of broadcasting, however, the immediate political imperatives led the British to keep control of broadcasting as a department of central government rather than a corporation advocated by John Reith. Gupta (2002: 466) noted that the constitutional mandate on provincial autonomy in the GOI Act of 1935 was designed as a 'divide and rule' strategy

> to deflect the energies of politically conscious Indians from all-India nationalism towards provincial politics, and thereby accentuate the cracks in the nationalist front. That political broadcasts could aid the divisive purposes of imperialism was fully understood by Conservative politician in London, though not by a seasoned bureaucrat in New Delhi.

To this end, Elangovan (2016: 66) argued that by formulating the constitutional provisions in terms of 'territorially distributing competing claims of sovereignty, the British government hoped to simultaneously strengthen the Empire and devolve power to the native population'. Although the *Report* did not proffer explicit political arguments about the nationalist movement, it employed the constitutional principles of the GOI Acts of 1919 and 1935 for the spatiotemporal organization of broadcasting in terms of a two-tiered structure, development of low-power, short-wave transmitters; provincial radio stations, and so on. The GOI Act of 1935 placed the institution of broadcasting under the central authority which remained unchanged in the 1950 postcolonial

India's Constitution. Evident in the spatiotemporal structure of broadcasting is a hybrid and peculiar mixture of power and authority, intermeshing elements of sovereignty and governmentality where several 'repertoires of authority' exist alongside administrative and bureaucratic technologies of power (Legg, 2016: 47).

As discussed above, whether one interprets the broadcasting experiments in terms of the 'instrument-effect' of bureaucratic-institutional penetration (Ferguson quoted in Sinha, 2008) or 'vertical encompassment' (Ferguson and Gupta, 2002), the spatial modalities and logics of such a discourse is materially produced. For instance, one of the first postcolonial broadcasting experiments, the RRFs, launched in 1954 as part of the national community development programmes, borrowed the colonial idea of 'zones of broadcasting circles' (Fielden, 1940: 41) that covered 150 villages in the Bombay State spanning 5 districts (Poona, Ahmadnagar, Nasik, North Satara, and Kolhapur). The colonial practices of linguistic and demographic analysis, population densities, and the urban–rural distribution framed the policies and programmes of rural radio experiments.

Both the colonial and postcolonial practices drew upon a range of 'transnational' exchanges of ideas, concepts, policies, and resources. Within such exchanges, colonial and postcolonial administrators proposed and implemented broadcasting and community development schemes, shaped by what Sinha (2008) characterized as a 'transnational development regime' that operated through the 'institutional matrix' created by this regime, combining aspects of colonial, national, and postcolonial logics along with forces outside the colonizer–colonized binary as well. Therefore, following Sinha, I assert that both the spatial discourse of India's community development project along with several imperial, colonial, and nationalist ideas and practices influenced the RRF. The postcolonial Indian state, through radio and television, framed ideas of sovereignty and citizenship through a set of pedagogic practices. From 1947 to 1991, the period that I have identified as postcolonial (see Table 1.1), the pedagogic practices in the context of broadcasting and media policies were, in large measure, influenced by the discourse of national sovereignty and development, pointing to both continuities and changes from the colonial period. For instance, the Indian 'village', as a geographic and territorial unit, represented by the colonial broadcasting model, the anti-colonial nationalist movement, and the postcolonial state, was enfolded into the development project through several administrative and bureaucratic practices. The organizational hierarchy, programme production units, and community listening centres of

RRF drew upon the bureaucratic structures of India's community development project: villages organized into development blocks with block development officer and village-level workers overseeing the running of the programmes.

Although communication scholars pointed to rural radio forums as successful broadcasting experiments, the benefits of the RRF were unequally distributed in favour of landowners rather than the poor (Singhal, 2006). More importantly, the spatial 'power-geometries' of the RRF sought to reinforce class and caste-based divisions in the rural countryside despite the fact that several radio programmes were designed to address caste-based and other social issues. After a few years, while the RRF were discontinued in the face of the failure of the larger community development projects initiated by the Indian state, the administrative and bureaucratic procedures reappeared in the development of television.

State-run television, Doordarshan (in English, Distant Vision), was introduced in 1959 after a series of discussions on its relevance to the state projects of national integration and social development enunciated and enumerated in the Constitution and outlined by the National Planning Commission. The first television experiment initiated in 1961 and sponsored by UNESCO and Ford Foundation sought to explore ideas of community development and citizenship through its programming. As part of the developmental agenda of the Indian state, a pilot agricultural programme, *Krishi Darshan*, initiated in 1967 around Delhi, drew upon the 1930s colonial idea of 'broadcasting circles'. Conceptualized and implemented by technological and scientific experts, *Krishi Darshan*, unlike the radio forums, explicitly mobilized technology that would become key to India's television experiments in subsequent years (Shingi and Mody, 1976). Both the 1961 and 1967 television experiments demonstrated the need for broadening television's reach by establishing larger terrestrial transmitters and a range of regional centres (in Hindi *kendra*s).

In 1975, India launched the most ambitious postcolonial television experiment anywhere, the one-year Satellite Television Experiment (SITE), designed by India's technocratic–bureaucratic elite—in consultation with UNESCO, and a satellite loaned from the USA—worked through the already established colonial spatial discourse: terrestrial radio centres that became television production/broadcast units. SITE covered 2,300 villages spread over twenty districts of six States (Rajasthan, Bihar, Orissa, Madhya Pradesh, Karnataka, and Andhra Pradesh). SITE's spatial reach facilitated by satellite broadcasting followed the colonial construction of broadcasting space in terms of linguistic and geographic surveys. This is visible in the idea of treating regions with established radio stations and hastily set up television broadcast and production facilities as 'clusters' and 'units'. Chander and Karnik (1976: 15) outlined this in their report on SITE thus: 'Each cluster area covers 3–4 districts and each district on an average has about 1000 villages, so the problem was to select 400 out of about 4000 villages.'

An important argument for starting SITE related to the idea of television as enabling a 'participatory democracy' through several short skits and docudramas that mixed everyday issues with larger goals of family welfare, health, sanitation, social ills, and so on, and aimed at rural students, farmers, and women. However, the developmental ideologies of SITE reproduced the colonial notions of 'village uplift' through the pedagogic and moralizing stance. Embedded within the pedagogic imperatives was the idea that such programmes could lead to an attitude change among people. The concepts of participatory democracy and attitude change were unable to dislodge deeply entrenched feudal, caste, and class relations in the countryside.

Around the time the SITE project was being implemented, technocrats at the Indian Space Research Organisation (ISRO) developed a smaller and more focused rural community television project, the Kheda Television project, as a hybrid decentralized broadcasting project that covered around 350 villages in the Kheda district. Both SITE and Kheda projects pointed to different and overlapping models for rural communication. For the radio and television bureaucrats, SITE served as a model for expanding and facilitating a commercial television network with hundreds of urban television transmitters, whereas ISRO technocrats argued for transmitters to be located in rural centres. In fact, as Satish Poduval (1999) argued, the notion of rural television embodied in the Kheda project might point to an alternate history of television in India; however, one needs to be careful in interpreting television's discourse of rural development and urban commercialism. William Mazzarella (2012: 219) likewise indicated that the history of television in India should not be portrayed as a straightforward transition between 'statist' and 'consumerist' ideologies; rather we ought to pursue an analysis of how both have similarly framed broadcasting in 'representative' instead of 'constitutive' terms, that is, to consider 'television according to its ability to represent or address supposedly pre-existing publics, as opposed to its power to help constitute those very publics'. I argue that the entrenched colonial-imperial ideologies in the structures of broadcasting in India, coupled with modernization and developmental ideologies blocked the potentialities of broadcasting in bringing about a genuine sociopolitical transformation. The failure of rural television in India has to be understood in the context of peasant unrest and labour strikes in the 1970s that led to the imposition of Emergency in India (Rajadhyaksha,

1990). Both SITE and Kheda television projects ran concurrent with the Emergency rule in India. The hegemony of the Indian state, in the face of the sociopolitical unrest, gradually shifted from developmental and socialist policies to free market-driven economics.

SITE created a new spatial context for satellite television in India by creating the necessary conditions for India's INSAT (Indian National Satellite Television) programme in the 1980s that was designed, among other things, to expand and facilitate the rise of India's commercial television services. Indeed, studies have noted that the 1980s geographic expansion of television in India, spurred by the INSAT space programme and the establishment of hundreds of low-power transmitters across the nation, was a significant attempt by the state to deal with the sociopolitical tensions (Rajadhyaksha, 1990; Butcher, 2003; Roy, 2008). With these massive infrastructural changes, national programming for television was being put in place, particularly through Doordarshan that would begin broadcasting from Delhi. Several regional centres located in Bombay (Mumbai), Calcutta (Kolkata), Madras (Chennai), and Bangalore (Bengaluru), along with numerous local terrestrial networks in smaller cities, were connected to Delhi and each other through satellite and terrestrial links. For several years (1982–91), the regional and local centres transmitted Hindi language programmes emerging from Delhi during primetime, and regional language programmes from their respective centres at other times. Thus, the centralized spatial expansion of television network and programming enabled the state to create the presence of a televisual *nation-ness*.

While the postcolonial broadcasting initiatives such as RRF and SITE in 1954–55 and 1975–77 respectively were designed as decentralized systems, they nonetheless reproduced the spatial and temporal structures of colonial rural broadcasting and village programming. Despite the attempts in inscribing the 'community development' and 'rural reconstruction' schemes into the programming structures, the initiatives posited 'villages' as self-subsisting entities, and 'farmers' and 'villages' as recipients of development. A cursory glance at the RRF and SITE rural programmes reveals the pedagogic imperatives of 'reforming' the villages and rural audiences who are perceived to be steeped in superstitions and obscurantist beliefs.[15] Furthermore, the technocratic imperatives of SITE, for instance, ignored the persistence of caste-based power relations, entrenched politico-economic, and social inequalities in the countryside (Mazzarella, 2012). The broadcasting discourse in RRF and SITE sought to transform rural, agrarian, religious communities into citizens of the nation. It is instructive to compare the ideological ways in which the 'village' and 'peasants' are interpellated in broadcast structures and rural programming with that of the literary televisual representations of rural life-worlds, the village, and the peasants that I examined in *Godān*, *Mailā Anchal*, and *Rāg Darbārī* in Chapter 2. The literarature-based series interpret the village and the rural life-worlds in terms of the complex mediations of sociocultural relations, the presence of capitalist and casteist exploitative practices, and the intrusion of the late colonial and postcolonial state into the local worlds.

RECONSTITUTING AUDIENCE AND THE BROADCAST PUBLIC

According to Richard Butsch(2007: 3),

> The noun 'audiences' makes it appear—and often makes us think—that audiences is a situated role that people temporarily perform ... the role is situated in institutions of entertainment, news, and media that construct subject positions for audiences and, in so doing, represent audiences. Governments, moral entrepreneurs, and others outside this relationship too have represented audiences through their discourse and response to audience.

Against this backdrop, how might we consider the genesis of the idea of audience and the broadcast public of radio and television in India's context, its subsequent iterations and reiterations in mediatic discourse? The question, who is the 'audience' of radio and television continues to perplex even though the influential scholarly work under the moniker 'audience studies' has examined the dominant categories of audience circulating in media discourses and listener and viewer interpretations of programmes, exploring the congeries of identities and their intersections across class, gender, race, ethnicity, and so on, pointing to both the ideological and agential dimensions of audience. In the following section, I examine the concept of audience and broadcast public in India, and the particular administrative and governmental discourses through which listeners and viewers have been constructed.

In a provocative argument on the potential links and divergences between audience and public, Daniel Dayan (2001: 746) noted that the public has remained undertheorized in relation to audience. He asserted, 'Audience turns out to be a "bad object", or as Livingstone put it, an empty shell, whatever remains after describing the public ... in comparison with the negative connotations of the "audience", a "public" is defined by a series of positive attributes.' When we consider the audience–public dialectic in India's late colonial and postcolonial context, however, a different set of ideas and attributes have marked the categories that yield a chain of negative valences. A brief hermeneutic–philological excursus into their iterations and usages reveals a broader range of meanings circulating in sociocultural contexts. Indeed, such an endeavour has been undertaken in the European context but has largely remained limited to the dictionary construction of the terms (Meinhoff, 2005). I outline brief linguistic and semantic provenance of the terms, and will not pursue a detailed philological analysis of how words acquire meanings and fresh significations between/across different linguistic registers and sociocultural worlds. What I want to point out, however, in the brief outline are the religious–secular imbrications of audience and public.

Audience: In Hindi, *shrota*, from *srot*, the ear, the source, one who hears, hearer (in Latin, *audiere* is 'to hear'). *Shrota gan* refers to listeners; *preksha*, looking at, beholding, observing, seeing, sight, view, look; any public show or spectacle; a play, dancing; conception, understanding, intellect, circumspection, consideration. *Prekshak* refers to spectator; *darshak* is used for viewer or spectator;[16] from the root word *darsan*. In Urdu, *nazir* is observer; spectator is *nazzaragiyan*, *tamashai*; the word *tamasha* straddles across languages, thereby receiving semantic charge in its usages. In other Indian languages, the words for audience and public acquire similar associations.

Public: In Hindi, *janata*, from the root *jan*, *janmat*, and *praja* (for people). In Urdu, *log* and *awaam*.[17]

The NWFP rural broadcasting experiment 'interpellated' the villager and the peasant who would benefit from radio not only ending their drudgery by providing 'doses' of entertainment but also, more crucially, improving their farming practices, animal husbandry, health and hygiene, and so on. Some excerpts below illustrate the envisioning of rural broadcasting in terms of the prevalent colonial-imperial ideas about the villages and peasants.

According to Hardinge (1934: 619), 'The rural population of the vast country is in urgent need of enlightenment, so that their lives can be made less drab.' For Strickland (1934: 1–2),

> Broadcasting has several duties to perform. It should in the first place entertain and interest, giving the peasant a mixed diet of song and story, preferably of the well-known kinds; for the countryman does not always seek novelty, but has old favourites—religious, sentimental, and humorous—which he welcomes again and again.

Thus, for Brayne (1929), 'broadcasting is the ideal method of producing both the stimulus and the knowledge necessary to move the villager to carry out those simple changes in his habits and methods that will make all the difference to his health, wealth, and happiness'.

The British colonial-imperial tropes and ideologies which prefigured the rural audience, the villager, and the peasant deployed a range of negative attributes and characteristics: ignorant, unruly, backward, uneducated, steeped in religious superstitions, and so on. Although the rural radio experiments in the NWFP were short-lived, this early envisioning of rural audience channeling the colonial-imperial imperatives about the villages as repositories of authenticity marked the rural audience as the 'other' in relation to the urban city-dwellers.[18] Indeed, the prefiguring of the audience continued to have a long afterlife in later colonial and postcolonial construction of rural broadcasting. In subsequent formulations of audience, the *Report* (Fielden, 1940: 67–68) elaborated socioeconomic and cultural categories to frame the radio listeners thus: 'A representative group of listeners would, perhaps, consist of A. The European. B. The Westernized Indian. C. The Educated Indian. D. The Middle Call Indian. E. The Patriots. F. The Nationalist. G. The Provincial. H. The Democrat. I. The Separatist. J. The Litterateur. K. The Villager.' While there are no specific arguments proffered as to why the radio listeners have been grouped, we notice a clear delineation between/across political, economic, and social categories. The 'villager' remains at the bottom of the list, clearly marked off as the anachronistic 'other'. The subsequent discussion in the *Report* on rural audiences considered them as ignorant and 'empty shells' in need of reform.

The idea of an audience research unit for radio broached for the first time in 1940, in fact, stemmed from the British colonial-imperial concerns about the popularity of overseas broadcasting among Indian listeners who were tuning into the BBC, Soviet, and German radio broadcasts in the Hindustani language. To stall the foreign 'propaganda', a permanent cell for 'audience research' was put in place (Luthra, 1986: 135; Gupta, 2002; Pinkerton, 2008). Interestingly, the AIR's need for the audience research unit drew on BBC's strictures on audience in Britain under John Reith's leadership which produced authoritarian and 'anti-democratic' tendencies. What we notice in the *Report* and the subsequent iterations of 'audience' are a complex set of unwieldy arguments and policy guidelines that produce a rural-urban spatial split in the audience, where the village audience came to stand in for all that is anachronistic and backward in relation to the urban audience. In his study of the BBC, Nicholas Garnham (1978: 35) has argued that 'just as the technocrat of industrial corporations have used advertising to control consumers and so eliminate unwanted fluctuations in demand, so the broadcasters used the statistical weapons of audience choices ... the need to control the audience rather than serve it is a fundamental system characteristic'.

In contrast to the dominant construction of radio audience and broadcast public by the AIR, local amateur radio clubs in Madras and Calcutta offered an egalitarian envisioning of audience. In Madras, the radio broadcasts of gramophone music in public places such as parks and beaches were widespread and popular. Hughes (2002: 454), in his study of the 'music boom' in Madras, noted that 'by early 1930s, the new sound technologies of radio and loudspeaker broadcasting contributed to the increased public presence of gramophone music. New means of broadcasting and amplifying records opened urban spaces for public consumption as never before'. This restrictive conception of public, produced by colonial broadcasting and carried forward in the postcolonial period, was visible in the music and language debates. What we notice are two distinct approaches to the emerging radio audiences and publics. The reformist zeal of AIR is evident in the colonial and postcolonial interventions into what constituted 'Indian' music on radio (Weidmann, 2006).

For the colonial broadcasting, 'orchestration and harmony are foreign to Indian music' and 'Indian music today with its tradition of a single melodic line stands in very much the same position as European music 400 years ago' (Fielden, 1940: 23). Furthermore, the *Report* (Fielden, 1940: 22) goes on to distinguish Indian music into various categories—'classical', 'light', and 'folk'— arguing that 'the whole of art music has largely fallen into the hands of prostitutes and mirasis and from this association has sprung a general feeling that there is something inherently immoral about music itself'. This reformist zeal in 'cleansing' music continued into the postcolonial period under B. V. Keskar, Minister of Information and Broadcasting from 1950 to 1962, the 'major formulator of the musical ideologies and policies of All India Radio' (Lelyveld, 1994: 111), who developed the concept of the National Programme of Music that was framed by upper-caste Hindu morality (Jeffrey, 2006). Keskar followed the colonial injunction on Indian music, combining the orientalist perspective with his 'Hinduized' caste-based and religious ideas about what constituted 'classical' music.

The nationalists, who came to power in 1947, blamed the British for neglecting Indian music, that is, classical music, and sought to reclaim Indian culture, along upper-caste, class, and religious lines. Many north Indian women musicians were barred from performing on AIR because of their 'immoral' antecedents. In the 1950s–60s, the high point of nation building, Keskar banned commercial Hindi film music from AIR for its corrupting influence.

Thus, the brand of nationalism promoted by the ruling elite in the sphere of broadcasting stood in sharp contrast to the 'secular, reformist, mildly egalitarian, cosmopolitan' nationalism that the anti-colonial movement espoused in its struggle against the British rule (Kaviraj, 1998: 150). Instead of transcending the colonial forms of sovereignty visible in the construction of the 'public', the ruling elite incorporated ideologies of class, caste, gender, and religion in the radio programme formats. Keskar's bureaucratic strictures blocked the possibilities for radio to either engage with nationalism or to foster a dialogue with the people. Radio could only produce a staid bureaucratic form of nationalism couched in a Sanskritized form of Hindi that was far removed from the everyday world of ordinary Indians. This was in line with how the postcolonial ruling elite framed various cultural institutions as spatializing sites for enacting the discourses of sovereignty and citizenship.

Several issues in the articulation of nation with respect to broadcasting included language as the first to bother the Congress government in independent India. Under the British it was decided to introduce Hindustani, a combination of Hindi and Urdu, as a common language of broadcasting which certain sections of the Congress had supported. The key figure in the formulation of language policy for radio was Ahmad Shah Bukhari, director general of AIR in 1939 under British rule. After India's independence, a detailed compilation of terms and phrases was undertaken to produce a language for AIR. Sardar Patel, independent India's first Home Minister in 1947 and one of the main nationalist leaders who formulated national integration policies for broadcasting, dismissed Bukhari from his official position in a political controversy generated around the implementation of a standard language for AIR. Bukhari, a former academic, suggested the amalgamation of Hindi and Urdu languages. Most nationalists, and most prominent among them was Patel, argued for a Sanskritized form of Hindi as India's national language.[19] Apart from these aspects, the growth and development of radio (and later television) was outlined through the rational logic of *The Linguistic Survey of India* that the British devised for mapping the country (Lelyveld, 1993). The establishment of terrestrial transmitters of medium-band wavelengths sought 'to accommodate 125 separate languages and cultural regions in a network of highly localized transmissions' (Lelyveld, 1990: 52). Within such governmental exercise was the desire to integrate the distinctive dialects and languages and the vast geographical regions of the country into a singular unit for administrative tasks. In contrast to radio, several popular films of this period developed an interesting synthesis of Hindi and Urdu into a sort of 'Hindustani' language through which a variety of meanings associated with nationalism were represented (Khan, 2006; Lunn, 2015). More importantly, the audience, the cinema public, conceived in terms of Hindustani and the multiple linguistic registers of India, is distinct from the governmentalized and bureaucratic representations of broadcast audiences and public.

In the context of broadcasting, a major redefinition of 'the public' can be located in the 1996 Supreme Court of India's judgment that declared the airwaves as public property. Despite its perceived novelty, this legal and juridical redefinition of the public drew on colonial logics and imperatives that had reframed the *actually existing* multiple publics in the eighteenth and nineteenth century India.[20] In both instances, law and courts were crucial to the redefinition of 'the public'.[21] While the colonial administrative and juridical interventions into South Asian social practices were far-reaching in the sense that the British were engaged in constituting colonial forms of knowledge to control and rule ('juridical sovereignty'), the postcolonial legal intervention sought to 'recode' the public in the language of 'private property', that is, through the principles of neoliberalism and market governance. While not attributing straightforward connections between the colonial and postcolonial redefinition of the public, it is nonetheless crucial to note the common administrative and juridical epistemologies underpinning the notions of 'the public' and 'public interest'. According to Ritu Birla (2015: 412), colonial market governance in 1870–1930 forged a homologous relation between 'public utility' and 'the rule of law', wherein

> the very inscription of the market coincided with the production of an abstract all-India public, not a citizenry, but the object of the paternal civilizing project of colonial policy. Moreover, as the colonial state gave way to the developmentalist nation-state, it may be argued that the rule of law fortified, rather than limited bureaucratic-administrative authority, again in the name of public agency.

The compound phrases, 'public interest' and 'public utility' are invoked extensively by the Supreme Court in connecting the notion of audience, listeners and viewers of radio and television to the notion of public. In addition, the judgment yoked together numerous court decisions and legal discourses on broadcast media from the U.S., Britain, and European contexts.

As noted in the introduction, most journalistic and scholarly discussions of the Supreme Court's judgment have explored the Court's operative statement, 'the airwaves are public property', contextualizing it in terms of public service broadcasting and the creation of a statutory broadcast authority, the Prasar Bharati. The Court's reconceptualization of 'the public' via several prior Indian court decisions, legal and juridical arguments, rights discourse, and so on, have remained underexplored. More crucially, a study of the particular ways in which the public was embedded in prevailing governmentalized notions such as 'public good', 'public interest', and 'public utility' would reveal the ideologies undergirding the Court's notion of the public. In fact, a sole exception is Ashish Rajadhyaksha's (1999; 2011) work which offered a comprehensive exploration of the judgment's imagination of 'the public'. In a recent study, Rajadhyaksha (2011: 47, my emphasis) traces the genealogy of 'the public', noting that the Supreme Court judgment tethered the '"laws of free market" [and] manufacture of a largely fictitious "public" [to] autonomous commercial institutions from governmental control *in the name of this public*'.

For Rajadhyaksha, the Court's iterations of the public point to its problematic envisioning. The Supreme Court's judgement gleaned the idea of the public through its exposition of broadcast systems and law in the United States and Europe, broadcast regulations and policy guidelines, the embeddedness of free speech and rights, and so on. The judgment noted that

> broadly speaking, broadcasting freedom can be said to have four facets, (a) freedom of broadcaster, (b) freedom of the listener/viewer to a variety of views and plurality of opinion, (c) right of the citizens and groups of citizens to have access to broadcasting media, and (d) the right to establish private radio/TV stations.[22]

Rajadhyaksha (1999, 2011) explores each of the facets pointing to their potential pitfalls and conflicting ways on which the public is imagined. Indeed, 'having access to public', 'public property', 'public service', and 'public interest' that underpin the judgment sit uncomfortably in relation to each other. What we notice in the Supreme Court's construction of the broadcast public and audience, therefore, is a re-enactment of the history of broadcasting, audiences, and public produced through privatization of the public domain undertaken by legal and juridical discourses in the West. In the Indian situation, however, this becomes more complicated as colonial and imperial legacies continue to persist and get imbricated with neoliberal governmentality into the postcolonial period.

Media and communication studies scholars in the United States and Britain have noted that each of the iterations have complex genealogies and histories that have framed broadcast structures, audiences, and publics (Garnham, 1973; McChesney, 1990; Butsch, 2007). Butsch (2007: 85 and 87), for instance, noted that the Radio Act of 1927 in the United States had declared 'airwaves as public property' yoking commercial and private interests borrowing 'legal terminology applied to railroads, defining them as common carriers and requiring them to offer their services unbiased to the public generally'. Indeed, this notion of broadcasting in the public interest continued its journey through other acts and laws, especially when in 1954 the US Congress formulated the argument that 'the spectrum is a natural resource [to] benefit the public interest'. Butsch (2007: 87) asserts that

> after the passage of the 1927 Act, for example, the Federal Radio Commission interpreted public convenience in such a way as to prefer commercial over non-profit stations, which they called 'propaganda stations'. Thus, while the ideal of publics remained part of the discourse about radio audiences, institutions that might have a force for realizing the ideal of radio public sphere were systematically neutered.

Although there was a spurt in state-sponsored commercial programming during the 1980s, a significant number of programmes produced during this period dealt with separatist and subnational movements in Punjab, Kashmir, and the nationalist movement constituting the discourse of the state that sought to construct national culture on television. Therefore, the construction of nation via television was one way through which the state sought to cope with the cracks in its hegemony during the intervening years, 1982–91, before the arrival of private television. Empirical data on television during this period demonstrates the spatial consolidation of Doordarshan and the rise in sponsored commercial programmes indicating television's shift from state-led developmentalism toward market-based consumerism. Manjunath Pendakur (1991) and Abhijit Roy (2008: 38) noted the shift as a consequence of a particular ideological grafting of consumerism into pro-development television forms as a concrete instance of a 'certain negotiation between the State and the Market in the context of an emergent commercial popular in the 1980s'. The dialectic between state and market marks an important phase in television in India. While a certain form of entrenched state capital was visible in the development of broadcasting until 1982, the seven-year period 1983–90 and post-1991 demonstrate the rise of national and transnational capital, propelled by what has been commonly referred to as media globalization.

After 1991, as private television networks started broadcasts using satellite communication, the government expanded the range of programming by setting up four new channels through the Indian National Satellite (INSAT) system. The second channel, 'Metro Network', was initiated as a competitor to the private entertainment networks like Zee, STAR, Sony, and so on. As is well known, satellite television, unlike terrestrial and geographic-based broadcasting, breaks down boundaries between rural, urban, regional, and national borders, thereby complicating the notions of sovereignty and citizenship. In the following section, I offer a brief discussion of a few media policies in India by focusing on the spatiotemporal discourses of nation, citizenship, and sovereignty. This account of how spatiotemporal modalities inflected media policies can be traced back to the history of broadcasting in India that I examined in the previous sections.

SPATIAL DISCOURSE IN MEDIA POLICIES

The postcolonial Indian state, through a combination of coercion and consensus, has historically negotiated with broadcasting through a series of measures legitimated by the Constitution. The governmental documents, committee reports, inquiry commissions, and draft policies represent 'sites' where a 'spatial discourse of power' operates. This spatial discourse is represented by the way in which a series of policy decisions were implemented in the expansion of broadcasting, particularly television, during the early 1980s. The numerous laws, acts, and policies relating to broadcast media are instances of the coercive spatial strategies that embody the project of national integration and the construction of national culture (Prasad, 1998). The spatial discourse in media and broadcasting policies in the periods 1947–91 and post-1991 points to major shifts in the state and market dialectic. Broadcasting and media policies during 1947–91 were articulated in terms of two types of policies, cultural and communication. In the case of cultural policy, the 'state seeks to produce certain educational and aesthetic outcomes amongst the people' (Cunningham and Miller, 1994: 23), whereas a communication policy engages with questions around technology, ownership, and structure of a broadcast organization. However, with the rise of private and satellite television since 1991, it is through regulation/deregulation of communication media, and policy transfer mechanisms that sovereignty and citizenship have been reframed. For instance, since 1996, the formulations of media policies and legislation, assigned to transnational private corporations, can be located within a neoliberal policy regime where market-driven logic reconfigures sovereignty and citizenship.

In order to demonstrate the spatial discourse in media policies, I shall briefly focus on several committee reports and parliamentary legislations. The Janata Party government constituted a committee (hereafter Verghese Report) in

1977, with B. G. Verghese, a former newspaper editor, as its chairperson, to examine a series of issues that centred on granting autonomy to the state-owned broadcast media, radio and television. The Verghese Report, published in 1978, recommended the establishment of an autonomous corporation, Akash Bharati, under which radio and television were to be operated. The Congress Party, which came back to power in 1980, blocked the passage of the Verghese Report in the Indian parliament, with members arguing that the country was not ready for an autonomous broadcast media. Following this, many ad hoc structural and technological changes were undertaken to prepare Doordarshan for the Asian Games in New Delhi in 1982. As Doordarshan expanded its spatial reach across the country, it lacked the ability to produce regular commercial programming needed to fill the daily broadcast slots. Thus, after that sports spectacle, for which broadcast changes were undertaken, Doordarshan faced a crisis in the form of an acute lack of programming material for broadcast. In December 1982, the Government of India appointed P. C. Joshi as the chairperson of a committee (hereafter Joshi Report) to formulate 'a software plan for Doordarshan' (P. C. Joshi, 1984).

The Prasar Bharati Act passed in the parliament in 1990 sought an autonomous broadcast corporation for radio and television and offered several changes—structural, legal, financial, and technical—for the state-owned broadcast media. Many provisions of the Prasar Bharati Act, despite being ratified in the parliament, were not implemented for political reasons. In 1996, a comprehensive report, 'National Media Policy: A Working Paper', drafted by several members of the Indian Parliament, with Ram Vilas Paswan as the chairperson (hereafter Paswan Report), argued that satellite television threatens India's sovereignty and territorial integrity. A three-member committee with Nitish Sengupta as its chairperson (hereafter Sengupta Report) reworked and reformulated some core notions in the Prasar Bharati Act of 1990 (1–2), and argued that

> dramatic changes have taken place at a dizzying pace on the media front since the passing of the Prasar Bharati Act in 1990. The advent of satellite channels and their rapid proliferation has substantially transformed the environment [and] complete rethinking of the role, organization and functions of Prasar Bharati became necessary in a multi-channel scenario, mostly driven by market forces.

Most discussions within policies took up issues of sovereignty and citizenship and linked those with territoriality, particularly through the geographical metaphor. The deployment of a geographical imagination figured frequently in all policies but with differing emphasis on particular issues. For instance, both the Verghese and Joshi Reports argued that by setting up low-power transmitters across the country the Indian state sought, in geographic and linguistic terms, to provide radio and television a 'national' presence. To 'imagine' a nation, the Verghese and Joshi Reports argued, geographic and linguistic integration of places, people, and communities was a central mission. The Joshi Report (1982: 45) argued that cultural communities residing in districts could be reached through the use of low-power transmitters. This 'mapping' of India, by the use of terrestrial technology linking Doordarshan centres (called *kendras* in Hindi) into a network, would help to 'attain the national objectives of unity and development'. The Hindi term, *kendra*, is infused with social power, that is, it denotes a notion of power and authority that is centralized. The semantic and linguistic force of the term also designates it as a centre from where national development programmes are relayed, and that the transmitters would serve production of 'area-specific' programmes catering to the needs of the local population. Thus, the primary metaphor in the Verghese and Joshi Reports, geography—invoked in multiple ways through references to space, place, territory, borders, and boundaries—gives a 'hinge' to the idea of India as a nation. The nation's identity is constructed by linking geography with sovereignty, whether spoken in political, economic, or cultural terms. Protecting and securing borders and boundaries from 'outside' forces, whether from the 'evil' designs of neighbouring countries or cultural imperialism of the West, marked the language. The very title of the television system, Doordarshan (Hindi for 'distant vision') suggests a certain mythic and geographical imagination at work.

Furthermore, the spatial construction of India as a nation that underpins the notions of sovereignty and citizenship is represented in Verghese and Joshi Reports through the 'fabrication' of a putative past. Ideas of *essence* and *destiny*, *transcendence* and *continuity* are linked to the nation's imagination. Though the term 'Bharati' in Sanskrit refers to language, it also signifies 'India', that is, 'Bharat' (as in the nation's Constitution). This double inflection of the phrase is more than a semiotic twist, for it carries a particular spatial history that has informed the nationalist project (Goswami, 2004; Deshpande, 1998). The Verghese Report in naming the report *Akash Bharati* tries to reconstruct the nation in a mystificatory and exclusivist manner. The phrases 'national values', 'unity in diversity', and 'national goals' produce a particular conception of a nation whose identity is fixed in the past. The Joshi Report made similar assertions about the nation that is signified through several phrases and clauses that are used in conjunction with one or more discursive elements—of essence, destiny, continuity, and transcendence—which form a silent subtext to the arguments, suggesting that the main task of communication policy is maintenance and preservation of national values.

While the Paswan and Sengupta Reports drew upon the arguments of Verghese and Joshi Reports regarding the ideas of nation, they were directly concerned with the influx of satellite television into India and focused on issues of 'uplinking' from Indian soil. The ideas around territoriality and sovereignty are deepened due to the 'invasion from the skies'. This 'invasion from the skies', they argued, requires a laissez-faire doctrine for programme production and broadcasting (Sengupta, 1996: 11). What is needed, according to them, are a new set of juridical and legal instruments. The Sengupta Report contains an extensive discussion of these issues noting that 'the new technologies [satellite based] have demolished the monopoly of state-run electronic media and rendered redundant the regulations. Loosening of controls is a global phenomenon' (Sengupta, 1996: 69). As a result of its argumentation, the report concluded that terrestrial broadcasting should not remain a monopoly of the Indian state and that private broadcasting companies should be allowed into India. Although the Paswan and Sengupta Reports have gradually moved away from the absolute concept of national sovereignty, the spatial discourse in India's media policies indicates a realignment of state ideologies with market forces that have resulted in contradictory articulations of citizenship with the consumer-subject (Rajadhyaksha, 1999).

In 1996, India's Supreme Court ruled that airwaves are public property to be regulated by an independent public body, not by the government. Although the Court's judgment called for the creation of an autonomous zone mediating the interests of the Indian public, the underlying logic suggested a move toward a public being thought in terms of a free market consumer public, or more precisely the citizen-as-consumer. On the one hand, the parliamentary reports and the committees outlined strategies in regulating private satellite television and raising revenues through advertisements and commercial sponsorship, while on the other hand, they were ostensibly promoting private broadcasting.

CONCLUDING REMARKS

This chapter demonstrated how a spatiotemporal approach to broadcasting and media policies within a *trans*national framework enabled a better grasp of the changing power dynamics of sovereignty and citizenship in colonial and postcolonial India. In several broadcasting experiments and media policies, sovereignty and citizenship were produced in terms of hegemonic articulations of territoriality, geography, populations, and people. A closer examination revealed how spatial and temporal modalities inflected the changing configurations of nationalism, sovereignty, public, audience, and citizenship as part of a wider set of ideas that flowed among individuals and institutions as part of a 'transnational development regime' (Sinha, 2008: 57). Importantly, colonial spatial and temporal practices significantly shaped anti-colonial nationalist movement's ideological programme as well as the postcolonial Indian state's broadcasting experiments. Although my study dealt with India, I argue that a sustained examination of broadcasting and media policies in postcolonial societies, particularly in the context of the increasing presence of information and communication technologies (ICTs), the Internet, and the various 'new' media modalities offers substantive analytic insights into the spatial materialism of how localities and places—urban cities and rural towns—intersect with the spaces of media flows—regional, national, and transnational (Hay, 2001). Furthermore, in much of the postcolonial world, economic globalization has precipitated the rise of neoliberal forms of governance that has influenced broadcasting and media policy-making in a variety of ways. The ongoing developments are also leading to new kinds of alliances between state and private—local as well as transnational—corporations in regulating and controlling the media environment. The widespread deployment of 'policy transfer' discourse underpinning the formulation of media policies is reconfiguring the notions of sovereignty and citizenship. While most studies in media and communication have understood the reconfiguration of sovereignty in terms of its diminution, some scholars considered sovereignty as being 'disaggregated' and 'unbundled' into multiple components of power, and pointed out that, in fact, nation-states reassert their authority through a range of political, legal, and economic strategies (Ruggie, 1993; Ong, 2006). However, missing from such studies is a sustained examination of state and neoliberal spatialities with respect to broadcasting, media policies, and ICTs, and the concomitant reshaping of sovereignty and citizenship.

NOTES

1. The notion of spatial discourse will be sketched out in greater detail in the theoretical section. Broadly, it is understood in terms of what Henri Lefebvre (1974) characterized via his triadic formulation of space embedded within politico-economic and material contexts of production, distribution, and circulation. The notions of

'national' sovereignty and governmentality as two modalities of power referring to broadcasting and media policies will be discussed in the theoretical section.

2. From an international communication perspective, Kaarle Nordentreng and Herbert Schiller's (1979, 1993) two-volume collection of essays explored national sovereignty and media systems in the 'third' world contexts. A recent book edited by Morris and Waisbord (2001) on media globalization and state offered an interesting set of essays on media and sovereignty. For a succinct elaboration and historical overview of the media debates around national sovereignty from the 1950s to the present, see Chakravartty and Sarikakis (2006).
3. According to Foucault, modern power operates through the triangle of 'sovereignty-discipline-governmentality', where discipline works through the bodily and mental techniques of the individual, sovereignty represents the language of rights, and governmentality, various techniques and strategies of managing populations.
4. In addition, Sinha (2012: xxvii) argued that Goswami's work does not pay enough attention to the precolonial developments, especially the overlaps between colonial and precolonial state practices; and inadequate analysis of roads, railways, transport and communication as well as post and telegraph which are crucial to the formation of the colonial state space. Citing Chowdhury's study of the telegraph in late colonial India, Sinha argued for considering roads, railways, and post and telegraph as potential areas of research. In a similar vein, Pinkerton (2008: 2) noted that 'the developments of the railway, the telegraph and uniform postage during 1850s may have instituted India's "nineteenth century communications revolution", but it has also helped spark the touch-paper of early Indian nationalisms; the improved state of transport and communications allowing latent ideas and attitudes to travel and ferment into broader political movements'.
5. It is worth quoting Bayly (1996: 25) in full here: 'Following Foucault and Said it is often taken as axiomatic that the influence of a knowledge or a discourse both reflects and substantializes the political "weight" of its authors. Yet we shall suggest that in pre-colonial and colonial times the emergence of systems of knowledge could equally well reflect the weaknesses of power and legitimacy, or situations of intense social competition. Assertive "knowledges" might grow up on the troubled margins of power. This apparently challenges Foucault's main theses, but it is consonant with his historical account of the emergence of "insurgent knowledges," from the margins of post-war French life'. See also Pinch (1999: 376–77) on Bernard Cohn and Chris Bayly's relationship to Foucault's work.
6. Through a hermeneutic and philological register, Bayly unpacks the prevalence of multiple meanings of 'information' and 'knowledge' in India languages: for instance, information interpreted/understood through words such as such as *khabr*, *suchna*, knowledge in terms of *ilm* and *vidya*, and also in its spiritual context as *gyana* or *jnan*. Throughout his study, Bayly explores the multifarious senses in which information and knowledge congeal and circulate.
7. There is a general agreement that British colonial administrative, bureaucratic procedures, and politico-legal frameworks have influenced the postcolonial Indian

state practices. Partha Chatterjee (1993: 204) noted that 'the new [postcolonial] state chose to retain in a virtually unaltered form the basic structure of the civil service, the police administration, the juridical system, including the codes of civil and criminal law, and the armed forces as they existed in the colonial period'. With regards to broadcasting, see Lelyveld (1990).

8. According to Goswami (2004: 4) Indian nationalism 'yoked together the demand for *swaraj* (self-rule, independence) with the developmental ideology of *swadeshi* (indigenous manufactures)', by frequently drawing upon a range of ideas, idioms, metaphors, and symbols from European as well as nativist contexts.
9. The lineage of the RRF and SITE can be traced to mixed parentage; across the colonial–imperial, nationalist, international, and global. RRF drew on Canada's Farm Radio Forum experiments of 1941 (see Neurath, 1962), and SITE was mobilized through the efforts of Indian Space Research Organization (ISRO), Ford Foundation, NASA, and UNESCO (see Chandar and Karnik, 1976; Sanjay, 1989).
10. A main argument of the utilitarians and colonial liberalism was that the British should pursue projects of 'moral and material improvements' (Mill, 1858) in India. Such ideas percolated into the early envisioning of rural radio experiments involving a diverse set of actors, all united in a singular 'civilizing mission' (Mehta, 1999).
11. According to Legg (2016: 45), the genealogy of the political term 'dyarchy' is derived from 'diarchy', that is, 'government by two rulers', which was how the British designed the structure of the provincial governments in India. While this is also referred to as leading to the devolution of powers, dyarchy or dual government originated in East India Company's 'diwani' rights in Bengal. For Partha Sarathi Gupta (2002), the constitutional idea of dyarchy was manipulated by the British to institute 'divide and rule' policies.
12. In fact, the projects and discourses of 'rural development and reconstruction' and 'community development' in India involve multiple institutions and social actors. For a discussion of the history of the 'village' in India, and its production as a conceptual idea, see Thakur (2014a and 2014b).
13. The global political currents, and more specifically the rising all-India popularity of anti-colonial nationalist movement, forced the British to implement constitutional reforms. Although the notion of provincial autonomy was embodied in the Government of India Act 1935, it was used before as a political strategy of 'divide and rule' to counter threats to British authority. For a splendid account of the development and politics of radio broadcasting, see Partha Sarathi Gupta (2002).
14. The provincial elections of 1937 in which the Congress took part were themselves devised to break up the unity of the nationalist movement by dividing authority and governance along class and caste lines, and to curtail Gandhi's increasing popularity with the peasants (see Muldoon, 2009).
15. See Mathur and Neurath (1959), especially pp. 30–38, for a list of RRF radio programmes, and Chander and Karnik (1976: 34–37) for a list of SITE's television programmes.

16. According to Luthra (1986: 434), the word *darshak* was coined by J. C. Mathur, director-general of AIR in 1959 for television viewer (the word 'Doordarshan' [Hindi for 'distant vision'] for state-run television was also coined by Mathur.
17. See the Digital Dictionaries of South Asia, available at http://dsal.uchicago.edu/dictionaries/platts.
18. On 'othering' of the farmers in the radio discourse in 1920s America, see Patnode (2003).
19. After formal independence from the British in 1947, Sardar Patel was the most prominent nationalist leader who was in charge of integrating various provinces and regions as part of India. The second phase of the reorganization of provinces and territories as states in the Union of India was based on language. Patel's views on 'India' come dangerously close to right-wing ideology that seeks to frame the nation within a dominant Hindu perspective. Several scholars have pointed out to the disagreements between Patel and Jawaharlal Nehru after India attained independence in 1947. Patel has been popularly called as the 'Iron Man' of India. Patel died in 1950 but his ideas continued to shape broadcasting reforms under B. V. Keskar, who served as the Information and Broadcasting minister for a long period.
20. Scholars have pointed out to the existence of multiple publics that overlapped with diverse narrative traditions and theatrical forms in precolonial and colonial India such as the 'bhakti publics' (Bayly, 1996; Bhandari, 2006; Novetzke, 2007; Orsini, 2009; Agrawal, 2012; Dubrow, 2017), an expanding reading audience and public of serialized fiction (Ratan Nath Dar's Urdu novel, *Fasana-E-Azad* and Devaki Nandan Khatri's Hindi novel, *Chandrakanta*, for instance) in the late colonial period. For a discussion of multiple publics, see the Epilogue.
21. It was through the legal and juridical apparatus that the British sought to engage and intervene in the religious domain and the public. David Gilmartin (2015), and before him Bernard Cohn (1996), argued that colonial courts and law were central in reshaping 'the public' in binary relation to 'the private'—a category that was problematic in South Asian context because the public–private distinction did not apply. For Gilmartin (2015: 375), '"religion" was reconfigured as a category as religious authority came to be subject to colonial litigation'. See Barton and Ingram (2015) and Freitag (1991: 2015) on public and religion.
22. The Secretary, Ministry Of Information and Broadcasting vs Cricket Association Of Bengal & ANR on 9 February 1995, available at https://indiankanoon.org/doc/539407/, p. 88 (accessed on 1 March 2018).

the televisual reconfigurations of myth and realism. Indeed, in the present moment of globalization and 'neoliberal' conjuncture in India, and in the larger contexts in which scholars have characterized television as part of the machinery of capitalism, it is crucial to develop critiques to *engage with forms of television*. This chapter offers such a critique by exploring specific forms of literary-based televisual narratives.

To develop such an analysis, I engage with Paul Ricoeur's philosophical hermeneutics, and certain strands of neo-Marxist and postcolonial perspectives.[1] Ricoeur's work, largely ignored in cultural and media studies, offers productive avenues in examining multiple temporalities in television narratives in terms of the stories, plots, and the intersubjective webs of relationships between and among the characters and their life-worlds.[2] In the British context, a discussion on television and narrative forms, on the question of realism and melodrama, largely shaped by the film studies–based *screen theory* perspective, focused on the processes of televisual identification, narrative space, strategies of gaze, and so on. On the one hand, this discussion, influenced by a reading of Marxist and Freudian formulations, had opened up a significant area of inquiry, while on the other, it also pointed to several theoretical conundrums in analysing television. Although such studies might consider the narrative structures, semiotic codes, psychoanalytic identification, and narrative voice, I argue that Ricoeur's hermeneutic approach enables a better analytic grasp into the televisual construction of myth, realism, and melodrama. More specifically, this chapter brings Ricoeur's concepts of narrative identity, temporality, and imaginary into a productive dialogue with postcolonial scholarship.

To pursue the connections between television and narrative form, I invoke Raymond Williams's (1977) work on realism that sought to provide a historical and contextual understanding of how realism is indeed a mediation of various cultural forms. If realism, following Williams, were to be understood as a highly variable and multi-textured concept, inflected by specific articulations of myth and melodrama, then the notion of development realism would be one among several other kinds of realisms. Scholars have pointed out that a slew of serials on the state-run television network, Doordarshan, particularly during the years 1983–91, articulated aspects of postcolonial Indian state's developmental ideologies embodied in ideas of family planning, education, progress, modernization, and so on. Indeed, with respect to cinema, the postcolonial Indian state had earlier mobilized several filmmakers to produce films depicting the state's development ideologies. Some of these filmmakers were later enlisted to produce television programmes for Doordarshan. While a majority of programmes represented the state's development realism, a significant number of television series—*Charitraheen*, *Darpan*, *Godān*, *Kayar*, *Kathasagar*, *Kirdār*, *Mailā Anchal*, *Mujrim Hazir*, *Rāg Darbāri*, *Neem Ka Ped*, *Panchlight*, and single adapted plays, *Jazeere* and *Pita*, based on literary works from various Indian languages and the West, and part of Doordarshan's programming, complicate our understanding of televisual narrative forms in terms of realism alone, and indeed open up the possibility of productively engaging with what Bisnupriya Ghosh (2004) noted as the significance of the vernacular literatures and idioms in consolidating postcolonial epistemologies.[3]

A study of television programmes based on literary works—novels, short stories, and plays—offers insights into how these are adapted for television, raising questions of aesthetic and formal techniques that underpin the transformation of 'form' from the literary to the audio-visual. The 'forms of television' discussed by Williams (1974) demonstrate how television combines various cultural forms like theatre, newspaper, magazine, radio, cinema, and so on, and at the same time alters these to fit the televisual modalities.[4] By incorporating the formal and aesthetic elements of various cultural forms, television changes the graphic organization of these forms; however, the communicational modalities of earlier forms remain salient. Thus, television analysis must begin with a consideration of how, and in what specific ways, the aesthetic and formal elements shape the forms. Williams' work, situated within the Marxist materialist approach, is not a call to a formalist analysis; it is, rather, a first step towards examining the form–content dialectic in television.[5] Indeed, such an examination is similar to what Fredric Jameson (1981: 98–99) had outlined—through his third horizon of analysis of individual text or cultural artifact—as the 'ideology of form', wherein 'form' is apprehended as content.

Jameson (1981: 98–99) indicated that 'the study of ideology of form is no doubt grounded on a technical and formalistic analysis in a narrower sense, even though, unlike much traditional formal analysis, it seeks to reveal the active presence within the text of a number of discontinuous and heterogeneous formal processes'. More importantly, in the Indian context, Jameson's notion of the 'ideology of form' enables us to grasp how the literary and televisual text contains 'the dynamics of sign systems of several distinct modes of production'—particularly the imbrication of pre-capitalist, mythic, and popular elements with the capitalist ones in television series (1981: 99). While it is useful to study how the different 'modes of production' co-exist in the text, it would be more productive to examine, following Ricoeur, how, and in what particular ways, narrative, temporality, and social imaginaries reveal about human action at the level of narrative.

Discussions of television in India have been framed in terms of the singular concept of 'development realist' aesthetic underpinning state-initiated broadcast policies and programming. In the Indian context, the origins of several television forms can be traced to the late colonial period, 1920–47, when British administrators and bureaucrats sought to create radio formats and schedules for broadcasting. For instance, colonial broadcasting's centralized control, programme formats, and the construction of audiences through essentialized cultural categories were in tandem with the postcolonial state's upper caste–class Hindu ideologies. Overall, several postcolonial television programme formats—based on the development realist aesthetic—followed the ideas espoused by Hardinge (1934: 619), a colonial bureaucrat, who pointed out that the 'peasant needs short daily talks of a homely nature upon rudiments of hygiene, sanitation, child welfare, improved agricultural methods and marketing, and similar helpful subjects leavened with entertainment'.

Since the 1970s, several programme formats of Doordarshan incorporated British colonial notions of rural development and the United States brand of modernization. This is evident in the one-year Satellite Instructional Television Experiment (SITE) and the Kheda rural communication project—designed by India's technocratic–bureaucratic elite, in consultation with UNESCO, and with the help of a satellite loaned from the USA—where programmes incorporated developmental ideologies within pre-capitalist narrative forms. An important argument for starting SITE was based on the idea of television as enabling a 'participatory democracy' through several short skits and docudramas that mixed everyday issues with larger goals of family welfare, health, sanitation, social ills, and so on, and aimed at rural students, farmers, and women. However, the developmental ideologies of SITE reproduced the colonial notions of 'village uplift' through a pedagogic and moralizing stance that assumed that such programmes could lead to an attitude change among people. The concepts of participatory democracy and attitude change, however, were unable to dislodge deeply entrenched feudal, caste, and class relations in the countryside.

Doordarshan initiated *Hum Log* (We People, 1984–85) and *Buniyaad* (Foundation, 1985–86), designed and produced as the televisual serial-mode of composition, and touted as 'progressive melodramas' which marked an important shift from the state's development realist aesthetic even as it embodied colonial and postcolonial developmental ideologies.[6] Indeed, as Roy (2008: 38) noted, 'One of the major sites of negotiation between the developmental state's pedagogic project and the emergent commercial popular was the "progressive melodrama"'. The arrival of commercial programming on Indian television in the 1980s and the subsequent rise of satellite television in the 1990s led to the spread of a whole range of consumerist-based programme formats.

In addition to the various programme formats discussed above, television in India has incorporated the formal language of commercial Indian popular cinema in developing specific televisual forms that adapt the cinematic techniques in programme production or directly draw upon the content of the films—as in song and dance sequence, cinema scenes or talk shows, and so on. The borrowing and reworking of film music on television and the increasing pastiche of film-based television programmes may point to television's constant thirst for content.[7] Madhava Prasad (1999: 127) noted that 'apart from the readymade forms of the sitcom, the soap opera—the Indian television has borrowed from elsewhere, there are signs in some quarters of formal innovations that can be traced to the specificity of Indian film history'. Unlike in Britain and elsewhere, Doordarshan has been unable to draw upon the various Indian theatrical and dramatic aesthetics in developing hybrid televisual forms. While Veena Das (1995), among others, noted that aspects of aesthetic and pre-capitalist elements from Indian dramatic traditions have found their way into several television programmes, they have not shaped the television's narrative forms in any significant way.

Developing a series of interconnected arguments on the ideological features of television and nation, Roy (2005) persuasively argued that studies of television in India have not paid attention to the debates concerning television 'form'. Roy situates his analysis by drawing out the idea of 'flow' in Williams' work. Indeed, the question of how various popular performative practices and traditions—from the pre-capitalist to the capitalist—have influenced television 'form' in India remains central to studying the evolution of the medium of television in India. Indeed, as Roy points out, a few studies of Indian films offered original insights into aesthetic and pre-capitalist traits in Indian film form. However, what is more interesting to the purpose of this chapter is Roy's attempt to engage the materialist contexts of the televisual apparatus in India. For instance, he notes,

> The television form is replete with traces of capital affecting the production process, that it can hold the ideologies of both the state and the market in such a manner as to make each one of them capable of *representing* the other, can we say that the televisual form does incline towards an ideology of real subsumption? (2005: 9)

Overall, I agree with Roy's argument that television can hold the ideologies of the state and the market, but would add that there are other ideological elements that may or may not fall under the sway of capital or state power. However, certain narrative forms of television are capable of either disengaging or reorganizing the dialectic of state and market to produce complex ideologies. Indeed, television series transmitted on Doordarshan developed such a complex set of ideologies ranging from conservative to radical. And as Williams (1977) and Brian Longhurst (1987) indicated, there are different kinds of realisms that televisual texts are capable of articulating.[8] Therefore, the mythic and realist elements in the television series identified above can be apprehended as narrative forms in terms of the aesthetic, formal, and political levels. Furthermore, Kapur (1987: 106) noted that the issue of realism 'must be continued to be debated, especially in the third world, where realism as a genre has proved to be so hospitable, spawning all manner of realisms that replicate and reify the "given"'.

While studies of television soap operas and serials and the overlapping of realism and melodrama reveal interesting aspects of television forms, a hermeneutic exploration of television narrative forms informed by Paul Ricoeur's concepts sheds light on how television narratives are constituted, thereby providing a better grasp of the overlapping of aesthetic, formal, and structural modes of graphic and visual composition. In contrast to the various textual and narrative approaches that use semiotic and psychoanalytic concepts, Ricoeur's analytic posits four dimensions—the formal, the historical, the phenomenological, and the hermeneutic—and provides a comprehensive framework for examining a variety of literary and cultural texts, ranging from an 'almost infinite variety of narrative expressions (oral, written, graphic, gestural) and the narrative classes (myths, folklores, legends, novels, epics, tragedies, drama, films, comic strips, etc.)' (Valdes 1991: 27). Ricoeur's formal and historical dimensions enable a better grasp of the aesthetic and technical aspects through which television narratives are constructed.[9] On the one hand, they accord importance to the various technical and semiotic codes that structure the televisual narrative and on the other, retain the important distinction between the semiotic and semantic levels.

Pursuing the key questions underlying hermeneutics, 'what is the meaning of being human' (Garcia, 1997: 81), and how does a 'being/subject' come to interpret itself, Ricoeur posited that the meaning of 'being/subject' is mediated through the process of interpretations—cultural, religious, political, historical, and scientific (Kearney, 2004).

Through his numerous critiques of structural linguistics, semiotics, and psychoanalytic approaches to language and subjectivity, Ricoeur argued that philosophers need to pay attention to the 'fullness of language'—since symbols, myths, metaphors, and even words constituting language carry traces of history and experience that cannot be revealed through structural analysis of texts via lexical codes and deep structures. In contrast to the structuralists, Ricoeur developed a theory of language through his philosophical hermeneutics by maintaining a distinction between semiotics and semantics: semiotics with its elaborate signifying system built on lexical codes and binaries, and semantics, where the sentence lives and words accrete new meanings, thereby acknowledging the speaking/listening subject with his/her history. To overcome the antimony between the semiotic and semantic, Ricoeur (1968: 126) places the 'word' between structure and event:

> Words are signs in speech position. Words are the point of articulation of semiology and semantics, in every speech event. The sentence, we have seen, is an event: as such, its actuality is transitory, passing, vanishing. But the word survives the sentence. As displaceable entity, it survives the transitory instance of discourse and holds itself available for new uses. Thus, heavy with a new use-value—as minute as this may be—it returns to the system. And in returning to the system, it gives it a history.

The presuppositions of structural linguistics, as Ricoeur states above, excludes the act of speaking, the speaking subject, and, along with these, history is subsumed to structure. Thus, through his several critiques of French structuralism, associated with the work of Roland Barthes, Claude Lévi-Strauss, Louis Althusser, Ricoeur questioned the underlying linguistic model that constructed language as an object to be investigated scientifically through an elaborate system of codes and signs that work in terms of relations of mutual dependence. Thus, to overcome the structuralist inadequacies, Ricoeur developed a theory of language through his philosophical hermeneutics. Ricoeur's distinction between the semiotics and semantics thus opened up a path toward exploring the speaking/listening subject.

Referring to a 1967 essay of Ricoeur where he presented his critique of structuralism and outlined his approach to language, Andrew (2000: 58) noted:

> His [Ricoeur's] brilliant and characteristic move in this essay was to interpose a term between the dyad 'langue/parole' of Saussurian linguistics; that term, 'mot,' carries thick traces of theology and history, complicating what he saw as

> too simple a distinction. Every word, Ricoeur points out, bears in its etymology the sediment of prior uses that amount to a history of experience. History can be accounted for neither by structural rules (langue) nor by an accumulation of individual events (parole). Words—les mots—especially in their evolution, are what bear tradition, heritage, and the credit human beings can draw on for a shared future. Structural analysis of texts may be indispensable to an explanation of their power to make meaning, but it is completely inadequate to the task of comprehending their import and consequence.

Following Émile Benveniste, Ricoeur argued that meanings constituted beyond the sentence can be grasped at the semantic level, since it is here the subject of utterance and subject of enunciation 'live', and where words and sentences return to history bringing polysemy to language. Subsequently, Ricoeur began to examine the semantic plane and developed original insights into the nature of language and meaning, interpretation, subjectivity, and human action. It is in this context that he brings his philosophical hermeneutics in dialogue and debate with other disciplines.[10]

A significant feature of Ricoeur's work has been its ability to engage with diverse philosophical movements. However, as the Marxist theorist, Fredric Jameson (2009) noted in his critique of *Time and Narrative*, Ricoeur ignored the Marxist tradition in his discussion of historiography and historical narrative.[11] While admiring the ambition of Ricoeur's *Time and Narrative*, Jameson (2009: 487) notes: 'What is bold in the ambition of the work itself is not only the vindication of narrative as a primary instance of the human mind, but also the equally daring conception of temporality itself as a construction, and a construction achieved by narrative itself.' Jameson's critique of Ricoeur is wide-ranging, and touches upon its many strengths and weaknesses. As Jameson (2009: 494) points out, 'Despite his brilliant appropriation of Heidegger's complex temporal analyses, Ricoeur is apparently unwilling to entertain any possibility that human time has in late capitalism undergone a kind of structural mutation.' While Ricoeur's notion of multiple temporalities does not account for late capitalism and the postmodern moment, it does provide significant analytic possibilities in examining heterogeneous times, at the level of history, narrative, and selfhood.

The Hindi novels *Mailā Anchal*, written by Phanishwarnath Renu in 1954, *Rāg Darbārī*, written by Srilal Shukla in 1968, and *Godān*, written by Munshi Premchand in 1936 are popular literary fictions that draw upon nationalist and historical topics, characters, and events from late colonial and postcolonial period. The multi-textured literary realism of the novels structured by their respective aesthetic forms and narrative strategies both subvert and expand the self-evident logics of realism to understand colonial domination and postcolonial power. In their literary and fictional writing, Premchand, Renu, and Shukla refigure and 'emplot' historical characters and events through the narrative. While it is well known that literary fiction makes explicit use of narrative, there has been a controversy among historians about the role of narrative in writing history.[12] Ricoeur (1984) provided a powerful argument that history-writing takes the form of narrative, and that historians draw upon the techniques of literary fiction in ordering and conveying their arguments and ideas. Maintaining the distinction between 'fact' and 'fiction'—especially the truth claims about what constitutes 'fact' and 'fiction'—Ricoeur brings back the crucial role of 'plot' in historical and fictional narrative discourses. In the three novels and their televisual adaptations under discussion, therefore, the refiguration of myths and tradition is not just an ideological exercise; it is, rather, a creative and critical interpretation of aesthetic forms at the level of narrative.

Focusing on the impoverished conditions of rural landscapes and villages, the failure of 1920s–30s anti-colonial nationalism (as in *Godān*) or the 1950s–60s postcolonial nation-state (as in *Mailā Anchal* and *Rāg Darbārī*), the novels portray the impact of local and national politics on the life-worlds of the peasants. The novels *Rāg Darbārī* and *Mailā Anchal*, narrated from multiple character positions, deal with the quotidian life in rural villages of India. Combining the mythic–realist forms and mixing genres, the novels present an evocative blend of local politics and culture, the pervasive presence of state institutions and bureaucracy with the developmental and nationalist discourses. In *Rāg Darbārī*, *Mailā Anchal*, and *Godān*, the actions are centred in the village with the arrival of the 'outsider'—from the big town or city—as an important part of the story. While in *Godān*—organized around a 'social-realist' aesthetic that presents a searing critique of capitalism and hence is of a different order from *Rāg Darbārī* and *Mailā Anchal*—the arrival of Gobar, Hori's son, happens at the end of the story, *Rāg Darbārī* and *Mailā Anchal* begin with the arrival of Ranganath, nephew of Vaidyaji, and Dr Prashant.

In his Marxist reading of Premchand's text, Michael Sprinker (1989) notes that Premchand reproduces the agrarian structures prevalent in northern India during the 1930s and develops an accurate narrative of how the larger socio-economic forces lead to the plight of poor peasants. Pointing to the Marxist orientation of Premchand's narrative, Sprinker (1989: 65) adds,

> Premchand's understanding of the elementary fact of social life is registered more immediately in the text's overwhelming concentration on the intricacies of finance, which dominate the action and occupy most of the mental exertions of nearly all the characters, from the poorest like Hori and his family to the wealthiest like the Rai Sahib and Khanna.

In Sprinker's (1989: 75) reading, *Godān* is understood as signalling a transition from feudalism to capitalism, and is considered as 'an authentically naturalist novel'. There is more to Premchand's literary form than Sprinker suggests. For instance, in early 1930, in a conversation with the Hindi writer Jainendra, Premchand delineated his literary style in terms of a 'complex' realism: one that is attentive to its own deficiencies and those of idealism and naturalism.[13] Explaining the development of Premchand's literary writings, Sudhir Chandra (1982) indicated that the delineation of nationalism in Premchand could be tracked in terms of the historical events surrounding anti-colonial nationalism.[14] In his analysis, Jagdish Lal Dawar (1996) identified a Gramscian strategy in Premchand's work, particularly through the critique of 'common sense'. For Premchand developed this 'from within the oppressed groups without being inculcated by the nationalist intelligentsia' (Dawar, 1996: 117). There is no educated leader organizing the peasants: Hori, the main protagonist and the peasant, encumbered by huge debt, attributes the reasons for injustice and social inequalities in terms of actions preformed in the previous life, unlike Gobar, his son, who provides a critique to Hori's common sense.

Renu's *Mailā Anchal* and Shukla's *Rāg Darbārī* provide an evocative demonstration of how language operates on the semantic level, where words, as Andrew (2000: 58) stated, 'carry thick traces of theology and history', thereby enabling sentences to 'return to history', and where language and form conjugate in the development of narrative form. Indeed, as Ricoeur (1968: 126) argued,

> words are the point of articulation of semiology and semantics, in every speech event. The sentence, we have seen, is an event: as such, its actuality is transitory, passing, vanishing. But the word survives the sentence. As displaceable entity, it survives the transitory instance of discourse and holds itself available for new uses. Thus, heavy with a new use-value – as minute as this may be – it returns to the system. And in returning to the system, it gives it a history.

Consequently, Ricoeur's hermeneutic philosophy identifies the polysemic nature of language, while at the same time acknowledging the presence of heterogeneous time. In the following pages, I explore Renu and Shukla's work through Ricoeur's hermeneutic approach.

Phanishwarnath Renu's *Mailā Anchal*, considered the most significant literary work after Premchand's *Godān*, is set in a northeastern rural region of Bihar. Although Renu spoke the Maithili language of the region and was conversant in Khari Boli, Bengali, and local dialects, he wrote primarily in Hindi. Kathryn Hansen (1981) noted that Renu developed a particular style of the Hindi language based on rural speech and idioms and grafted words from one language to another (Sanskrit, Hindi, Khari Boli, and Maithili), and integrated prose and poetic forms to render multiple temporalities. In *Mailā Anchal* several Sanskrit words are phonetically altered to make it intelligible for the rural readers. Hansen (1981: 281) points out that 'Renu reveals a linguistic virtuosity unrivaled in modern Hindi literature. The patchwork of diverse ethnic groups that constitute the population of Purnea District, far in the northeastern corner of Bihar bordering on Nepal and West Bengal, has been recreated in the linguistic texture of his fiction'. By bringing the oral traditions, Renu assimilates *Mailā Anchal* with indigenous techniques of storytelling. The mixing of story genres, the most pronounced being the *katha*, *qissa*, *git*, and *gatha*, creates different temporalities within the novel. Indeed, these are the sedimented forms that Ricoeur argued as central to the history of narratives. Ricoeur (1996: 163–64) referencing Benjamin points out, 'Walter Benjamin recalls that, in its most primitive form, still discernible in the epic and already in the process of extinction in the novel, the art of storytelling is the art of exchanging *experiences*'.

Srilal Shukla's *Rāg Darbārī* is built around a series of interconnected events in an imaginary village, Shivpalgunj in Uttar Pradesh. The stories are organized around Vaidyaji (an Ayurvedic physician, hence the name), who as a local politician and a self-professed devotee of Gandhi embarks on spreading development and democracy in the village. Through multiple overlapping layers of narratives of village life—vignettes from the everyday chatter and gossip, the machinations in local governance institutions, the village farmers cooperative, and so on—Shukla provides sociopolitical commentary. Written as a comical satire of village politics, the novel is peopled with characters throughout the interlinked stories. In Rupert Snell's (1990) account, *Rāg Darbārī*'s genre and style combine disparate linguistic elements where Hindi words are mixed with English ones. Since English is not comprehensible in village settings, 'its incomprehensibility makes it an iconic symbol rather than a means of communication; it develops a semiotic potency equivalent to that of the Sanskrit *sloka*' (Snell, 1990: 164).

Indeed, as in *Mailā Anchal*, *Rāg Darbārī* demonstrates the significance of the acoustic effect created by the juxtaposition of words from different languages on the ears of the people. Shukla's recourse to irony, humour and satire, the references to Indian aesthetic and religious idioms and metaphors, imbued with realistic representations of characters, events, and happenings, enable him to develop a kind of 'comic realism'. As Ulka Anjaria (2006) notes, through the politics of 'ulti batein'—that is, the inversions of conventional realistic descriptions, presenting effects before causes, appearances before essences—imbued in the plot structure of the novel, Shukla undertakes a critique of the postcolonial state.[15] Anjaria (2006: 4797) points out to one such inversion from the novel by way of example: 'In our ancient books of logic it's written that wherever there is smoke there is fire. To this should be added that wherever there's a bus-stand, there's filth.' Throughout *Rāg Darbārī*, 'the language of refractions, bends, travesties and inversions captures the abject experience of the state …' while noting the failed promises of nationalism and the Nehruvian state.

Ricoeur's hermeneutic insights on narrative, temporality, and social imaginaries allow us to discern how language, words, and speech in the television serials acquire an aural–visual density, wherein the identities of the characters and protagonists, tied to various social practices—via actions, performances, and events—are structured around a whole repertoire of idioms, imaginations, symbols, and 'ways of being' marked by the presence of multiple temporalities. Indeed, the social imaginaries in *Mailā Anchal*, *Rāg Darbārī*, and *Godān*—in their novel form as well as the television adaptations—occupy a 'fluid middle ground between embodied practices and explicit doctrines', most notably ideologies, and the idioms of imaginaries are 'expressed and carried in images, stories, legends, and modes of address' (Gaonkar, 2002: 10). To this end, the notion of social imaginaries opens up an important avenue for studying narrative identity and temporality in the novels and their television adaptations. Therefore, the notion of social imaginaries developed in Ricoeur's writings, and by the postcolonial scholarship, enables a creative and critical interpretation of how in the three novels, tradition is refigured at the level of aesthetics and not as an ideology alone. Premchand, Renu, and Shukla through particular linguistic strategies decode a range of 'mythic-realist' elements. In doing so, they make narrative and human action interchangeable. Although the televisual representations of the actions and events translated from the novels lose the radical edge, there are a significant number of moments in the serials that stand out.

2 | Doordarshan, Literary Drama, and Narrative Identity

It has been over half a century since television was instituted in India. Although scholarship on Indian television has provided valuable insights into its structural, textual, and reception contexts, a sustained examination of its narrative forms, for the most part, remains unexplored. In addition, a significant number of television serials translated from literary works have not been studied. In this chapter, I argue that a critical study of television's narrative forms that looks at how its repertoire of cinematic codes, techniques, and styles involve a complex overlapping between myth, realism, and melodrama will enable a better theoretical understanding of Indian television. In what follows, I discuss the television serials *Mailā Anchal* (1987–88, dir. Ashok Talwar), *Rāg Darbārī* (1986–87, dir. Krishna Raghav), and *Godān* (2004, dir. Gulzar) transmitted on the state-run television network, Doordarshan. These serials, adapted from literary works, deal with questions of late colonial and postcolonial identity in the countryside in terms of the dialectic tensions between the forces of tradition and modernity, local politics, nationalism, development, encroaching capitalism, public life, and more specifically, on the human condition. They frame the various issues through complex 'mythic-realist' narrative forms. For instance, the literary adaptations look at the effects of the process of development—through local (rural) politics, state institutions, and bureaucracies—in the lives of ordinary Indians, mostly peasants and working class. Both a critique and valorization of anti-colonial and postcolonial nationalism, the television serials portray the stories and plots in terms of a complex interplay between religious beliefs and practices and the secular vocabularies of public institutions. The main focus of this chapter is to explore the 'ways' through which the literary works (novels) are translated for Doordarshan and the presence of pre-capitalist performative practices in

While the television adaptations of *Rāg Darbārī* and *Mailā Anchal* reproduced the novel's narrative forms, maintaining fidelity to the plot structures of the literary works, the naturalist principles of the television medium define the unfolding realism in the serials.[16] This dominance of naturalism tends to dissipate the critical force of irony and humour. However, significant moments in both *Rāg Darbārī* and *Mailā Anchal* represent a break from this sort of naturalism as their language and form and mixing of story genres disrupt it. For instance, *Rāg Darbārī*'s 'ulti batein' reverses the logic of realism and frames the comic moments as satire. In *Rāg Darbārī*, while the actions, events, and plots are organized around the characters Vaidyaji (Manohar Singh), Ruppan Baby (Veerendra Saxena), and Ranganath (Om Puri), they retain fidelity to the novel's language of 'comic realism'. Similarly, in *Mailā Anchal*, words and sentences acquire colloquial and visual density, frequently transferring meanings from one linguistic register to the other. The idiomatic grammar of Renu inflects the speech of the characters in the series, particularly the protagonists Doctor Prashant and Kamili, and many others. Unlike in the novel, the emotions and affective states of the characters are enacted and become visible in the televisual version as bodily gestures. Renu's strategy of grafting words and idioms from one language to another (Sanskrit, Hindi, Khari Boli, and Maithili) and the integration of prose and poetic forms to shape the narrative structure of the novel enabled him to develop a sharp critique of the workings of the newly independent Indian state.

In *Mailā Anchal*, Renu mixes genres like *katha*, *qissa*, *git*, and *gatha* into the novel form.[17] He invokes pre-capitalist and mythic narrative forms like songs and ballads that predate and militate against a quintessentially modern genre—the novel. These storytelling modes embody a different concept of time (cyclical and heterogeneous time) as against the linear, homogeneous time of the nation. Indeed, what we notice in Renu is that the idea of a linear time is broken up with the introduction of multiple events that run across the narrative as digressions from the main one and in the process elaborates a composite set of tales within tales. This is further enhanced by Renu's ability to work across linguistic idioms and multiple story formats such as *katha*, *qissa*, *git*, and *gatha*. To this end, Hansen (1981: 290) noted:

> Using traditional storyteller's method, Renu breaks down the linear concept of time and creates instead a feeling of time's cyclical nature and the simultaneity of events. The Western concepts of time and causality (B happens after A and because of A) which were inherited with the nineteenth-century novel form are here being replaced, in part, by the traditional Indian view of time.

> In the Indian concept, time is structured in large units and subdivided over and over until one reaches the human timescale … One tale contains another, which contains another, and so on. Time is also infinitely expandable and is patterned in cycles.

Thus, Renu is able to bring multiple temporalities into play in his work. How does one, then, explain the presence of heterogeneous time? Dipesh Chakrabarty (2000), developing his critique of Benedict Anderson's (1983: 24) account of nation as an 'imagined community' located in 'homogeneous empty time', argued that social and religious practices in India cannot be grasped by remaining within the ambit of a linear and singular conception of time; in fact, these practices belong and emerge from an uneven and dense 'heterogeneous time'. In his philosophical mediation on narrative, Ricoeur (1984) noted that narratives embody two dimensions of temporality: a chronological, episodic dimension, where a story is made up of events, and a non-chronological, configurational dimension, where the plot organizes significant wholes out of scattered events. Whereas the episodic dimension is marked by a linear representation of time, the configurational points towards 'within-time-ness', a phenomenological notion of time that is experienced in terms of past, present, and future. The linear and phenomenological conceptions of time, Ricoeur argued, are integrated, and that it is narrative which has a capacity to explain the complex interplay of time. Against the singular conception of the 'homogeneous empty time', I argue that Hansen's, Chakrabarty's, and Ricoeur's works offer a way forward in understanding the multiple temporalities through which a given people imagine their collective social life.

The identities of various characters and protagonists in the televisual *Mailā Anchal*, *Rāg Darbārī*, and *Godān* can be analytically grasped through what Ricoeur (1992) has characterized as a person's narrative identity. Ricoeur (1992: 113–68) has argued that a person's narrative identity can be approached via two interconnected and overlapping notions of identity: *idem* (sameness) and *ipse* (selfhood). While *idem*-identity refers to 'sameness of body and character, our stability illustrated by genetic code', *ipse*-identity pertains to our 'selfhood, the adjustable part of our identity', and furthermore the two kinds of identities—of sameness and difference—offer coherence to the self and the possibility for change and reflexivity. In the televisual *Rāg Darbārī*, the identities and life-worlds of the main protagonists, Vaidyaji, Ranganath, and Ruppan Babu, in *Mailā Anchal*, Doctor Prashant and Kamili, and in *Godān*, Hori, Dhaniya, and Gobar as well as their wide network of relationships with peasants and rural community are layered with phenomenological detail.

Their embodied identities become visible in the unfolding actions, events, and plotlines that centre around Vaidyaji's machinations in *Rāg Darbārī*, Hori's plight in *Godān*, and Doctor Prashant and Kamili's relationship in *Mailā Anchal*.

In the Indian situation, several pre-capitalist performative practices and traditions, along with the colonial, postcolonial, and capitalist discourses, have shaped the development of broadcast and televisual forms. In the televisual adaptation of the literary works, the narrative forms of the novel undergo significant changes, particularly through the formal procedures of the audio-visual medium. The televisual adaptation of *Godān* by Gulzar follows the main thrust of Premchand's critique, but the director prefigures and 'emplots' specific aspects of the literary work, and structures it to fit the audio-visual format of the medium. Talking about this, Gulzar noted: 'I have designed these two stories [*Godān* and *Nirmala*] as full-fledged films because the episodic structure of a television serial would have affected the continuity of the novels.'[18] By taking creative liberties with Premchand's *Godān*, Gulzar restructures particular narrative elements from the novel to fit the televisual form of the miniseries. Indeed, the filmmaker took out a portion of the novel, focusing on the story of Hori and Dhania in the village, ignoring the city segments in which they are absent. For Gulzar, the aesthetic and formal decision to structure the novel for the televisual also has a political intent: 'The state of our villages has only worsened. Farmers still commit suicide and starving women are forced to sell their children for a pittance. We must therefore listen to Premchand's timeless voice' (Chatterjee, 2004: 2).

In the televisual version of *Godān*, the plight of Hori and his family is represented through a realist form shaped largely by the formal elements of the television medium. The 'radical' realism of Premchand's text is substituted by a 'progressive' realism of Gulzar's televisual rendition. However, Premchand's novel *Godān* and its televisual adaptation by Gulzar are shaped in relation to different and interconnected political conjunctures. Premchand's work engaged the inability of the 1930s anti-colonial nationalist politics in the face of increasing encroachment of usury forms of capital and debt financing structured by the semi-feudal and colonial relations, whereas Gulzar sought to relate this to the postcolonial situation of peasants in rural India. In fact, John Caughie's (2000: 109) elaboration of 'progressive realism' in the context of British television presents some ideas that may be relevant to Indian television, particularly the development of aesthetic and cultural forms for the televisual medium:

> Television's progressive function may indeed be to bring the world into the home in ways which sometimes escape the order of institutional discourse—and sometimes don't. At the same time, within the more conventional and conservative forms of representation (whether they be naturalistic, realistic, or modernistic) the new elements of social discourse may enter the stage of public visibility, as if they have always been there, adding to social discourse without transforming it or moving it on. Content which is innocent of form guarantees nothing—but neither does form alone.

Several Indian filmmakers and television producers have experimented with the televisual form in adapting novels, short stories, and plays.[19] Mani Kaul's *Ahmaq* (Fyodor Dostoevsky's *The Idiot*) is an instance where the naturalist, realist, and modernist elements are deployed in reworking the formal, aesthetic, and narrative form of the novel for television. James Monaco (2000), referring to the development of television forms in the American context, points out that the series as a basic unit of television enables the development of plot and character, and it was the miniseries or novel-for-television style that revived television programming as serial format. The literarature-based serials discussed earlier in this essay and adapted from novels, short stories, and plays reveal such interesting reworking of the narrative forms that point to an emergence of a particular style/genre in the Indian context where the pre-capitalist performative traditions overlap with the realist, melodramatic, and modernist forms.[20] A few serials point to a creative 'refiguration' of tradition combining critical and progressive force of the various aesthetic forms.

Although the preceding discussion for the most part has been preliminary, my modest attempt has been to explore possible points of convergence between Ricoeur's philosophical hermeneutics and neo-Marxist and postcolonial approaches in examining televisual narrative forms. The serials adapted from literary works constitute an important group of narratives that stand out from Doordarshan's programming 'flow' and yield several important insights in thinking about the relationship between postcoloniality and television. Although this chapter explored the embeddedness of religion and secularism in various television series, and the particular ways in which they get amplified through the dialectic relations between the literary and the televisual, the next chapter will take up the concept of religion and secularism as embedded imaginaries in much more detail. I indicate how religion and secularism in televisual narratives reveal a complex overlapping of the secular principles with sacred idioms and motifs, one that stands in sharp contrast to broadcasting discourse on religion and secularism, and the postcolonial Indian state's ideological project that consider them as distinct and insular categories.

NOTES

1. Geeta Kapur (2000: 233) interpreted myth in terms of Ricoeur's philosophical hermeneutics. Through an examination of two films, *Sant Tukaram* and *Devi*, she outlined several crucial narrative forms that emerge, and are built upon myth: 'Recuperation of tradition is not just an ideological operation; that it must be perceived at the level of aesthetics proper. We should recognize above all the narrative strategy of such transformations whereby an inherited iconography is decoded and sometimes radicalized. For the narrative move is most closely analogous to, indeed interchangeable with, human action.'
2. Andrew (2000, 1984) and Stadler (1990), among others, noted this lack of attention to Ricoeur's work in film and television studies. However, there have been some analyses of films that engaged aspects of Ricoeur's work (Andrew, 1993; Rosen, 1993). In her recent book, Caroline Bassett (2007) developed an interesting analytic framework that combined aspects of Ricoeur's narrative model of mimesis with Jameson's narrative approach to study how new media narratives are shaped by a range of discourses.
3. Discussing Amitav Ghosh's English novel *The Calcutta Chromosome* and building insights from Dipesh Chakrabarty and Amitav Ghosh's correspondence on the question of vernacular literary and religious traditions as crucial resources, Bisnupriya Ghosh develops an interesting argument regarding how Amitav Ghosh 'grafted' a larger vernacular tradition of fiction writing (Rabindranath Tagore and Phanishwarnath Renu) onto his English novel. I would suggest that the televisual adaptations of literary works on Doordarshan be considered in terms of engaging vernacular literatures and idioms as well.
4. From a different perspective, the American film scholar and philosopher Stanley Cavell (1982: 84), contrasting cinema with television, indicated that 'if television's aesthetic practices are located in the serial-episode mode of composition then an investigation of the fact of television ought to contribute to understanding why there should be two principles of aesthetic composition'.
5. Tracing the beginnings of television series and serials in the naturalistic drama of Henrik Ibsen and August Strindberg, and nineteenth and twentieth century serialized fictions, Williams (1977: 54) noted that the longer formats proved particularly useful to television programme planners. However, this television 'form' was also shaped by other constraints for writers and producers who 'usually find themselves writing within established formation of situation and leading character, in what can be described as collective but is more often a corporate dramatic enterprise'. Williams' discussions of television relate to Britain and the United States in the mid-1970s, and indeed are pertinent to the current moment of media globalization within which television 'flows' and 'forms' circulate with

increasing frequency between and across North America and the rest of the world. A majority of television serials and soap operas have formulaic storylines and plots, and in many instances, writers script individual scenes in terms of 'beats' to hold the attention of audiences/viewers. The serials are infused with consumer sensibilities and are embedded as commodity-forms within the larger 'flow' of programming. See Newman (2006) and Altman (1986).

6. The first televisual serial-mode of composition for Doordarshan was initiated in 1976 with a serial called *Aisa Bhi Hota Hain*. I thank Abhijit Roy for bringing this to my attention. However, it was with *Hum Log* that the serial-mode of composition became a regular feature of television programming. For the design and implementation of the serial-mode structure, *Hum Log* drew upon Mexican and other Latin American 'pro-development' genre of programmes as well.
7. During 1978–82, when Doordarshan began its broadcasting services on a limited basis all over India, films became a significant part of the programming. On Saturdays, 'regional' language films were transmitted from the respective regional networks, and on Sundays, a song and dance episode (*Chitrahaar*) followed by a Hindi film on the National network. Since the 1990s, however, the film-based programming has evolved into numerous genres/shows: movie clips featuring dialogues, comedy acts, specific music forms, interviews with film personalities in the form of talk shows, and a whole gamut of programmes.
8. Within television studies, realism is understood as the defining aesthetic of television based on the medium's institutional and journalistic modalities. John Corner (1992) notes that the influence of film theory also shaped the centrality of realism to television. Williams' discussion of television as a combination of various cultural forms along with the medium's own mixed forms offers important analytic possibilities in pursuing the connections between realism and television.
9. A narrative analysis ought to begin with the study of the formal properties of the story and discourse before interpreting the meanings embedded within the narratives. Narrative is broadly composed of a story and a discourse: story is comprised of *events* and *existents*, which in turn are made up of *actions*, *happenings*, *characters*, and *settings*. The discourse, on the other hand, is elaborated through the *narrative transmission* and *manifestation* of the components of the story in specific ways. Thus, the examination of story and discourse reveals the ideological tasks of the narrative. Television programmes are constructed through collaboration among several people—producers, directors, camera persons, set designers, script writers, editors, artists, technicians, and so on. These people deploy various strategies of storytelling that are encoded at the formal and ideological levels.
10. Dudley Andrew's (2000: 44–45) essay and review of Francois Dosse's French biography on Ricoeur offers a brilliant commentary on Ricoeur's work—the formative influences, intellectual development of his thought, and the remarkable philosophical career. According to Andrew, 'To calculate the impact of his workaday ethic, it is enough to note that Ricoeur directed the thesis or served as mentor to Jean-Luc

Nancy, Jacques Derrida, Jacques Rancière, Vincent Descombes, Jean-François Lyotard, and Michel de Certeau.'

11. Andrew (1984, 1993, 2000) notes that both within Marxism in general and film theory in particular, Ricoeur's writings were ignored as well: 'Film scholars who flirted with structural and psychoanalytic methodologies and yet who worried lest these approaches utterly smother the films they sought to interpret, could have used Ricoeur as a staunch ally. This became perfectly evident in 1977, with the appearance of *The Rule of Metaphor*—whose heart beat to the vibrant but unpredictable rhythm of creativity and art. Ricoeur was again timely.'
12. Hayden White (1978) had offered a similar perspective regarding the relationship between history and narrative; however, there are significant differences between Ricoeur and White. Discussing the question of the reality of the past, postcolonial scholar Prasenjit Duara (1993) demonstrated the importance of Ricoeur's discussion of how history and fiction emplot or refigure events.
13. Here is Premchand from Madan Gopal's biography (1964: 395): 'If life were to be portrayed as it actually was, it would become only a photograph of life. For the writer, unlike the sculptor, it is not necessary to be a realist, even though he may attempt to be one. Literature is created to enable humanity to march ahead, to elevate its level of existence. Idealism has to be there, even though it should not militate against realism and naturalism. Naked realism would be more than a police report, and naked idealism no more than a speech from a pulpit. What is needed is a blend of the two.'
14. Chandra (1982: 612–13) presents a cogent discussion of the complexity of Premchand's work and its critique of nationalism: 'But Godan offers no hope; not even contact with nationalists, for whatever it is worth. Considering that Godan was begun in 1932 and continued during the kisan agitation launched by the UP Congress, the political insulation of Semari and Belari cannot be related to the contemporary political situation. A more likely explanation seems to be Premchand's determination—evidenced by the sustained austerity of the rural portions of the novel—to permit no false hopes this time. The lone occasion when some hope is offered is when Gobar, the rebellious son of Godan's protagonist, returns to the village from Lucknow. But the angry young man can achieve little beyond an impotent vent of collective anger in a hastily put up farce. And he, too, goes back to Lucknow. So complete, in fact, is this insulation that even when people like Prof. Mehta and Miss Malati, who are politically active and alive in the city, visit these villages, they do so for either recreation or social service.'
15. In his essay on narratives of corruption, Akhil Gupta (2005) considers Shukla's literary novel *Rāg Darbārī* as an evocative and quasi-ethnographic representation of village life. Through his contextual analysis of the representations of corruption in Shukla's literary work, and F. G. Bailey's ethnographic research on Orissa's village, Bisipara, Gupta demonstrates the workings of local institutions, bureaucracy, developmental and nationalist discourse in two different genres of writings. In an interesting discussion on the close relationships between literary fiction and

anthropological research on development, David Lewis et al. (2006) demonstrate the significance of literary representations in relation to the scholarly ones.

16. I am using the term 'naturalism' broadly and as outlined in television aesthetics and production handbooks. Williams and Caughie noted that television has a propensity toward naturalist–realist method since the formal language and graphic design of the medium embody the naturalistic principles as a mode of composition. For Williams (1977) and Caughie (2000), television in the West developed by drawing upon drama and various cultural forms. Television dramas in India have not inherited the shared legacies as in Britain. Major aesthetic influences have been radio and cinema. For an interesting discussion of how radio and television shaped Urdu drama in Pakistan, see Desoulieres (1999) and Alain (1999).
17. The word 'narrative' as Hayden White (1980) had suggested is derived from its Sanskrit root *gnā* ('know') and subsequently fused together with the Latin *gnārus* ('knowing') and *narro* ('to relate'). The Indian storytelling tradition has a long lineage, from its roots in Sanskrit to other languages of India, Hindi, Persian, Arabic, and Urdu. For instance, Visnu Sarma's *Panchatantra*, the *Jatakas*, and *sloka*s from the Upanishads, the Vedas, and so on, are rendered as oral narratives. The writings of Raja Rao and R. K. Narayan have also drawn extensively on these traditions. Scholars have noted that *dastan*s and *qissa*s have influenced the works of Devki Nandan Khatri (*Chandrakanta*, 1988) and Munshi Premchand. See Sankaran (1991), Sharma (2002), Orsini (2009), and Khan (2015).
18. Gulzar's interview with Saibal Chatterjee in *The Tribune*, 'Gulzar's Vision of Timeless Classics', 15 August 2004.
19. As noted earlier, during the 1980s, Doordarshan enlisted several filmmakers to produce programmes on the nationalist movement. Most of these programmes were propagandist, serving the government's interests. The noted filmmaker Kumar Shahani, who was unable to get his documentary—produced for the Madhya Pradesh government—screened on Doordarshan, pointed out that 'many of our film-makers—some well-known names included—have compromised and started making "slottable" films to suit the needs of the system'. However, Shahani did acknowledge that several good programmes were transmitted for a brief period. See Shahani (2002).
20. While I provide examples of television serials based on literary works in Hindi transmitted on Doordarshan's National network, there are several other serials in various Indian languages that have been transmitted on the regional television networks as well. Anupama Rao (1995) examined a serial based on the Marathi novel *Paulakhuna* transmitted on Bombay Doordarshan.

3 | Televisual Representations of Socio-Spatial Conflicts, and the Religious–Secular Imaginaries

Secularism, perhaps more than any other category or concept, has increasingly become entangled with religious practices in several postcolonial societies (Majid, 2000). Although most political and religious conflicts in this part of the world have their beginnings in this entanglement, various responses to these conflicts have generally taken two approaches: they either assume the resurgence of religious identities as a result of an encroaching secularism, or consider secularism and religion as two opposing and incompatible value systems.[1] However, events of the last few years, especially 9/11, the subsequent 'global war on terror', and the rising violence from Darfur to Somalia underscore the importance of engaging religion. It should be noted that in certain manifestations religion and secularism can become tyrannical, and one needs to be vigilant against the violent epistemologies of both.

The postcolonial scholar Dipesh Chakrabarty, reacting to the secular intellectual incredulity towards religious beliefs and practices, urges that we pay close attention to 'the importance of faith in guiding contemporary imaginations of the political' (Chakrabarty, 2004: 462).[2] To *engage religion* in terms of a critical inquiry or 'political theology' is to explore the practices of ethics and tolerance among various religions, and to identify points of conversation with secularism. In a similar gesture, William Connolly (2006) argued that religious practices and secular principles ought to be brought into a productive dialogue.[3] Furthermore, Chakrabarty and Connolly point out that pursuing religion and secularism as *binaries* may be theoretically untenable and practically unsustainable given the fact that in most postcolonial and non-Western contexts—and, perhaps, even in the Western world—religion and secularism frequently overlap.

Similarly, Jose Casanova (1994), in his comparative historical work on religious movements, pointed out that along with the rise of religious fundamentalisms of various hues, there have been important conversations across the boundaries of the religious and the secular:

> The religious revival signaled simultaneously the rise of fundamentalism and its role in the resistance of the oppressed and the rise of the 'powerless'. Ali Shariarti, the intellectual father of the Islamic revolution, in translating Frantz Fanon's *Les Damnes de la Terre*, chose the resonant Koranic term *mostaz'afin* (the disinherited) ... Gustavo Gutierrez, the father of liberation theology, effected a similar transvaluation from the secular back to the religious categories when he turned the proletariat into the biblical *los pobres*. (Quoted in Jakobsen and Pellegrini, 2000: 13)

If, indeed, Jakobsen and Pellegrini (2000: 14), following Edward Said, assert that one can find the 'religious in the secular and vice versa', then it is obvious that the two can be pursued as embedded imaginaries, rather than binaries. Taking a cue from these arguments, this chapter posits an analytic strategy that considers religion and secularism as *embedded imaginaries*. The concept of 'imaginaries' offers a better account of the multiple, overlapping meanings—for instance, the dialogic relations and ideological imbrications between the religious and the secular—and opens up some fundamental questions about modernity, tradition, and belief from a postcolonial angle. More importantly, it provides a nuanced elaboration of religion and secularism within national and cross-national settings.

One such setting, India, with its sheer diversity of religious faiths, provides a powerful expression of the overlapping of the religious with the secular, and offers a baseline for exploring these as embedded imaginaries on the state-run Indian television, Doordarshan. The last two decades in India have increasingly witnessed the gradual attenuation of the concept of secularism from political discourse in the face of numerous sectarian conflicts.[4] This chapter examines two genres of television programmes—documentary and drama series—on Punjab and Kashmir to demonstrate the overlapping of religion and secularism as these get enacted and performed in terms of stories, plots, characters, and their life-worlds.[5] To analyse the modalities of this overlapping, the chapter extends the concept of 'imaginaries', via the interlinked notions of imagination, temporality, and narrative by drawing insights from—and seeking common ground between—Dipesh Chakrabarty's postcolonial critique, the hermeneutic philosophy of Paul Ricoeur, Margaret Somers' theory of narrative identity, and television studies scholarship (discussed in the second section). The essay argues that Indian state-run television mediates tensions between religion and secularism that offers interesting possibilities for understanding not only *how* the characters in the television narratives appropriate from multiple temporalities to constitute identities, but also *what* sorts of conversations are possible across secularism and religion.

While secularism and religion have typically been perceived in terms of two distinct conceptions of time—secularism in terms of a linear, chronological, 'homogeneous empty time' and religion as non-chronological and sacred time—this chapter resists such an approach; instead, it posits a complex overlapping between religion and secularism where the two temporalities are integrated, and not separate. A related purpose of the chapter is to offer a theoretical elaboration and outline a preliminary analytic framework for engaging religious and secular imaginaries in view of contemporary global realities. I argue that television narratives are an important location to examine the embeddedness of religion and secularism. These enactments might reveal the links between the religious and the secular, or, in Casanova's parlance, point to the possibilities of 'transvaluations' of religious and secular categories and vice versa. More specifically: How must one characterize the relationship between television and the religion–secularism dynamic? What meanings of secularism emerge in the programmes, and how do the narrative subjects secure these meanings? How do class–caste, gender, and other identities inflect the religion–secular dynamic? And, finally, how do these televisual versions of secularism and religion define the discourse of the nation?

Television is a suitable context for the study for two main reasons. First, the beginnings of the crisis of secularism coincided with the massive growth and expansion of the state-run television.[6] To deal with this crisis, the Indian state deployed television to frame the discourse of national integration.[7] Consequently, numerous symbolic representations of secularism dominated television programming. Although most of the programmes promoted state-based conceptions of secularism, a significant number pointed to interesting overlaps between the religious and the secular. Second, the various studies of secularism and religion on Indian television have typically pointed to the aberrations and deviations from state policies disregarding the modalities through which religion and secularism may indeed overlap.[8] The chapter is divided into four sections. In the first section, I discuss several television programmes in the context of nation, secularism, and religion. The second section provides a theoretical context for my study and presents the analytical framework for studying television documentaries and fictional drama series. In the third section, I analyse the selected television programmes. Finally, in the fourth section, the conclusions are situated against the background of the findings.

TELEVISION AND THE NATION

Although studies of television in India have examined the dominant historicist constructions of nation in terms of the discourses of modernization, gender, and right-wing politics, other modes of imagining the nation, particularly through the interplay between secularism and religion, have not been fully explored (Mankekar, 1999; Rajagopal, 2001). In the following discussion, I sketch some main lines of the trajectories of nation vis-à-vis television programmes[9] before I bring the topic of my chapter to a sharper focus. During the period 1982–96, a range of programmes—fictional drama series, current affairs, and documentaries—on the state-run television, Doordarshan, drew upon and related to the larger historical changes from the point of view of the Indian nation-state: nation-building, secularism, citizenship, and social development become visible as key themes on various television narratives.

The first drama series, *Hum Log* (We People), sought to address the middle-class national community through state discourses of family planning, literacy, public health, and other social issues; another popular drama series, *Buniyaad* (Foundation), dwells on the partition of the country into India and Pakistan, and its consequences for some families. In each of these programmes, the nation remained the central signifier. *Hum Log* and *Buniyaad* elaborated ideas on culture and community as key to the nation's identity. The titles of the series themselves serve as powerful tropes for the nation. The representation of family values in *Hum Log* were moulded in line with the state's developmental ideologies, and Veena Das (1995: 172) points out that *Hum Log* 'weaves many quotidian images from everyday domesticity into itself … [and] this tradition has not continued on Indian television'. However, during 1982–96, there have been a significant number of television narratives that sought to represent the postcolonial everyday and, more importantly, provided interesting examples of the intertwining of the religious with the secular.

The Hindi–Urdu literary adaptations—*Rāg Darbārī*, *Darpaṇ* (Looking Glass), *Kirdār* (Deed), *Neem Ka Ped* (Neem Plant), and *Daane Anār Ke* (Pomegranate Seeds) explored the everyday lives of Indians. *Rāg Darbārī*, the television adaptation of the 1968 Hindi novel by Shrilal Shukla, looks at the process of development—through local (rural) politics, state institutions, and bureaucracies—in the lives of ordinary people. Both a critique and valorization of postcolonial nationalism, the televisual *Rāg Darbārī* is about how individuals construct narratives of corruption and citizenship, frequently drawing idioms and metaphors from their religious life-worlds. Similarly, the multi-textured realism of writers from various Indian languages, adapted for television as a programme series called *Kirdār* by Gulzar, portrays the stories and plots through a complex intertwining of the religious and the secular. Another television series, *Neem Ka Ped*, based on Rahi Masoom Raza's novel, depicts Muslim *zamindari* and *lambardari* (a system of landholding and revenue collection by feudal landlords and proprietors) as a crumbling edifice in early postcolonial India, and its impact on both the landlords and the poor labourer, Budhai Ram. Here too, there is a complicated interplay between the religious beliefs and practices with the secular vocabularies of the public institutions.

Most television programmes were inscribed with national integration themes and did hegemonic work of the nation-state. For instance, the religious 'mythological' series popular during 1985–91, *Ramayan*, *Mahabharat*, *Sri Krishna*, *Chanakya*, among others, consistently drew upon a repertoire of images of *rāstra* and *desh*—that is, state and nation—throughout the narratives. These 'epic' narratives constructed an idealized past and provided ideological mediations of contemporary India, which was beleaguered by regional politics and separatist movements raising questions about the character of the Indian nation-state. Arvind Rajagopal (2001) convincingly argued that the telecast of *Ramayan* engendered the rapid rise of the right-wing Hindu politico-religious movement, and Purnima Mankekar's (1999) study of how women viewers interpreted and constructed meanings of the Hindu religious epics, *Ramayan and Mahabharat*, on television is instructive and raises important questions around faith and belief. Refusing to offer facile explanations of secularism and acknowledging the centrality of religion in the lives of the women viewers, Mankekar asserts that that the left and liberal critics were unable to engage with people's faith and reduced the questions of religion to instances of sectarian conflicts.[10]

In the mid-eighties, especially around the time when 'separatist' and subnational movements in Assam, Punjab, and Kashmir were threatening the project of national integration, a slew of programmes were produced on themes of national and religious harmony. A major impetus for the political movements stemmed from uneven development of the regions, hence broadly socio-spatial in nature. Of these three states in the Union of India, Assam is part of the Northeast region, which has received very little developmental assistance and is considered as having a 'backward' economy despite being the largest producer of tea in India. Punjab in the northwest of India, the largest producer of food grains, is considered the 'granary' of India, and Kashmir, created in the northernmost part of India after an 'accord' was reached between the ruler of the state and India's first prime minister, Jawaharlal Nehru, in 1947–48, enjoys a special status.

Several drama series, *Choli Daman*, *Chunni*, *Dil Dariya*, and *Doosra Keval*, and a few documentaries on Punjab, *Doosra Adhyay* and *Punjab 1983*, were broadcast. Kashmir was represented through the drama series *Gul Gulshan Gulfam* and news-based documentaries such as *Kashmir File*, *Freedom from Fear*, *Beyond the Haze*, *Kitne Aurangzeb*, and *Ek Duniya Sarhad Ki*. At first glance, the television programmes on Kashmir and Punjab seem to crudely present state-based ideological notions of secularism and national integration, but a closer look reveals an overlapping of the religious and secular practices.[11] To study the modalities of this overlapping, a critique of the idea of imagination, temporality, and narrative, and a discussion of imaginaries from a hermeneutic perspective is a necessary first step.

IMAGINATION, TEMPORALITY, AND NARRATIVE: HERMENEUTIC DETOURS

The concept of 'imaginaries', first developed by Cornelius Castoriadis, and later reworked by Paul Ricoeur and postcolonial theory, 'refer[s] broadly to the way a given people imagine their collective social life'. More significantly, however, imaginaries occupy the 'fluid middle ground between embodied practices and explicit doctrines', most notably ideologies. Furthermore, the idioms of ideological and non-ideological imaginaries are 'expressed and carried in images, stories, legends, and modes of address [that] constitute a symbolic matrix … embedded in the habitus of a population' (Gaonkar, 2002: 4, 10). From a postcolonial perspective, this notion of imaginaries opens up important avenues for interrogating imagination, temporality, and narrative that has significance in understanding how religion and secularism may indeed overlap (Göle, 2002).

Dipesh Chakrabarty (2002) developed an important critique of imagination and temporality that is complementary to Partha Chatterjee's articulations on the postcolonial nation. Chatterjee (2004), developing his critique of Benedict Anderson's account of nation as an 'imagined community' located in 'homogeneous empty time',[12] argued that social and religious practices in India cannot be grasped by remaining within the ambit of a linear and singular conception of time; in fact, these practices belong and emerge from an uneven and dense 'heterogeneous time'.[13] Chakrabarty (2000: 174) complicates the understanding of the term 'imagination' by suggesting that inscribed within it are two contradictory modes of 'seeing' the nation in India: one, a historicist-realist that sought to engage the political in historical time, and the other, a romantic organized around the practices of *darsan* located outside the linear and singular conception of time. While the notion of *darsan* has Hindu religious connotations and broadly refers to seeing in the presence of a deity (or more appropriately, *mūrti*) as a form of knowledge, it mediates seeing and experiencing the sacred and profane in their relationality. Chakrabarty's critique pointed out that the term 'imagination' in Anderson's usage does not explain the plural and heterogeneous ways of seeing around which the nation has come to be imagined in India.

Although Chakrabarty is careful not to reduce the complexity of *darsan* and discusses the aesthetic and religious modalities, he relies almost exclusively on the centrality of 'vision' to imagination. Chakrabarty's insights can be broadened by drawing upon Paul Ricoeur's (2004) idea of the hermeneutic imagination. Ricouer not only offers a critique of the subject-centred philosophies of imagination, but also focuses on the creative role of imagination that extends beyond the visual to the linguistic, symbolic, and narrative dimensions.[14] According to Ricoeur (1992: 140, emphasis in original), his 'hermeneutic philosophy has attempted to demonstrate the existence of an opaque subjectivity which expresses itself through the detour of countless mediations—signs, symbols, texts and human *praxis* itself. The hermeneutic idea of subjectivity as a dialectic between the self and mediated social meanings has deep moral and political implications'. This 'detour of countless mediations', of myths, symbols, and metaphors within the rubric of imaginaries, enables the 'grasping together' of heterogeneous time and modes of seeing with secular time and ideologies. For Ricoeur, the key locus for such mediations is the narrative.

In an important theoretical move, Ricoeur (1980) had pointed out that narratives embody two dimensions: a chronological, episodic dimension, where a story is made up of events, and a non-chronological, configurational dimension, where the plot organizes significant wholes out of scattered events. Both episodic and configurational dimensions have specific conceptions of temporality. Whereas the episodic dimension is marked by a linear representation of time, the configurational points toward 'within-time-ness', a phenomenological notion of time that is experienced in terms of past, present, and future. Ricoeur (1998) argued that in human experience, the linear and phenomenological conceptions of time are integrated, and that it is narrative that has a capacity to explain the complex interplay of time. Without going into Ricoeur's philosophical arguments regarding narrative and time, it is safe to posit that most studies of television narratives have ignored the complex experience of linear and phenomenological conceptions of time. My analysis of television narratives draws upon this temporal complexity to explain how the various characters and protagonists and their identities are tied to the sacred and secular practices—via actions and performances—structured around a whole repertoire of idioms, imaginations, symbols, and 'ways of being', marked by heterogeneous time.

Television studies scholarship has produced several illuminating analyses of the ideological dimensions of programme narratives, but none broached the complex issue of multiple temporalities.[15] A notable absence from critical television studies, the hermeneutic approach offers productive avenues in examining multiple temporalities in television narratives in terms of the stories, plots, and the intersubjective webs of relationships between and among the characters and their life-worlds. In his critique of the structuralist approaches to narratives, Ricoeur (1980: 170) argued that 'both anti-narrativist epistemologies and structuralist literary critics have overlooked the temporal complexity of the narrative matrix constituted by the plot ... the emphasis on nomological models and paradigmatic codes results in a trend that reduces narrative component to the anecdotic surface of the story'.[16]

John Fiske (1987) and Seymour Chatman (1978), focusing on televisual and cinematic codes and rules, developed the notions of narrative and ideological representation in empirically productive ways. Fiske sought to bridge the gap between ideological and narrative dimensions of television, with specific emphasis on the 'encoding-decoding' modalities. Televisual material, Fiske argued, gets inscribed through particular codes at three levels: reality, representation, and ideology. For instance, an event before it gets televised is already framed through 'social codes', which is transformed on television through 'technical codes'. These processes occur at the level of 'reality'. The event inscribed in the narrative structure of television undergoes further transformation through 'representational codes' before they get organized into specific ideologies through the 'ideological codes'. Chatman's methodology for studying narrative structures in literature and film considered narrative as broadly composed of a story and a discourse; story is involved with the *what* question and discourse is *how* the story is told. These two levels, story and discourse, are interrelated, that is, what really happened (the content of the narrative) and how what really happened is told (the expression of the narrative). This distinction, while maintaining the form and content dialectic, indicates that 'story' comes wrapped in social codes, and 'discourse' elaborates and transforms these social codes. The examination of a story and discourse, Chatman argues, reveals the ideological tasks of the narrative.

To examine religion and secularism as embedded imaginaries, and to probe particular modalities of their overlapping, this section outlines a preliminary analytic framework from a hermeneutic perspective. I integrate certain aspects of Fiske and Chatman's models, particularly their enunciation of the ideological and representational dimensions of television narratives in terms of the larger concept of imaginaries. Following Ricoeur (1992: 143), imaginaries are understood as complex 'detours of mediations' via the idioms of myths, metaphors, stories, symbols, and ideologies. Although Chatman and Fiske's discussion features chronological time, their model is compatible with and opens up possibilities for developing a framework that examines chronological and non-chronological conceptions of time. Margaret Somers's (1994) reformulation of narrative identity provides two useful heuristic concepts that link Chatman and Fiske's model with Ricoeur's hermeneutic perspective. Somers (1994: 625, emphasis in original) pointed out that 'narrative identities are constituted by a person's temporally and spatially variable *place* in culturally constructed stories composed of (breakable) rules, (variable) practices, binding (and unbinding) institutions and the multiple plots of family, nation, or economic life'. Somers (1994: 618) specifies four different types of narratives: *ontological, public, meta, and conceptual.* According to Somers (1994: 619), ontological narratives are 'the stories that social actors use to make sense of—indeed, to act in— their lives'.[17] In short, ontological narratives are about individual selves and their identities. Public narratives, on the other hand, are 'attached to cultural and institutional formations larger than the single individual, to intersubjective networks or institutions', where publicly shared set of beliefs get reproduced. In developing the analytic framework, I draw upon ontological and public narratives, as these are consistent with Chatman, Fiske, and Ricoeur's formulations.

The television programmes in this study, as narratives of Kashmir and Punjab, span a wide range of stories and plots around a set of interconnected themes mediated through religious and secular practices. These can be considered as public narratives that get entangled with the ontological narratives of various individuals and families within the programmes. An examination of the intersections—at the level of stories and plots—provides insights into how the religious and secular identities are co-constituted and constructed. A preliminary examination of the television narratives revealed four interrelated themes: mythical recuperations of the past; religious life-worlds shaped by secular ideals; symbolic articulations of artifacts, objects, and things in terms of geographies and territoriality; and the constitution of class–caste, gender, and citizen-subjects.

RELIGION AND SECULARISM AS EMBEDDED IMAGINARIES

Scholars have identified the copresence of religious and secular symbols in India's public spaces but considered these as mutually incompatible value systems. I argue that televisual discourses of nation on Doordarshan, structured through particular conceptions of secularism, are overdetermined by religious idioms and metaphors, thereby indicating that religion and secularism can be seen as embedded imaginaries rather than binaries. The study of religion and secularism elaborated via television narratives indicated the persistence of certain spatial and temporal themes that not only reveal the presence of the dominant discourse of nation and nationalism, but also point to the co-imbrications of religious and secular practices. As I shall demonstrate in the following sections, the dominant discourses of nation become visible at the surface of the television narrative, whereas religion and secularism as embedded imaginaries can be tracked in the multiple plot lines and the intersubjective webs of relations between the characters and communities. The interplay of public and ontological narratives mediated by linear and phenomenological notions of time constitute several micro and macro events within the unfolding plots of the television narratives. The brief summaries of the television narratives set up the context for the ensuing analysis.

The 13-episode television series *Choli Daman* (henceforth *Choli*), directed by M. S. Sathyu and telecast in 1989, was set in Punjab in the early and mid-1980s. M. S. Sathyu earlier directed the acclaimed movie *Garam Hawa* (Hot Winds, 1973), based on Ismat Chugtai's short story that probes the travails of partition on a Muslim family in India. While the television series cannot be compared in a similar vein to the movie, the series does offer several deeper reflections on the question of the religious and the secular. *Choli* sketched the relations between a Hindu and a Sikh family in a small town near the cities of Amritsar and Jullundar in Punjab. The direct allusion to the sociopolitical situation during the early to mid-1980s in Punjab binds the unfolding story.

The two families remained friends, but the social and political tensions began to affect their interpersonal worlds, and their relationship becomes strained and the various characters in the story deal with the tensions in different ways.

The 43-episode television series *Gul Gulshan Gulfam* (henceforth *Gul*), directed by Ved Rahi and telecast in 1990–91, unlike *Choli*, is disengaged from the sociopolitical tensions of Kashmir.[18] The series was written by a prominent Kashmiri writer and dramatist, Pran Kishore, who recently wrote a novel based on the same name.[19] As the story unfolds, and the trials and tribulations of Haji and Aziza, the ambitions of their children, and the lives of their grandchildren are interspersed with everyday concerns of securing a decent livelihood. Tensions between tradition and modernity are sketched out through the life-worlds of the characters. More importantly, the relationship of Kashmir with India, questions of nation and belongingness, and of culture and identity punctuate the narrative. Both programme series—*Choli* and *Gul*—can be considered as 'consensus' narratives (Thorburn, 1987) that are largely silent on the underlying causes of political unrest and violence in Punjab and Kashmir. Although politics remains in the background, and state violence is glossed over in favour of certain intercommunal and interreligious discourse, the micro-stories and specific plotlines in the respective series directly confront questions of conflict and violence. While a benign realism operates, sometimes lapsing into naturalistic and sentimental melodrama, the two series, however, foreground the problematic of religious–secular discourse that this chapter investigates.

The television programme series *Kashmir File*, produced by Arun Kaul and telecast once a week from 1995 onwards, combines features of a documentary and a news magazine. The programme series provides explicit political commentary on the Kashmir issue through various topics. The people who speak in the programme are government representatives, bureaucratic officials, and other political elites. Nalini Singh, an independent journalist, produced the documentary on Punjab, *Punjab 1983*. The main focus of the documentary on Punjab began with the usual investigative formulation of the question: 'Why did the sad tragedy happen in Punjab?' The question refers to the 1983 slaying of Hindu passengers in a bus by Sikh terrorists in Punjab, and the documentary probes the status of Hindu–Sikh relations in Punjab in the wake of this event.

Secular Ideals and Religious Life-Worlds

In *Gul*, an example of the idea of secularism unfolds when the boatman, Haji, is travelling back to Kashmir on a train, after spending a few weeks in Bombay in search of his third son, Ghulam Qadeer, who has fled his home. In the train, Haji's fellow traveller is Nityanand, a devout Hindu *sadhu* (priest). The contemporary tensions in Kashmir, though not referred to in the entire series, remain the crucial hinge on which the narrative is built. Haji and Nityanand locate each other as belonging to Kashmir. The train conversation between them is underlined by two kinds of narratives: an outwardly visible public narrative that infuses their discussion with messages of 'unity in diversity' and *hum sab ek hain* (we are all one), along with a deeper ontological narrative grounded in their personal and community identities marking their 'habitus'. Haji, with his dress and cap, and Nityanand, with his saffron robes, have well-defined religious identities. Haji's attire marks him as a Kashmiri, unlike Nityanand. Haji is portrayed as a devout Muslim whose life-world is built around Islamic practices. Some of these become visible through his physical characteristics: mark on the forehead indicating that he prays regularly, the cap, and other gestures, all symbolic markers of his religious identity. One can be tempted to argue that the symbolic markers are a deliberate strategy to foreground Haji's 'Muslim-ness', a sort of visual stereotyping. This could, perhaps, be a plausible interpretation. However, I resist such an interpretation and look beyond to see the interplay of religious idioms and imagination with the secularist ideals.

After becoming familiar with each other, and as the conversation continues, Nityanand points out that he is a frequent traveller to Kashmir and is dedicated to the teachings of Swami Vivekananda. Haji, aware of Vivekananda's teachings, having been introduced to them years earlier by a foreign visitor to his houseboat, says that after he learned about Swami Vivekananda's teaching, it became clear to him that all religions teach the same principles of love. Nityanand's response acquires a double tone when he says—referring to religious bigots (could be read as Kashmiri or other Muslims living in India)—that those who understand the soul of their religion do not criticize other beliefs. Haji, then, concludes that Kashmir is a living witness and that the soul of all religions is one. A cursory 'reading' (or 'viewing') of the conversation shows that it is layered with several religious idioms and metaphors. Although Haji and Nityanand develop the public narrative of secularism, their conversation evokes a far greater social power than in translation. The translated version may suggest a linear and empirical reality, but the Hindi (as also Urdu) conversation works through several metaphors. These utterances trigger numerous collective memories—of Hindu–Muslim relationships, of partition of India and Pakistan, the Kashmir conflict, religious strife, and communal violence. In short it represents, in an encapsulated form, a history of communities in conflict in postcolonial India. These collective memories are recuperated not in terms of a linear or 'empty homogeneous time', but in terms of heterogeneous time constituted out of the narrative fragments grounded in certain 'religious hermeneutic imaginations of the political'. Haji marks his day by prayer time rather than clock time or in terms of 'duration', but as heterogeneous time represented through his *iman* (faith) and *ibadat* (worship).[20] Connolly (2006: 77–78) suggested,

> In traditional Islam, *iman* typically translated into English as 'faith', is not a singular epistemological means that guarantees God's existence for the believer. It is better translated as the virtue of faithfulness toward God, an unquestioning habit of obedience ... a disposition that has to be cultivated like any other.

The same applies for *ibadat* as it dissolves the distinction between the sacred and the profane. Further, the private–public division secular time seeks to create (freedom of private belief and participation as abstract citizens) is incommensurable in understanding the centrality of *iman* and *ibadat* for Haji. The same problem arises in understanding Guna's conceptions of secularism she seeks to engage with through the idea of *bhakti*. Indeed, what we notice here is the sort of 'transvaluation' of the religious and the secular ideals that Casanova (1994) indicated.

Guna's personal reflections on the lack of inter-community co-existence and the several exchanges with her husband, Ram Lal, daughter, Roshni, and son, Vinod, emerge from deeply held religious beliefs. Her bemoaning the loss of Hindu–Sikh unity and of the infusion of *siasat* (bad politics) in the holy shrines reflects her anxieties. These very anxieties provide Guna a context for nuanced elaboration of religious tolerance that cuts across not just the Hindu–Sikh relations but also with Muslims. At an obvious level, Guna's observations on the mixing of religion with politics point to the secularism of Nehru as *dharma nirpekshata* which espouses the separation of religion from politics. But Guna's personal reflections, muttered when seeking *darsan* of the deities, foreground the Gandhian version of *sarva dharma sambhava* where religion and politics become intricately linked. Here politics is shaped by ethical and moral conduct. Guna's personal reflections via the process of *darsan* in the form of the intrapersonal modality of communication with the divine enable her to overcome the subject–object distinction that is visible in her interpersonal exchanges with family members.

In *Choli*, the presence of a nameless senile woman, though outside the narrative, performs a crucial role in constituting secularism. The 1947 partition of India and Pakistan and the subsequent violence and trauma—as represented by the senile woman who lost her daughters in the violence along with her sanity—is mapped onto the contemporary Hindu–Sikh tensions. The woman seems to embody a secular voice that has been injured. Her recurring statement, 'I will write a letter to Nehru', is evocative of the loss of Nehru's idea of secularism, particularly in the 1980s. Jawaharlal Nehru, the absent signifier, triggers several ideas. The invocation of Nehru's name by the senile woman, suggesting that he will bring the Hindus and Sikhs to their senses, draws upon not only the loss but also the need for Nehru's conception of secularism that seems to be absent from the narrative of *Choli* and, by implication, from sociopolitical life in 1980s postcolonial India.

In the documentary *Kashmir File*, secularism appears through an inherent claim to factuality and objectivity in representing the Kashmir issue by invoking Hindu mythology and connecting it with history. In fact, there is a persistent switch between mythology and history. The visual rendering of landscape, lakes, houseboats, and *shikara*s along with arts and artefacts, and the recitation of Sanskritic verses along with Kashmiri music, organize the expression of secularism and connect it to national culture. According to the presenter, 'This one word, *Kashmiriyat*, represents the history, sufi traditions, rishi thoughts, and this flowery valley's *gunga-jumni* face—an exemplary thing which is unique in itself', while the former Governor of Jammu and Kashmir, General K. V. Krishna Rao, suggested that 'Kashmiriyat is quite consistent with the Indian ethos of composite culture and unity in diversity'. Here Kashmir is considered an embodiment of secularism and thus, through secularism, Kashmir gets bonded with the nation. *Punjab 1983*, on the other hand, enunciates secularism quite differently due to its investigative nature that seeks to elicit people's views on the Punjab situation. The interviews with the middle class traders suggested that Hindu–Sikh relations have remained cordial despite the ongoing violence. The secular character of the Hindu and Sikh communities is further explained by the presenter through interviews of Sikhs who have helped their Hindu brethren in the face of threats to their own lives from terrorists.

Invocations of the Past

The titles of both fictional series are suggestive of a metaphorical relationship in terms of a family. 'Gul Gulshan Gulfam', the names of the three houseboats, is evocative of a filial bond. 'Choli Daman' invokes the metaphor of blood and belonging through a reference to a particular form of clothing, the 'choli' (a jacket, bodice) that is used to cover a woman's body, or more precisely, the 'daman'. This metaphoric valence draws upon a repertoire of everyday language–sedimented understanding—where 'choli' is incomplete without the 'daman'. The evocative suggestion here is a close relationship—*choli daman ka saath hona*—between Hindus and Sikhs. The narratives work around a series of threats posed to the metaphorical notions and the subsequent resolution of the threat.

The past is evoked within these two fictional narratives through several textual strategies. The opening sequence of both *Choli* and *Gul*—a montage of visual shots with songs and music—prefigure certain notions of 'Kashmir' and 'Punjab'. In *Gul*, the visual shots show the houseboats, *shikaras*, Dal Lake—all standing in as significations of Kashmir. Then, the voiceover introduction, as the visual depictions continue, affirms that Kashmir is a 'heaven on earth', symbolizing the state as an idealized and a beautiful place. Despite the common introduction, both fictional narratives exhibit some crucial differences. While Kashmir is referred to in feminized terms, emphasizing its natural beauty and idealized state, a set of stereotypical signifiers project a martial character of Punjab and its people. Common to both the opening sequences is the marking of the specific identities with particular cultural designators such as Kashmiri garb, Muslim 'fez' caps, houseboats, *shikaras*, Sikh turbans, gurudwaras, and so on, that bear the signature of religion.[21]

In the documentary *Kashmir File*, the past is recuperated through a set of textual strategies that work upon, and inflect, the social ideologies embedded within the first theme. The presenter's references to the river Vyeth (Jhelum), drawing upon the authority of the Hindu scripture Rigveda—along with a Sanskrit verse on the river rendered through music—come together with visuals of art pieces, scriptural paintings, deities, and so on to organize the opening narrative sequence and to introduce the program series:

> According to Kashmir's oldest scriptural book, Neelmad Puran, God Shiva brought Parvati to Earth from the nether world. In Verinag, at a place Vyeth-butur, he struck his trident in [*sic*] Earth and created a water fountain. This has been called Vyeth. Kashmir has rich resources of water in the form of ponds, lakes and rivers. Vitasta has been called a great holy river. Kashmir has been called Vyethastika.

First, at the verbal level, several tropes are deployed. The conflation of Kashmir into Vyethastika through explicit Hindu categories and the coding of Kashmir in terms of a religious metaphor—that is, a holy river created by a divine force outside history—mythologizes it. The series of montage shots of houseboats, *shikaras*, lakes, and ponds, along with religious places of worship—temples and mosques—draw upon common motifs from the social imaginary of nation in postcolonial India. These visuals, known collectively as referring to India's nationhood, explicitly stress territory and geography.

Symbolic Geographies and Territoriality

A range of symbolic meanings, from ideologies of territoriality and sovereignty to implicit understanding of objects, places, and things framed the various television narratives. The symbolic evocations of everyday objects not only provide interesting intersubjective mediations of religious and secular practices but also point to their overlaps. *Gul*, *Choli*, and *Kashmir File* begin with an explicit marking of space and place in the introductory sequences. In fact, a common feature is the manner in which the programmes begin and end by drawing upon broad geographic metaphors. The narrative of *Gul* has an extensive coding of geographical features. The idea of geography in *Gul* can be discerned at two mutually interacting levels. First is the geography of place, rendered through the visual imagery of the landscape, locales, towns, cities, and so on. These visual depictions link the particularities of Kashmir, such as the lakes, houseboats, *shikaras*, *chinars*, and so on, to the nation. The social and symbolic meanings of the Dal Lake, houseboats, and *shikaras* provide a sort of 'geographical family' relationship. For instance, the Dal Lake, besides its natural beauty, gives the houseboat and the *shikaras* an identity. One does not exist without the other. This geographical family is tied to the human characters, their families, and the unfolding drama that 'enact' particular representations of the nation. Second, interspersed within the *Gul* narrative, typical Kashmiri everyday objects and artefacts constitute a 'household geography'. The *kangdi*, *kahwa*, *murghabi*, *sargam gosht*, *pashmina* shawls, *wazawan*, apple orchards, and so on, mark out this space.[22] The social function—and signification—of these objects locate it within the collective familiarity with the motifs of the nation.

In one particular episode of *Gul*, Narayan Joo is dying and Haji is by his bedside. He utters, 'I don't care about leaving the world, but I am sad that I am leaving Kashmir. This land! This air! These lakes! I can't imagine living without all these.' Narayan, as he slowly loses his breath, asks Haji whether these things will be available where he is going and reminds him of the time they spent together under the *chinars* and *badam* trees (a certain species of trees particular to Kashmir). As he says this, his face slowly dissolves and blends with the landscape and *chinar* trees. Narayan's identity as a Kashmiri pandit is, then, linked with Kashmir when he says, 'Tell me dear friend, how can a Kashmiri pandit live without all these things?' Within this segment, Narayan Joo draws upon a particular geography of Kashmir—the landscape, the *chinar*s, and the *badam* trees. These are central to his identity. The reference to another identity, of a Kashmiri pandit, is significant as it marks the geographic space created by Narayan Joo, but it also evokes the nation via politics: the sociopolitical situation in Kashmir led to a large scale forced migration of Kashmiri pandits, a minority Hindu community, to New Delhi during the late 1980s. Narayan Joo's last reflections indirectly allude to the politics of Kashmir.

References to geography and place in *Choli* were not as emphatic as in *Gul*. The opening introductory sequence, common to all episodes, frames Punjab with typical geographical characteristics, that is, landscape, towns and streets depicting a mass of turbaned Sikhs, tunes of religious Punjabi hymns, wedding songs and dances by men and women. This audio-visual montage locates Punjab in terms of a distinct social and cultural identity. An element that stands out, and also defines the cultural aspects, is geography.

Religious geography also punctuates the narrative in terms of Sikh and Hindu shrines. The suggestive visual evocation of the exterior of gurudwaras, and the slow camera movement into the inner precincts of the shrine to make the religious symbols and icons visible distinctively locates Punjab vis-à-vis the nation. The figure of gurudwaras, in fact, becomes crucial in the narrative because apart from drawing upon a collective identity of Punjab, it represents a crisis of identity for Guna, especially as she cannot visit the holy place. The tensions around Roshni's, Vinod's and Ram Lal's lives were mediated by gurudwaras.

In *Kashmir File*, the mythological coding of Kashmir through the deployment of the Hindu past linked geographical aspects like the origins of the Jhelum River named 'Vyethastika'. Kashmir gets conflated with Vyethastika here. The story of 'Vyetha-gatha', as the epic story of the holy river (*vitasta*), the presenter says, stands as 'a mute witness to the tragedy being written on its shore'. The tragedy here refers to the political unrest in Kashmir. A series of visual images of Kashmir's landscape and rivers, flora and fauna, temples and mosques symbolically pull together these locales and places into a condensed set of social meanings that designate Kashmir and link it to national culture.

Class–Caste, Gender, and the 'Other'

The opening voiceover synopsis of the *Gul* cast of characters emphasized the Kashmiri identities of individuals in terms of their beliefs, values, and attitudes.

As the narrative progressed, this preliminary sketch of identities acquired distinctive and concrete class, caste, gender, and religious manifestations that had a bearing on the way citizen–subjects were constituted. The strong Kashmiri identity of Haji and Narayan Joo became a locus of their existence, and it was a threat to this identity that disrupted the narrative.

In *Gul*, two kinds of outsiders visited Kashmir. For the tourists on the houseboats, Kashmir became an object of desire and fantasy, almost like a fairyland away from their own, perhaps, tension-filled world and lives. The upper class–caste backgrounds of houseboat tourists Bhosale and Rathinder Singh, perceived through their family names and occupation, bestowed a certain 'symbolic power'. Bhosale, a customs officer from Bombay, and his family represented upper–middle class citizen-subjects. Rathinder Singh's descent from the erstwhile rulers of Rajasthan provided him a particular 'gaze' through which he experienced Kashmir, that is, through the lens of nostalgia and loss that linked him with his ancestors through collective memories of Kashmir. William, a benevolent outsider from England, is visiting the houseboats to relive memories of his grandfather, who, for years, had journeyed to Kashmir—and Haji's houseboats. The Victorian glorification of nature and beauty (a common colonial trope) through which William's grandfather glimpsed and wrote about the *chinar*s, provided a symbolic identity to Kashmir. William's language, while retaining a dominant Victorian motif, turns it around a bit by lacing it with environmental concerns.

Representations of gender in *Gul* did not significantly inflect the ways in which Kashmir and, through it, the nation was articulated. Operating within a broad set of patriarchal relations, gender was located in terms of home, domesticity, passivity, and so forth. Aziza's role and place within the family, though assertive, was depicted through familial melancholic situations, and mostly visible in the kitchen either preparing food for the family or doing household chores. Unlike *Gul*, gender representations in *Choli* displayed a direct engagement with the nation through references to the Hindu and Sikh relations. Guna and Roshni articulated these in particular ways. The characters in *Choli*, besides deploying a nation-as-family metaphor, revealed facets of nation and citizenship through particular class, caste, gender, and religious identities. As the tensions began to affect the relationship between the two families, Ram Lal expressed an ambivalence that turned to bitterness as the narrative unfolded. Vinod, on the other hand, demonstrated his firm anti-Sikh resolve through his verbal duels with others as he questioned Sikh patriotic virtues. Vinod's deep-seated anti-Sikh views surfaced in his attitude towards his sister's relationship with a Sikh man, Joginder.

The repositioning of Kashmir in *Kashmir File* (as Vyethastika) informed the narrative of nation being worked out through the invocation of a menacing 'other', either Pakistan or the terrorists who posed a threat to the nation. Through such a rendering of the 'other', human rights violations and subsequent violence in Kashmir were explained (and justified). The arguments assembled about Kashmir and the exposition of these through the narrative structure at multiple, overlapping levels—presenter's comments, voiceover narration, interviews, songs and music, visual images, and so on—connoted a middle-class, upper-caste framing of the nation. *Punjab 1983*, based on a series of interviews with middle class individuals and a few peasants and women, displayed marked differences from *Kashmir File*. The presenter's comments and voiceover narration provided a gentle critique of politics in Punjab, but the documentary operated within the mainstream perspective in which the nation stood outside of critique.

CONCLUDING REMARKS

The television narratives pointed to the persistence of the dominant discourse of nation and secularism (public narrative of the state) along with the interplay between religious and secular idioms, metaphors, symbols, and practices (ontological narratives of individuals and communities). Despite the middle and upper class–caste backgrounds of the characters that reproduced aspects of the public narrative, certain 'transvaluations' across the religious and secular categories pointed both to the problems and prospects for secularism in India. The religious idioms and metaphors through which borders, boundaries, and symbolic geographies became visible in fictional series and documentaries revealed territory and identity as primary constitutive elements of the nation.[23] While the documentaries framed discussions of territorial integrity of India in explicit Hindu categories, the fictional series drew upon a range of interreligious ideas that tended to reproduce the dominant strands of territoriality, but also pointed to some alternatives.

The television narratives revealed two distinct modes of narrating secularism. First, the state-based notions with their stereotypical trappings through which universal values of different religions were stressed. This was more pronounced in documentaries but also present in the fictional series. Second, in the fictional series, certain secular ideals were espoused through the life-worlds of the characters suffused with religious beliefs and practices that articulated ideas of interreligious harmony and tolerance. Several religious principles and practices, expressed in terms of *bhakti*, *darsan*, *iman*, and *ibadat*, can be considered as the hermeneutic imaginations of the political, where the sacred and the profane, the private and the public come together in some sort of a productive tension. Aijaz Ahmad (2005: 5–6) pointed out to some examples of interreligious conversations when certain 'traditions of anti-caste devotional theism which arose from inside Hinduism opened-up themselves, profoundly, to strands of transgressive devotionalism in certain dissents within Islam ... the Sufi's hatred for *Sharia* seemed familiar to the anti-brahminical *sant*, so that historically novel kinds of syncreticism were born out of the encounter'.

For the past several years, particularly after the events of 11 September 2001, the return of the religious, in quite unexpected ways, has shaped contemporary global discourse. Along with the rapid growth of television and other media in the non-Western world, there has been a concomitant rise in the representations of religious and secular practices. Through the study of Indian television narratives, this chapter in a preliminary manner demonstrated that a theoretical formulation of religion and secularism as embedded imaginaries, with a focus on multiple temporalities, could be usefully employed in other postcolonial and non-Western settings. An immediate gain from such an approach is the possibility of identifying concrete 'spaces for dialogue' between religious and secular practices akin to what Ahmad outlined above.

NOTES

1. It is difficult to see religion and secularism together because most accounts suggest these terms name oppositions and that 'religion is merely a historical trace of that which has been overcome by secularism ... Secularization is at the heart of the intertwined Enlightenment narratives of modernization, rationalization, and progress, all of which depend on the overcoming of religious dogma by reason ...' See Jakobsen and Pellegrini (2000: 2–3).
2. In an earlier discussion, Chakrabarty (2002b: 22–23) asserted that 'religion is a major and enduring fact of Indian political life ... But Indian historians—the best of whom today are of a Marxist and Left-liberal persuasion—have never been able to develop any framework capable of comprehending the phenomenon'.
3. Connolly (2006) provides a brilliant exposition of secularism and religion drawing from Talal Asad's work and developing arguments about a 'minor tradition' in Europe regarding multidimensional pluralism. In an earlier work, Connolly (1999) argued for an *ethos of engagement* between religious and secular notions.
4. Several major social and political issues in different regions—Northeast (Nellie violence and other killings), Kashmir (state repression), Punjab (state repression and Operation Bluestar), communal riots (Moradabad, Meerut, Mumbai, Delhi,

Hyderabad, Ahmedabad, Ayodhya), and Dalit killings (in various parts of India)—were ignored, misrepresented, or erased from Doordarshan (Singh, 1984). Some of these issues, particularly those related to Punjab and Kashmir, reappeared as televisual narratives. The 'epistemic' state violence is located within the hegemonic conception of national culture that the government of India has constructed through various modalities—constitutional statutes, legislative enactments, policies, collective histories and biographies, and so on—since Indian independence in 1947. In the last three to four decades, particularly, large-scale violence had state and governmental involvement and the right-wing Hindutva forces, for instance, the massacre of Sikhs in Delhi and northern India in 1984, Muslims after the destruction of the Babri Masjid in 1992, and in Gujarat in 2002. In addition, caste violence and killings of Dalits ('lower-caste' Hindus) has been a common feature of sectarian killings in postcolonial India. See Das (1985), Mathur (1992), Basu and Subrahmanyam (1996), and Vanaik (1997).

5. I use the concept in its hermeneutic sense, that is, 'as lived' and constituted through social practices and beliefs in terms of stories and narratives.
6. The debates in India about the relevance of broadcasting to national development and social change began as early as 1966, but the year 1982 brought a major break with previous government policies. 'Television went through major changes under what has been called, in the official language, *The Special Expansion Plan for TV*, an important state initiative in reorganizing television during the 1980s' (Sinha and Asthana (2004: 1175).
7. National integration refers to a wide variety of processes associated with the project of nation-building and state formation. As a political project of the postcolonial Indian state for forging disparate religious and socially backward constituents of the society into a nation, it operates through various subjective and objective processes—emotional, spiritual, moral, cultural, economic, and political integration—usually carried out through the state's various institutional apparatuses.
8. In the early history of broadcasting in India, religious-based programmes were avoided due to a certain interpretation of secularism, which was defined by the absence of religion from state and public discourse. However, since the mid-1980s, state-run radio and television allocated a significant portion of the programming for religious events and festivals. This idea of secularism—equal representation to all religions—was inscribed as a broadcasting code. See Rajagopal (2001: 75–86).
9. It is difficult to separate television programmes of the 1980s into distinct genres for a number of reasons. For instance, almost all programming during this period was dominated by developmental and national integration themes. Programmes arbitrarily categorized into groups by state-run television displayed certain generic characteristics, but frequently overlapped. For example: drama, mythological, historical, patriotic, film-based, comedy, detective, children, youth, literature, classical music, and so on. Some programmes that became popular with the audiences included comedy and humour series such as *Yeh Jo Hai Zindagi*, *Wagle Ki Duniya*, *Mr. Yogi*, and *Mungeri Lal Ke Haseen Sapne*; the detective series *Karamchand* and *Byomkesh*

Bakshi (adapted from the Bengali writings of Sharadindu Bandopadhyaya); drama series such as *Khandan*, *Nukkad*, *Sansar*, *Humrahi*, and so on. There were numerous literary adaptations that included *Ek Kahani* and *Katha Sagar* based on short stories from Indian languages, *Charitraheen* and *Mujrim Haazir* from the Bengali classics of Sarat Chandra and Bimal Mitra, *Mulla Nusruddin* from the Arabic language that was based on the famous Sufi mystic and jester, and *Malgudi Days*, R. K. Narayan's English short stories. In recent years, the famous Hindi–Urdu literary figure and filmmaker Gulzar adapted Munshi Premchand's works for Doordarshan.

10. What is termed as sectarianism in Western societies refers to communalism in India (and South Asia). Communalism, then, is the name for religious hatred and violence. In 1989, during the Ayodhya mosque–temple dispute, Purushottam Agarwal, political activist of an anti-communal organization, created a slogan—*kan kan mein vyape hein Ram, mat badkao danga lekar unka naam* ('Ram permeates every particle of the universe, do not instigate riots in his name')—to counter the Hindu right-wing stridency and the looming violence. Mankekar points out that the left and liberal intellectuals were hostile to the slogan. Agarwal argued that he created the slogan to 'strategically acknowledge and appeal to the everyday religiosity of Hindus and enable them to resist Hindu nationalists' rhetoric'. See Mankekar (1999: 198–200).
11. I undertook several visits to Doordarshan's main headquarters in New Delhi in 1999, 2000, and 2001 to talk to programme executives and to procure some of the series and documentaries. They told me on condition of anonymity that the Ministry of Home and internal security of the government of India created separate units and 'cells' on Kashmir, Punjab, and the Northeast regions and that any interviews on the subject and access to internal files are out of bounds.
12. The concept of 'homogeneous empty time', first enunciated by Walter Benjamin and later extended by Benedict Anderson in his classic formulation of nation as 'imagined community', refers to a teleological, historicist idea of time in which modernity and progress are perceived as linear and singular.
13. According to Chatterjee (2004: 7), 'People can imagine themselves in empty homogeneous time; they do not live in it ... many examples from the postcolonial world [that] suggest the presence of a dense and heterogeneous time. In those places, one could show industrial capitalists delaying the closing of the business deal because they hadn't yet heard from their respective astrologers, or industrial workers who would not touch a new machine until it had been consecrated with appropriate religious rites ... To call this the co-presence of several times—the time of the modern and the time of the pre-modern—is only to endorse the utopianism of western modernity.'
14. Ricoeur's hermeneutic formulation of symbols in terms of 'double intentionality' suggests that meanings are not given intuitively to the subject but are rather mediated. Although Ricouer's primary references are the Judaeo-Christian sources, his ideas can be extended to other religious traditions as well. See Kearney (1989).

15. Todd Gitlin (1979: 254) studied the 'hegemonic process' in American television entertainment and suggested that it supports the larger hegemony of the capitalist state. Gitlin stated that on American television, 'hegemony is reasserted in different ways at different times, even by different logics' and notes 'some of the forms in which ideological hegemony is embedded: format and formula; genre; setting and character type; slant and solution'. In their 'ideological readings' of the news and current affairs British television programme *Panorama*, Stuart Hall, Ian Connell, and Lidia Curti (1981) examined the contexts in which news produces the 'hegemony of the state' by representing elite interests as general interests through a plurality of messages that affirm state power.
16. Although Ricoeur critiqued the structuralist approach to narrative for the neglect of the non-chronological dimension of temporality, he acknowledged their indispensable role in uncovering the ideological aspects of narratives. He advocated combining the ideological analysis with a hermeneutic one. A critique of ideology may be embraced therefore as 'a view through which any kind of mediation of faith must pass. To smash the idols is also to let symbols speak'. See Richard Kearney (2004: 82).
17. The term 'ontological' used at an individual level may suggest essentialized and fixed self, but Somers (1994: 618) argues, 'Ontological narrativity, like the self, is neither a priori nor fixed. Ontological narratives make identity and the self something that one *becomes* … Ontological narratives are, above all, social and interpersonal.'
18. The first fifteen episodes of the television series was shot on location in Kashmir in 1989; but due to the ongoing violence in the Kashmir Valley, the production crew had to move to Bombay (Mumbai) to shoot the remaining episodes.
19. Pran Kishore's novel published by Harpers Collins which was written based on his original writings for the television series was featured in popular media in 2017. See Awaasthi (2016) and Naqash (2017).
20. Singh and Bhargava (2002: 631) have pointed to the Marxist misreading of the religious in Anand Patwardhan's documentary *Bombay: Hamara Shehr* (Bombay: Our City), where Patwardhan interviewing a mill worker asks a series of questions about when they would fight back against the oppressive conditions in the factory. The worker uses the metaphors of prayer and worship in Hindi, *voh aadesh denge tab na,* which is translated in the documentary as 'he will bless us', instead of 'we will fight when he commands us'. According to Singh and Bhargava, this is not just an issue of mistranslation but rather a larger problem surfacing as an 'epistemological gap between Patwardhan and the Worker 1. The statement made by Worker 1 is at loggerheads with everything modern secular rationality from European Enlightenment onwards has taught us to believe in'. My argument is similar in that we need to be attentive to the particular histories of ways of being without discounting these as some anachronistic practices.
21. Shahid Amin (2004) talks about how the Indian Muslim (Musalman) was stereotyped through the Turkish cap in popular representations of 'unity in diversity' in government produced posters.

22. *Kangdi* is a small earthen pot used to warm oneself during winters. *Kahwa* is a green tea prepared with a flavour of saffron. *Murghabi* is a species of bird particular to Kashmir. *Sargam Gosht* is a type of meat. The material of the Pashmina shawl comes from the underbelly of a goat called *Pashmina*, and *wazwan* refers to the ritualistic feast served to a guest.
23. Sankaran Krishna (1999: 242–43) argued that the geographical narration of the nation has been a powerful impulse within the postcolonial nationalist imaginary. The internal dynamics of this imagination in postcolonial India has shifted over the years, but the notions of territory and identity have remained consistent, and that 'the recent history of South Asia suggests that every attempt at forcibly aligning territory and identity has unleashed ethnonationalist movements and violence ... the fiction of homogeneity reigns hegemonic over both the managers of nation-state and many insurgent movements fighting against them'.

4 | Patriotism and Its Avatars

Tracking the National–Global Dialectic in Music Videos and Television Commercials

In recent years, discussions in social sciences and postcolonial studies have identified *cosmopolitanism* and *post-nationalism*[1] as two major notions that seek to surpass the nation-state. As a framing device for the paradigm of globalization, certain components of the post-national thesis have indeed proved influential in explaining the gradual erosion of the old certainties of nation-state, but do not adequately explain how the nation-state itself is accommodating globalization to preserve, and thereby strengthen, its hegemony. Interestingly, the ascendancy of such ideas has been accompanied by the gradual dislodging of materialist critiques of capitalist expansion (read: globalization) in the postcolonial world. One can discern a certain disquiet that prevails behind the sophistications and subtleties through which the contemporary moment of globalization is being theorized. In postcolonial India, the two 'cultural systems', nationalism and globalization, have an enduring influence, and it would be theoretically significant to trace their mutual effects in the context of the music video genre, particularly the procedures through which ideas of patriotism get articulated.

Leela Fernandes (2000: 612) probed the post-national thesis by examining 'the ways in which "globality" is invented through the deployment of nationalist narratives', while pointing out to the 'hybrid' relationship between the national and the global, and the place of gender in such configurations. In addition, Arvind Rajagopal (1998: 16) noted that the national and the global were increasingly being shaped by Hindu themes and idioms, which coincided with the expansion of state-run television thereby creating a single mediated visual regime from the late 1980s. Indeed, for Rajagopal, the confluence of several forces such as economic liberalization facilitated the rise of right-wing politics in India. For Rajagopal, therefore,

> [the] visual regime was largely shaped in a struggle between the Hindu Right and its secular opponents, where, it is fair to say, the Hindu Right gained most ground. It was from this reformulated political consensus that advertising culture drew its fundamental understandings of the mode of signifying relations between the diverse classes and communities that comprise Indian society. Through advertisements we can see the reflected and changing shape of an increasingly Hinduized public.

In this chapter, I extend some of these key points identified by Fernandes and Rajagopal by formulating my task in a different way: showing how hegemonic articulations of the national and the global work along the axes of the visual, and the constitution of 'new' forms of patriotism. The visual is understood as a social and cultural practice (Foster, 1988) embedded within politico-economic and material contexts of production, distribution, circulation, and reception. The various references to visual in the chapter, unless mentioned otherwise, centre on television in general and the music video genre in particular. The concept of hybridity, despite its explanatory purchase in media and cultural theory, does not capture the full range of power dynamics and material coordinates of nationalism and globalization. Rather than rejecting hybridity tout court, I suggest a nuanced understanding of hybridity vis-à-vis a dialectical approach. Instead of asking whether the power of the nation-state is eroding under the impact of globalizing forces, it would be useful to examine the 'internal structures'—the space constituted by the ideological cementing of the discourse of the national and the global—that are ambivalent and contradictory and seem to reactivate patriotism.

There are deeper issues at stake in the national–global representations in music videos, which this chapter will identify and explore. For instance, some of these issues centre on mobilizations of middle-class/upper-caste subjectivities and contradictory articulations of gender and religious identities in the media. I probe the issues through a set of interrelated questions. How do the national and global representations in selected music videos interact to produce particular conceptions of patriotism? How does the visual in the selected music videos generate notions of patriotism vis-à-vis discourses of the national and the global? In what ways are citizen/consumer-subjects constituted through such representations in selected music videos?

The chapter is divided into five broad sections. In the first section , I trace historical notions of patriotism in select media forms and demonstrate the importance of media in producing nationalism. The second section provides a brief account of nation, globalization, and the visual. The critical discussion of various concepts here serves as a specific context for the study by pointing out the politically charged meanings that cluster around constructions of patriotism. The third section provides background information on the music videos, and lays out the methodological protocols for the study. In the fourth section, I analyse the selected music videos and engage in a theoretical discussion on the articulations of the national and the global and the construction of patriotism vis-à-vis the visual discourse. Finally, in the last section, the conclusions are situated against the background of the findings.

MYTHOLOGIES OF PATRIOTISM

Although the *Oxford English Dictionary*'s definition of patriotism refers to 'love and loyal support of one's country', and may sound rather innocuous, the term has a far greater semantic and emotive force—a range of meanings cluster around, charging it with significations always in excess than can be described. The congeries of meanings provides patriotism with the glue that makes the nation feasible. Benedict Anderson (1983: 141–44) puts this point quite nicely while pointing to the power of patriotism and its hold on people's imaginations:

> … it is doubtful whether either social change or transformed consciousness in themselves do much to explain the attachment that people feel for the inventions of their imaginations – or, to revive the question raised at the beginning of this text – why people are ready to die for these inventions … so too, if historians, diplomats, politicians and social scientists are quite at ease with the idea of 'national interest,' for most ordinary people of whatever class the whole part of the nation is that it is interestless. Just for that reason it can ask for sacrifice.

After India's independence in 1947, patriotism also meant participating in the tasks of nation-building, development, and modernization, the three rhetorics of the postcolonial nation-state. The articulation of patriotism during the 1950s–60s, a period marked by the *nationalization of the private*, or, in the words of Ravi Sundaram (1999), a time when 'the space of the nation was bracketed and fissured from global space' (Ravi Sundaram, 1999), was characterized by a strong language of destiny, mission, progress, and purpose. According to Satish Deshpande (1993: 25), production and work become central to articulation of patriotism during this period, and 'the protagonist of this model of national development is the producer-patriot'. The Nehruvian state stands testimony to this grand vision that can be glimpsed through hydroelectric dams, irrigation canals, iron and steel industries, architectural projects and public enterprises, all imbued with the ethic of nationalist/socialist realism.

This modernist developmental aesthetic was the lens through which patriotism got refracted. The portrayal in media and cultural production—governmental apparatuses like radio, films division, publications division, commercial Hindi cinema, particularly films songs, as well as national songs—drew upon a wide variety of symbols depicting patriotic acts, feelings, and sentiments through Hindu religious and geographic metaphors. In addition to the all too frequent invocations of kinship, motherland, and blood and belonging, patriotism, in the context of India, is inflected with a religious and sacred duty, that is, devotion to one's country (*desh bhakti*). Popular articulations of patriotism, most notably in Hindi commercial film songs of the 1950s–60s, deployed the language of Nehruvian modernism along with religious, cartographic, and geographic symbols. I do not wish to suggest that a singular discourse of patriotism emerged in Hindi commercial cinema; rather, several films (*Dharti ke Laal*, *Neecha Nagar*, *Do Bigha Zamin*, and so on) portrayed the failures of the Nehruvian project. My interest here is in the songs of certain films (*Jaagriti*, *Sikandar-e-Azam*, *Naya Daur*, *Ganga-Jamuna*, *Kabulivala*, and *Haqeeqat*) that became popular and came to stand in, paradigmatically, as signatures of patriotism in postcolonial India.[2] These songs played at public places—*galli*s, *chauraha*s, *and mohalla*s[3]—on two major national holidays, 26 January (Republic Day) and 15 August (Independence Day), as well as on birth anniversaries of prominent national leaders, every year have had a powerful hold of people's imaginations. Along with these, various forms of print media—calendars, portraits, and posters—produced a set of symbolic representations of the nation that evoked patriotism and nationalism. For instance, the calendar images of *Jai Jawan*, *Jai Kisan* (Hail the soldier! Hail the farmer!)—pervasive in everyday India during the 1960s—refurbished patriotic virtues via the iconic figure of the peasant with sickle in hand and the soldier with a bayonet.[4]

Interesting counterpoints to the earlier representations of patriotism were the series of short programmes made by the state-run television, Doordarshan, during 1988–89. The visual discourse of patriotism makes a decisive shift from the Nehruvian modernist paradigm and the socialist realist imagery to one that has no clear ideological moorings. However, in the field of politics, the ideological bases of this shift can be understood as the nation-state has begun to move towards a neoliberal market regime from a developmental welfare one. The programmes were produced and broadcast on the nationalist movement and its struggles against the British, especially around the time when 'separatist' movements in Punjab, Kashmir, and the Northeast were threatening the project of national integration. These anti-colonial narratives included biographies of freedom fighters and national leaders, and these enactments were quite distinct from the earlier documentaries produced by governmental agencies like the Films Division. Several short films (around five minutes each), collectively titled *Mera Bharat Mahaan* (My India is Great), ostensibly under the name of 'public service advertisements' by a specially created division in Doordarshan, Lok Sanchar Seva Parishad (LSSP), were telecast on the themes of 'national unity' and 'unity in diversity'. Some examples include *Mile Sur* (Melodies Meet), *Desh Raag* (Country's Tune), and *Freedom Run*. The theme of patriotism was a central feature of these productions. *Mera Bharat Mahaan* featured several famous Indian classical music artistes to portray Indian *sanskriti* (culture) and instill a sense of love and pride for the country. *Mile Sur* was a montage of short musical sequences with the artistes performing (either on vocal or instruments) to the tune, 'Mile Sur Mera Tumara' (Let Our Melodies Meet). *Freedom Run* depicted school children with candles and various Indian sportspersons and film personalities jogging along with a torch (representing freedom and patriotism) and singing tunes, while getting in and out of trams and trains, of love and belonging. Patriotism meant a celebration of one's identity and 'Indianness', unlike the valorization of work and production by Nehru's 'producer-patriot'.

With economic reforms and liberalization in 1991, undertaken under instructions from the International Monetary Fund (IMF) and World Bank as part of structural adjustment, the government began to ease economic restrictions on private corporations through a series of policy measures. Though slow in the beginning, privatization soon became a buzzword among various intelligentsia—academics, bureaucrats, journalists, and politicians. The impact of privatization (the term used in most cases interchangeably with globalization) has been decisive during the past few years. In this particular conjuncture, television and Hindi commercial cinema generate their own discourse of patriotism that looks quite distinct from earlier ones. Indeed, this conjuncture is marked by what may be called as the *privatization of the nation* and the *nationalization of the private.* The distinctive feature of this sort of patriotism displayed most notably in films like *Pardes* (Abroad), *Taal* (Tune), and *Yaadein* (Memories), to name few, is that it is driven by liberalization and private media technologies as well as commodities and consumerism. It offers visions of India/nation that seems to rework East/West and home/abroad dichotomies, thereby reinscribing nation within a new set of discourses.

NATIONAL, GLOBAL, AND THE VISUAL: THEORETICAL DETOURS

At a broad level, globalization refers to 'the intensification of economic, political, social and cultural changes across borders' (Holm and Sorenson, quoted in Holton, 1998: 11). Despite the rhetoric about globalization, if there is one field that has decisively influenced contemporary questions around globalization, it is media and cultural production. Frederic Jameson (1998: 55–56) suggests, '... globalization is a communicational concept, which alternately masks and transmits cultural or economic meanings.' What is also interesting here is that Jameson understands the process of globalization as a particular stage of capitalist expansion—the third or multinational stage. According to Stuart Hall (1991: 27), it is within this third stage that contemporary globalization is 'dominated by television and by film, and by the image, imagery, and styles of mass advertising'. Hall's characterization of globalization in terms of cultural processes marked by de-territorialization of experience, identities, places, products, and services plays out in particular ways in India. Pankaj Mishra (1995), referring to India's 'shabby' modernity in his travel accounts in small towns of India, writes about the pervasive presence of these cultural symbols—satellite television, global products, goods and services—in shaping the everyday life in the towns. Sunil Khilnani (1997: 145) distinguishes between 'garbled' modernity represented by small towns and a 'cosmopolitan' sensibility of large Indian cities. Khilnani argues that the 'Indian city had entered a new post-national stage ... and most big city opportunities for consumption are available in [these] small towns: Maruti car salesroom, hotels and fast-food restaurants, shops selling Reeboks and Proline, Titan watches and Videocon electronics ...' I argue that in contemporary India, these processes are increasingly visible through the entanglement of the national and global, and globalization has inflected the nation state in a specific way leading to the reconsolidation of the hegemony of the nation-state and a construction of 'new' nationalism. Thus, the cosmopolitanism and post-nationalism described by Khilnani does not represent the full range of the material shifts indexed by capital remobilization and privatization.

Partha Chatterjee (1998), responding to Arjun Appadurai's (1996) essay, remarked that the time of the 'post-national' (and the cosmopolitan) is not yet on the horizon in postcolonial India. Geeta Kapur and Ashish Rajadhyaksha (2001: 30) caution us 'that there is a complicity evident in the way the globalizers and the political right-wing are able to produce a neo-nationalist address from a combination of market commodification and chauvinistic nostalgia'. Furthermore, Aijaz Ahmad (1995: 12, emphasis in original) outlined a specific relationship between the national and the global. He argued, 'The structural dialectic of imperialism *includes*, in other words, the deepening penetration of all available global spaces by the working of capital *and* intensification of the nation-state form simultaneously. This dialectic produces contradictory effects in the realm of culture and ideology.'

Against these developments, Benedict Anderson's (1983: 15) definition of nation as an 'imagined community' despite treating nations as 'cultural artifacts' is restrictive for three reasons. First, following Philip Schlesinger (1991: 164), it can be argued that Anderson does not explain the consequences of electronic communications on ideas pertaining to the nation in a globalized environment. Second, Anderson's concept of the nation is bound within the confines (in a geographic and sovereign sense) of the nation-state. Third, as we shall see, Anderson lumps together the construction of nation as an outcome of 'print capitalism', without attending to the specificities of colonial and postcolonial societies, which do not follow a similar trajectory of capitalist development. In the context of India, several precolonial and pre-capitalist cultural practices (visual and vernacular) have shaped the conceptions of the nation. The discussions of 'modular' national imagining (or the nationalist model) that the non-European bourgeoisie exported in their own struggles against colonial powers leaves out these precolonial and pre-capitalist cultural practices that shaped the construction of the nation through the visual 'idiom' (Chatterjee, 1993; Pinney, 2001).

The visual is one site where the relationships between the national and the global in the articulation of patriotism can be tracked. Appadurai and Breckenridge (1996: 12) suggest that the contours of the visual can be grasped through a notion of 'interocular field' which, organized in terms of 'the substantive transfer of meanings, scripts, and symbols from one site to another (in surprising ways), is a crucial feature of public culture in contemporary India ... In general, the coevolution of these experiences ... is a crucial part of the emergence of the new Indian consumer-citizen'. Kajri Jain (1995) explains that pre-capitalist image-based cultural practices exist alongside and intersect with mass mediated images. In her study of pictorial calendars in everyday contexts, Jain states that the traditional and the modern elements get mixed up in urban India. In bringing the formulations of these scholars together, on the one hand, I point to their common motifs about the 'intermeshing' of various modes of visualities, and on the other, show the cursory references to television without outlining concrete characteristics of how images have become an index of material significations. To grasp these broader changes and shifts, it would be useful to characterize the visual in terms of a *visual regime*. As a theoretical construct, a visual regime explains the various modalities in and through which particular discourses (national and global) organize and structure 'ways of seeing'. Thus, a visual regime in postcolonial India, especially in media and cultural production, draws upon a range of ideologies and social practices—precolonial, pre-capitalist, modern, and capitalist.[5] It is analytically important, then, to position and situate the idea of a visual regime in material contexts rather than treating it as an anthropological construct or an ontological category, something that can be apprehended a priori. As a starting point of the analysis, I extend these ideas against the backdrop of my findings to conduct a theoretical discussion on the shifting modalities of the visual regime vis-à-vis patriotism and national–global dialectic.

ANALYTICAL FRAMEWORK

As outlined earlier, the research questions deal with how national and global representations in selected music videos interact to produce particular conceptions of patriotism, the procedures through which the visual generates notions of patriotism vis-à-vis discourses of the national and the global, and the constitution of citizen/consumer-subjects through such representations. An analysis of the music video genre is undertaken to explore such questions. This genre is a significant site for study over other formats—documentaries, entertainment series, talk shows, game shows, and so on—for two reasons. First, historically, in India, the music video genre, whether through Indian commercial films or televisual music videos, has successfully produced nationalistic sentiments and patriotism and has been very popular with the audiences. Secondly, in the contemporary period, the music videos, as a 'hybrid' televisual genre, are structured by consumerist principles. Hence, it would be significant to explore the various procedures through which nationalism and globalization get deployed in constructing ideas around patriotism. The videos chosen for study are 'Vande Mataram' (Hail Motherland!), 'Apna Desh' (Our

Country), and 'Kho Jaane Do' (Let Me Get Lost). The music videos (around 4–5 minutes each), marketed and released in 1997, in the 50th Independence Day celebrations in India, were a regular fixture on all major television channels (state-run, private, local cable, and transnational networks) for the major part of 1997, the year of the celebrations, and thereafter. These videos mobilized aspects of nationalism, globalization, and consumerism in generating ideas around patriotism. In addition, I examine two Bajaj scooter commercials aired on the state-run television during the later 1980s, and in the early 1990s.

As indicated earlier in the chapter, the short animation clips and music videos depicting the nation, national integration, and so on, on state-run television in the early 1980s, drew upon and reworked the repertoire of Nehruvian socialist–realist visual imagery for the televisual medium. The earlier Doordarshan incarnations of *Mile Sur* short videos gradually acquired a commercial and commodified character. More crucially, however, the televisual commemoration of the fifty years of India's independence, and the impending Kargil conflict with Pakistan, precipitated a corporatization and commodification of the nation and nationalism on private television networks as well as on the state-run television.[6] Srirupa Roy (2001; 2002), in her study of the commemoration of the 50th anniversary of Indian independence in 1997 examined a short music video, 'Anjani Raahon Mein' (On Unknown Roads), produced by BharatBala and commissioned by Coca-Cola India, as part of the *Vande Mataram* collection. Roy (2002: 254) noted that such 'corporate initiative tied concepts such as "independence", "freedom" and "Indian identity" into a sign system of a market economy, with print and television advertisements throughout the 1997 deploying these signifiers as brand endorsements and adopting what they termed as a 'freedom-positioning mode of commercial advertising'.

A significant feature of the televisual representations of nation was the ways in which ideas of 'patriotism' were tethered to the mediated cultural regime. For Kumkum Sangari (2009: 6), '… the coverage of Kargil in 1999 the site of India's war with Pakistan, which quite literally competed with the World Cup cricket series and materialized as sport and sport as war. War was sanitized; cricket, especially the India–Pakistan match, already a part of televisual nationalism became deadly'. To this end, Daya Kishan Thussu (2002: 210) noted that the television networks, private as well as the state broadcaster, Doordarshan, were selling a militarized version of nationalism in the 'supermarket of jingoism'. Indeed, what emerged in the new televisual environment, then, was a new jingoistic patriotism that diverged from the earlier renditions of patriotism:

the Nehruvian patriotic citizen-worker anchored in production is reincarnated as a commodified, patriotic-consumer (Deshpande, 1993).

The music videos 'Apna Desh' (hereafter 'Apna') and 'Kho Jaane Do' (hereafter 'Kho'), part of the series of eight music videos, were put together in the album titled *Meri Jaan Hindustan* (My Love, India) directed by the film producer Mani Shankar. The album was sponsored ('dedicated to the nation') by the multinational soft drink company, Coca-Cola. The music and songs were composed and sung in 'pop' style by some prominent musicians, film actors, and pop music artists, and featured famous models and cricketers.

The music video 'Vande Mataram' (hereafter 'Vande'), based on India's national song written by Bankim Chandra Chattopadyaya in Bengali, may be literally translated as 'Hail Motherland!'. The music video, translated into Hindi-Urdu with some changes, was conceived and produced by BharatBala and features the popular film music director/singer A. R. Rahman from Chennai (formerly Madras). A series of music videos and audio tracks have been produced since 1997. Some of these are 'Vande Mataram II', 'Desh Ka Salaam', and 'Gurus of Peace'. 'Vande' is the most popular in that series.

The chapter draws upon an eclectic set of writings in neo-Marxism, postcolonial theory, and media and visual studies to outline a model of critical visual analysis. The works of Roland Barthes (1977), John Berger (1972), Stuart Hall (1973), and Judith Williamson (1978) provide a basis for sketching the critical model. In this chapter, then, the critical visual analysis focused on three interrelated levels—formal, verbal, and visual—through which particular representations of the national and the global are articulated. The formal level, the level of denotation, deals with 'technical' and 'symbolic' aspects like camerawork, editing, sound effects, composition, costumes, dress 'codes', settings, and so on. The verbal level deals with language use, words, vocabulary, and sentence construction. Together, the formal and the verbal levels construct and mobilize an image, or a set of images, which in turn constitute the visual. Thus, the verbal and visual operate in the realm of culture and ideology. It is, thus, crucial to focus on the three levels to examine and understand the symbolic representations of the national and the global.

Following Stuart Hall (1993: 251), the national and global can be considered as discourses mediated by various 'institutions, symbols and representations'. The concept of representation, Hall says, involves the 'constructivist' approach to the study of media. Against this background, national and global articulations may illustrate the interlocking relations between discourse, ideology, and hegemony. Hall's (1986: 29) definition of ideology as 'the mental frameworks—the languages, the concepts, categories, imagery of thought, and the systems of representation' is useful in probing the national and the global. Hall (1977: 24) states that 'ideologies do not operate in single ideas; they operate in discursive chains, in clusters, in semantic fields, in discursive formations', and ideology should be understood in terms of 'articulation of different elements into a distinctive set of chain of meanings' and further, 'ideologies "work" by constructing for their subjects (individual and collective) positions of identification and knowledge'.

A preliminary look at the various music videos revealed that various ideologies, themes, and tropes were pervasive. I am using ideologies, themes, and tropes to suggest that the various modes through which national and global are 'imagined' and constructed may be considered relationally. More importantly, it does not reduce all the material changes to the ideological level. For analytical purpose, then, national and global may be considered as discourses that are constituted of several ideologies, themes, and tropes. The various themes that connote the national include patriotism, national integration, secularism, and so on. For example, national integration is structured by themes like 'unity in diversity' (in Hindi, *Ek Mein Anek*) or 'composite culture'. The global is understood in relation to the following themes: foreign, imported, international, the West, non-resident, diaspora, cosmopolitan, post-national, and so on. Further, national and global also get 'flagged off' through several tropes that draw upon notions of a nostalgic past, geographical and territorial imagination, 'us' and 'them' (process of 'othering'), and so on. These themes and tropes, through a series of articulations and interpellations, get constituted as ideologies and organize the discourse of the national and the global.

MODES OF REPRESENTATIONS, CIRCLES OF COMMODITIES

An analysis of music videos and television commercials reveals the following distinguishing features that mark various facets of patriotism. First, a cosmopolitan sensibility gets refracted through the nationalist optics, whereas patriotism is worked through global metaphors and symbols. Second, the processes of de-territorialization and re-territorialization of various practices punctuate it. Third, as a consequence of the shifts indicated above, one can discern a dissolving and gradual erasure of conflicting and contradictory articulations of class, caste, gender, religion, and regional identities. Fourth, there is a powerful and enduring presence of the nation-state in the form of flags, air force, army, soldiers; and finally, these various features are embedded in a densely structured visual field that simultaneously draws upon earlier ideologies and practices as well as contemporary media forms and technologies. In the following analysis, I unpack these arguments and demonstrate how the various features work in particular media forms.

NATIONALIST FERVOR, COSMOPOLITAN SENSIBILITY

Let us consider how 'Apna' deploys nationalism and patriotism through the painter–singer protagonist Nagarjuna, a popular actor from south India who made a considerable impact in Hindi commercial cinema during the early 1990s. He gets a vision of Gandhi's assassination, first glimpsed through the last words of Gandhi, 'Hey Ram' (O God!), etched in Hindi on an epitaph, followed by some archival documentary footage of Gandhi participating in the freedom struggle, and the assassination scene from Richard Attenborough's film (shown in black and white). This causes a considerable degree of anxiety and distress in the painter as he is standing in front of a painting aisle waiting to put his cosmopolitan aesthetic sensibilities to use. In the first several frames, it is established that this young painter's repertoire is quite wide—painting fashion models in urban settings that represent Khilnani's post-national city—thereby signalling his cosmopolitanism. In a moment of agitation, he picks up colour from the palette with bare hands and dabs them on the painting surface on the aisle to create the tricolour, the Indian flag. Then, he steps back, stares at the painting, picks up a pistol, aims, and shoots in the direction of the aisle. Next, we see the phrase 'Hey Ram' carved at the centre with a red drop indicating blood dripping from the centre of the flag. In the following sequences, the painter's works, mostly of fashion models, are put up on a display in an exhibition. While all these paintings fetch a decent price, the flag painting is not for sale. In the closing shot we see a tag, 'Not for Sale', written on the painting.

The video began with the painter serenading and playing a trumpet and a piano, dancing around in green fields and landscapes a la Hindi film song. He is shown mingling with a group of rural (read: 'lower caste') women carrying water pots on their heads and driving around. The exoticization of tradition, represented through the rural women carrying pots of water on their heads and working in the fields, exemplify productive labour; the cosmopolitan settings, paintings of fashion models, and the exhibition indicate the display of consumption as a moment of celebration. The nationalistic fervour of the protagonist links the traditional and the cosmopolitan. The de-territorialization evident in the music video is largely a consequence of image-based technologies. On closer look, however, it reveals a re-territorialization, especially through re-imaging (or re-imagining) India along the vectors of national–global. This sort of re-imagining is quite explicit in 'Kho'. It is interesting to note that in 'Kho' the camera and photograph become a medium through which change during the fifty years (1947 to 1997) is enacted. First, we see the woman photojournalist, who sets her camera onto a self-timer, posing with a man shown as her husband across a cut-out with 1947 written on it. Both wear traditional Indian clothing, a dhoti and a saree. In the next frame, the same couple pose in front of a 1997 cutout, and this time dressed up in modern attire.

In 'Apna', the figure of Gandhi and the Indian flag exist alongside fashion models, commodities, and consumerism. In a rather uncanny way, the iconicity of Gandhi, the power of the image, is re-situated in the market place and has an exchange value. The nationalism of the protagonist painter is perfectly at peace with this sort of consumerism and globalization even if it violates Gandhi's distrust of unbridled capitalism and privatization. Similarly, in 'Vande' and 'Kho', nationalism can be glimpsed through the banal display of commodities and consumerism in specific ways. In 'Kho', the idiom of Hindi commercial film lyrics combine with 'pop' style music to produce nationalist sentiments. Thus, the national and global relation can be understood through the nationalism and cosmopolitanism of the subjects. I use the phrase 'subject(s)' in a double sense—to indicate subject as the construct that stands in for the narrative characters, and subjects as themes of the music videos.

The patriotic overtures get more pronounced in the popular 'Hamara Bajaj' campaign (Our Bajaj) and Bajaj Auto television commercials, even as they get narrativized through capital, commodities, consumerism, and nationalism. Although the 'Hamara Bajaj' campaign started as print advertisements in the 1980s, the television campaign was very popular with the audiences across class, caste, gender, and religious backgrounds (see Chapter 5). The recasting of patriotism, along the national–global axis, is accomplished by powerful lyrical tunes and a densely constituted montage of images packed within 30–45 seconds. Let us take a look at the first Bajaj ad. It opens with a shot of the famous 'Chetak' brand of scooter on a boat set against the backdrop of the Taj Mahal connoting the distinctiveness of the scooter like the monument; the next shot shows a lower middle class, small-town family, in their front yard assembled around a scooter with a woman performing *arati*—a form of worship done by circular movement of lighted camphor or oil in a lamp around an image or an object; shots of several people, both young and old, from different parts of India riding scooters; shot of a young man, obviously a Hindu hugging a Muslim, whose identity is revealed through his dress and cap, near a railway station with a Bajaj scooter parked nearby; shot of two young men riding a scooter carrying a television set; shots of young college girls chatting around a brand of scooters promoted for women; and a final shot of a boy on a Bajaj scooter with a small Indian flag in hand saluting the viewers. These numerous images are pulled together into a narrative by a song in Hindi that says: 'the pathways are open and the bliss and joys are unique ... the world is new and the heart tugs with passion ... all this has produced a new portrait, new India's new portrait ... our Bajaj.' The visual depictions and the song create a realist imagery of bountiful India where Bajaj scooters are part of the everyday life. What is being emphasized and heralded is 'newness', obtained as the country is marching along the road to a free market. Apart from the obvious connotation of Bajaj metonymically standing in for 'Bharat' (India), the ad points towards a horizon, a future that is yet to come alluding to the fruits of liberalization. The ad is imbued with national integration messages denoted through the Hindu–Muslim brotherhood as well as various depictions of people from different geographic and linguistic regions.

In the second Bajaj ad, the global manifests explicitly through the 'tradition-modernity' trope. First, we see a young man dressed in jeans and leather jacket with dark glasses riding the 'Eliminator' brand motorbike unlike the scooter from the earlier ad, which was a symbol of middle class India of pre-liberalization era. As this man approaches a Hindu shrine on the roadside, he slows down his vehicle, turns his head around, and bows in reverence; this is followed by a shot of young couple riding a motorbike passing along a residential city street. The woman is shown clasping her arms around the man's chest and upper torso. As they approach an elderly man walking along the sideway, the woman withdraws her arms as a mark of respect towards the elderly man; the next shot shows a young woman wearing a helmet and riding the 'saffire' brand of scooter. She stops her vehicle, takes off her helmet to reveal a red powder mark in her parting—the sign of a Hindu married woman; in the last shot a Sikh is riding on a motorcycle with a white woman who is wearing salwar-kameez, a traditional Indian dress. In the final shot, the two are shown in front of a Sikh shrine, the Golden Temple, and the Sikh man putting a scarf around the lady's head to suggest a mark of respect towards the holy shrine. Against these string of visuals, we hear music that blends Indian and western instruments. The lyrics of the song say that 'India is changing here ... tomorrow is new ... new India's ... rising India's new portrait ... our Bajaj'. In a very uncanny way, the ad has made some banal arguments by essentializing tradition and modernity. Here, India, its traditions, customs, and rituals are valorized even as the social life is moving towards modernity. The lyrics of the song, 'We are changing here', makes reference to the national that is accommodating the global.[7]

Although the Bajaj commercials invoke Hindu idioms and symbols in crafting the idea of India as Bharat, it would be premature to suggest that the visual imagery lends itself to the Hindu Right. In the 1980s, most print advertisements and television commercials borrowed ideas from the rich repertoire of 'unity in diversity' and 'national integration' themes circulating in the print and visual fields—calendar art, religious-based bazaar posters—to portray a much more nuanced understanding of the religious and secular themes, popular and vernacular cultural myths, idioms, and symbols that draw primarily upon Hindu as well as Muslim themes (Jain, 1995, 2003; Uberoi, 2002; Chatterjee, 2008). What we notice in the 'Hamara Bajaj' campaign is an extension of the religious–secular visual vocabularies that are essentialized for the televisual medium.

MOBILIZATIONS OF CLASS/ CASTE AND GENDER

The visual composition and editing techniques in 'Vande', 'Apna', and 'Kho' are influenced by the travel–tourist aesthetic, a la *National Geographic* visual mode, although some of the influences come from the music television genre. In 'Vande', for instance, in the opening shots, we see huge empty desert landscape accompanied by a synthetic musical score that is cut to shots of rural people in their natural surroundings. In terms of the editing devices, apart from the cuts, there are a few quick dissolves that show the people and the landscape. The soft focus lighting effect created to constitute the images is an intrinsic part of the composition. Here, the popular cinematic style that borrows from music video genres can be discerned. One shot has a group of rural children running with the national flag in hands, whereas another one has a girl child in medium close shot with a small flag fluttering in front of her. Then, there are a few shots of women in traditional Rajasthani attire with water pots on their heads walking across the frame. A few still shots of the men in their headgear form part of the visual narrative of the music video. It may be argued that the music video of 'Vande' renders the rural women, men, and children for middle class/upper-caste consumption and is symptomatic of how the visual itself is constituted on the principle of 'othering'. The rural people in the video do not have a clear identity and remain nameless, and yet are made part of the cultural nationalism espoused in the music video.

If the themes of nationalism clearly dominate every frame, the middle- class/ upper-caste desire of displaying its patriotism in the form of nation-as-mother along with strong territorialized depictions provides the context of the music video. In fact, the middle-class/upper-caste desire and pleasure gets 'written onto the body' of the rural poor (Dhareshwar, 1997: 125). This can be explained by drawing upon Vivek Dhareshwar's (1993: 121) persuasive argument about the nationalist and secular 'disavowal of caste [that] locked the lower-castes into their identities …' In terms of media, R. Srivatsan (2000: 18) suggested, 'By addressing the viewer as ideally (linguistically) literate, most photographic imaging in this country, in practice, norms the viewer as upper caste', and further, 'the notion of caste is a condition of visibility in India. It functions as a screen that without itself being seen makes the world visible in a certain way'. Interestingly, gender portrayals in both domains—modern (cosmopolitan) and traditional—point to contradictory subject positions; in the former, women either perform male-centred activities (photojournalists in 'Kho', for instance), or as fashion models (as in 'Apna'), while in the latter they are either engaged in some form of labour (carrying water pots or working in the fields in 'Apna', grinding chillies in 'Kho') or posing as inert carriers of tradition and national identities ('Vande').

'Kho' has two popular Indian female models acting as photojournalists. The music and lyrics, based on a typical Hindi film tune of the 1980s, refers to being lost on the plains of the river, among mountains, greenery, and so on, evoking images of nature. The visual images are organized into a narrative with the music as a backdrop. The two women photographers shoot different locales and people in small towns and big cities. The viewer-subject is positioned in relation to what the two photographers seem to do in their acts of rendering visible various spaces and places. This 'doubling-up' of the image that is, what the women are shooting and that which is being shot, together constitute the visual narrative. The performance that is enacted through these images almost immediately sets up a dichotomy between tradition and modernity which expresses itself through gestures, postures, manners, dress, contraptions, and other physical manifestations that constitute the mise en scène.

The opening few visuals show the two photographers taking pictures of the city, one of them travelling in a rickshaw (manually driven tricycle) along the streets in the city. A few pictures of three Indian cricketers who are dancing to music follow this. Then, there are a few shots of women bathing in a pond, while the photographers click their pictures. The next few images show one of the photographers, who appeared in the popular Liril brand soap commercial, splashing water around which is reminiscent of the advertisement. This is followed by a series of visuals of women on the terrace of an apartment manually grinding red chillies. A big satellite dish antenna is conspicuous in the frames. As the photographers are clicking pictures of this chore to the beats of the music track, the video shifts to a series of freeze frames in quick succession—giving the viewers a sense of what is being shot. The video now makes a transition where the two photographers, until now performing a perceived 'masculine' task of being photojournalists, visit their homes dressed in traditional clothes and behaving as daughters, and performing those domestic tasks which their women subjects were engaged in. These juxtaposition of images (as a montage) in the form of a tradition/modernity binary depicts the smooth passage of the English-convent-educated urban women from modern to traditional practices; reversing roles quite easily unlike their subjects of the photo assignment who remain within the traditional domain.

The presence of the power of the nation-state is quite explicit in 'Kho' and 'Vande'. One of the photojournalists in 'Kho' is shown taking pictures of an air force fighter pilot standing near a fighter aircraft followed by group images of fighter pilots, and a set of aircrafts flying past. In 'Vande', the final few aerial shots show the multitude of rural people who are shown hoisting the National Flag with the Indian Army helicopters hovering in the skies.

RECONFIGURATIONS OF THE VISUAL

The photographic technologies of representation have influenced the visual regime in some fundamental ways, reordering its vectors along consumerism, commodities, advertising, and capital. In the sphere of media and cultural production, this regime provides the Indian middle classes/upper castes a space to reconstitute their identities. The display of consumption as a site for negotiating and reinventing patriotism draws upon capitalist image-based technologies in three ways. First, there is the deployment of a *National Geographic* visual aesthetic that frames the overall structure of the images in the music videos. Second, the production process of the music videos deployed advanced cinematic and televisual techniques. Third, within the narratives of the music videos there is a pervasive presence of cameras ('Kho'), and documentary and film clips ('Apna') to render India visible. This fetishizing of the 'image', then, marks the 'newness' that is generated. This is part of the contemporary conditions in which the privatized media production is remapping the national along the contours of the global, variously indexed in terms such as abroad, the West, and diaspora that are significantly different from earlier notions like foreign and imported.

Thus, the visual regime that structures the music videos 'Vande', 'Apna', and 'Kho' is informed by middle class/upper-caste *perspectivism* that is drawn, in complex ways, from a range of interlocking forces, ideologies, institutions, and practices, which work across several 'sites' simultaneously. To fully understand the visual regime it is necessary to study the socio-psychoanalytic characteristics and the reception contexts of the middle class/upper caste subjects, a task that is outside the scope of this chapter.

CONCLUDING REMARKS

In a promotional programme on television that featured several multinational companies and their Indian counterparts, it was stressed (by advertisers and the music video makers) that the idea of *Vande Mataram* can be successfully marketed as a 'global mantra'. What this indicates is that the middle classes/ upper castes in India and their counterparts outside India, the non-resident immigrants, are part of this globalization 'pitch' of capitalist interests in India.

These, then, are the markers of the (new) consuming-citizen-subject of India, the pro-liberalization votary. According to Deshpande (1993: 163), 'The figure of the cosmopolitan is the unexpected or the "new" term, one that is relatively unprecedented in Indian ideological history. Its clearest representative is perhaps the ubiquitous figure of the Non-Resident Indian, the closest approximation to a modern mythological hero that the Indian middle-classes possess.' The mythology of patriotism in the music videos created a dubious cosmopolitanism to interpellate the middle classes/upper caste subjects. More crucially, the reincarnation of patriotism in the music videos is inflected with what one can term as a 'diasporic imaginary' that pulls Indian immigrants from North America, Europe, and elsewhere into its fold. These media narratives in the music videos do not look different from earlier representations of a putative and essentialized Indian identity and patriotic sentiments but differ in the way in which cosmopolitan settings become the sites on which patriotism gets enacted. This creates an interesting situation wherein a territorially bounded nationalism, the one articulated by the nation-state as well as middle class/upper caste citizen-subjects in India, interlocks with a diasporic nationalism espoused by Indian immigrants from North America and Europe. The powerful vectors of patriotism in both generate a complex discourse of nation and reactivates proto-fascist and recidivist nationalism.

NOTES

1. The concept of cosmopolitanism has been approached from a number of different theoretical angles. Timothy Brennan (1997) understands cosmopolitanism as a naive brand of nativism masquerading in a global guise. Bruce Robbins (1999) sees this as an emerging form of a liberal identity. It is interesting to note that the typical brand of cosmopolitanism, the one Brennan has correctly identified and critiqued, is articulated by advertisers, journalists, media gurus and film and television producers, and usually draws upon elements from Robbins' conceptualization. In contemporary Indian public culture, this sort of cosmopolitanism, with some interesting twists, gets refracted through nationalist frames. Arjun Appadurai (1996: 158), a leading proponent of post-nationalism, argues, '[W]e need to think ourselves beyond the nation' because nation-states have become obsolete, and new forms of identities and solidarities have emerged. This, according to Appadurai, leads to alternatives—in the form of 'resources', 'images', and 'ideas'—that contest the nation-state. As a result of such changes, several 'national forms' get de-linked from the territorial bounded states (168–69). There are a number of problems with this position, especially in relation to media in postcolonial India. I pursue the cosmopolitan and post-national in this chapter.
2. For instance, a powerful visual rendering in the song *'Aao Bachchon Tumhaen Dikhayaen Jhanki Hindustan Ki'* (come on children, will show you the tableau of India) evokes the nation-India-patriotism through a string of mythic elements drawn from Hindu geographic and religious symbols—words like *Mitti* (soil, land), *Dharti* (earth), *Vatan* (country), *Balidan* (sacrifice), *Azaadi* (independence), *Kurbani* (sacrifice), *Goliyan* (bullets), *Jallianwalla* (Jallianwala Bagh in Amritsar, Punjab (in 1919 hundreds of Indians were massacred by British colonial military), *Inquilab* (revolution), *Har Har Mahadev* (battle cry in Hindi), *Janmabhoomi* (birthplace) trigger strong emotional feelings. Likewise, in *Jahan Daal Daal Per Sone Ki Chidiya Karti Hai Basera* (golden bird roosting on branches). In India's national anthem, *Jana Gana Mana*, national song, *Vande Mataram*, and other alternate national songs like *Sara Jahan Se Ache Hindustan Hamara* (my India is better than the whole world), and *Hum Honge Kamyab* (we will succeed), patriotism is signified through similar procedures. Rukmini Bhaya Nair (2001) provides a good discussion of how national anthems work on people's imaginations in crafting patriotic feelings.
3. The Hindi-Urdu words, *galli*s refer to by-lanes; *chauraha*s, street corner; and *mohalla*, neighborhood.
4. For an excellent account of how the nation was imagined via postcolonial state's audio-visual discourses in terms of print and visual formats, annual commemoration of Republic Day displays and parades, see S. Roy (2007).

5. There are very few theoretical studies on the epistemology of the visual in India. Sandria Freitag (2001) outlines three realms through which the constitution of the 'visual' can be grasped—South Asian courtly culture, religious practices, and live performance traditions. She also mentions the influence of paintings, posters, photography, and early cinema in shaping the visual vocabularies. It is here one can discern an 'intermeshing' of the traditional and the modern.
6. India's Kargil conflict with Pakistan, the first major military confrontation between the neighbours since the war of 1971, lasted a little over two months (May–July, 1999). This conflict became the first televised conflict in the Indian subcontinent with television reporters and correspondents reporting from the frontlines, daily news briefings from the government, and a slew of programmes such as talk shows with military strategists analysing and discussing battle strategies, and television commercials blending patriotic themes into their products. See Thussu (2002) for a discussion on the television networks' representations of the Kargil war.
7. According to Rajagopal, the chairman of the Bajaj company was a member of the Hindu nationalist Bharatiya Janata Party and hence the Hindu imagery is not coincidental. See Rajagopal's (1998) analysis of the Bajaj commercial.

5 | Remembering Doordarshan

Figurations of Memories and Nostalgia on Blogs, YouTube, and in Oral Interviews

This chapter explores people's memories of Doordarshan in the 1980s; a decade which witnessed rapid expansion of the television network and the emergence of a wide range of programmes such as drama, classical and film-based music, historical, mythological, and fictional narratives, soap operas, sitcoms, serials, and so on. It is not unusual for people to have memories of their first encounters with television, the particular experiences of watching 'favourite' programmes, remembering advertisements, jingles, parts of programmes, television personalities, and so on. Should we dismiss these as nostalgic and sentimentalized accounts, the fragmentary moments of their lives and experiences that have no bearing on the present? I argue in this chapter that the idea of nostalgia is not a singular experience of the past, but rather, it contains alternative, generative, and productive modalities in the reconstruction and remembering of the past (Pickering and Keightley, 2006). The question, therefore, I like to consider is not whether memories are authentic, but rather how, and to what end, memories are mobilized in people's practices of remembering. Overall, the chapter foregrounds people's memories of the everyday experiences, and knowledge of television paying heed to the argument of Darian-Smith and Turnbull (2012: 1) that '... the everyday "informal knowledge" about television and its technology as experienced by those who are watching it has been displaced by the "formal knowledge" of those equipped with the appropriate fashionable theory to analyze it'.[1]

Although memory is crucial to individual and social identity formation, and some recent work in media and television research has explored television as 'memory-text', and the mnemonic practices it has engendered in the ideological construction of the past, the broader theoretical relations across television, memory, and history, particularly as they pertain to how people's memories shape their personal and social identities as audience, viewers, and the public remain unexplored. The chapter is organized in four sections. The first section is a critical discussion of recent work on television memories and 'memory studies', pointing both to their potential contributions and limitations in examining people's personal and social identities. I argue that Ricoeur's work on memory, history, and narrative identity offers productive analytic insights in studying the interplay of personal and social identities. In the second section , I examine people's recollections and reflections of Doordarshan in journalistic articles, online blogs, and YouTube collections. The third section analyses abstracts of interviews of people from the city of Hyderabad. I pay attention to congeries of identities such as class, caste, gender, religion, urban/rural at play in people's mnemonic uses of Doordarshan. In the fourth section, I discuss the significance of memory in interpreting television, and offer some remarks on how people's remembering offers insights into their constitution as audience, viewers, and the public.

TELEVISION, MEMORY, AND HISTORY

Several influential approaches to television have characterized the medium as abetting amnesia, generating forgetfulness, and collapsing the spatiotemporal dynamics that link the past to the present, in favour of the here-and-now. This constant 'nowness' of television, they argue, has led to 'the annihilation of memory, and consequently of history' (Doane, 1990: 227; Heath, 1990). While the long-standing suspicion towards television has persisted in scholarly literature, recent accounts of the medium have examined the mnemonic properties of television in the ideological construction of the past, thus bringing history, and subsequently memory, to the forefront of the debates (O'Sullivan, 1991; Anderson, 2000; Bourdon, 2003; Dhoest, 2007; Barfield, 2003; Holdsworth, 2010; Keightley, 2011; Darian-Smith and Turnbull, 2012; Lozano, 2013). Indeed, as Steve Anderson (2000: 16), drawing on the work of Mimi White, noted, 'History, duration, and memory are central to the any theoretical understanding of television's discursive operations as liveness and concomitant ideas of presence, immediacy, and so on'. Throughout the chapter, I understand 'television memory' as the particular ways in which the past is appropriated, reconstructed, and utilized by people, that is, the viewer recollections of television as an object, artifact, cultural form, symbolic resource, programmes, programme personalities, events, places, and so on.

Some studies explored people's recollections of television, from the arrival of the medium in their homes, their experiences of televisual texts, and the gendered nature of viewing practices. The everyday processes of remembering about television reveal a complex dynamic of individual, familial, cultural, and social forces that influence how people make meanings in their mobilizations of the past. Jérôme Bourdon (2003) argued that scholarly studies of television have theorized the relations between television and memory in terms of two models he identified as a 'destructive' model and a 'hyper-integrative' model: the former is seen as promoting 'forgetting', whereas the latter in shaping collective memory at the national and global levels. For Bourdon (2003: 6), the hyper-integrative model based on analyses of major 'media events'—rituals, ceremonies, funerals of heads of state, weddings, Olympic games, and so on—generate a shared viewing, thereby serving as a bridge 'between personal and collective history' as well as memory. Despite the increasing number of studies, however, the relations between television, memory, and history remain a fraught one. More importantly, perhaps, are the confusions stemming from specific usages of the terms 'collective memory', and the particular conceptualizations of the linkages between individual and collective memory.

The approach proposed by Wulf Kansteiner (2002) considers individual and collective memories as dialectically linked together and shaped by social dimensions, linguistic and narrative patterns, relying on a wide repertoire of discursive, visual, and spatiotemporal elements. Others such as Jan Assmann (2010) offered a broader notion of 'cultural memory' to signal the presence of 'cultural objectivations'—languages, institutions, cultural symbols, and images. David Leichter (2012: 116), referring to the work of Eviator Zerubavel (2003), points out that the '"norms of remembrance" and "mnemonic traditions" embodied in the ideology, narratives, and rituals that contain and transmit symbolic order'. Furthermore, research in the field of memory studies demonstrates the overlaps between individual and collective memory, suggesting that

> memory has a texture which is both social and historic: it exists in the world rather than in people's heads, finding its basis in conversations, cultural forms, personal relations, the structure and appearance of places and, most fundamentally ... in relation to ideologies which work to establish a consensus view of both the past and the forms of personal experience which are significant and memorable. (Bommes and Wright, 1982: 256)

Within the interdisciplinary field of memory studies as well as the scholarly literature on television memories briefly discussed above, the concept of 'collective memory', first proposed by Maurice Halbwachs in the 1950s, has been critiqued for ignoring the individual remembering subject (Pickering and Keightley, 2012). Halbwachs (1992: 43) had argued that 'no remembering is possible outside the frameworks used by people living in society to determine and retrieve their recollections'. To overcome the individual and collective memory conundrum, memory studies scholars proposed various models and conceptions of memory ranging from private or public memory, communicative or cultural memory, and social memory (Kuhn, 1995; Radstone, 2000; Kansteiner, 2002; van Dijck, 2004, 2007). While these studies offer productive analytic gains in exploring the dialectic between individual memory and collective memory, I draw on Ricoeur's (2003) work on memory, history, and narrative identity instead.

This chapter does not engage with television's role in the construction and production of history; rather, my goal is to examine the relations between television and memory in terms of what people remember about television, the recollections of their encounter with the medium, and the social, cultural, and political contexts of their memories. The chapter examines the relations between television, memory, and history, and more specifically, explores how people's recollecting, remembering and reminiscing about television as material object, a cultural form, and a symbolic resource opens up the space to investigate broader sets of relationships that centre on the following questions: What do people remember, and why? Do they share memories, if so, which ones? What patterns can be discerned in these memories? How does television shape individual and collective memories? A larger question stemming from the above, I pursue especially in the third section, through a direct engagement with Ricoeur's work where I examine extracts of people's interviews, pertains to the 'politics of memory', that is, how do people draw upon their televisual memories through selective remembering, glossing over, and/or active forgetting of media events, as well as the social and cultural forces.

The analysis in the second and third sections is situated in terms of three overlapping themes that emerged in people's memories of television: (*a*) childhood, (*b*) spatiality and temporality, and (*c*) programmes. For instance, in most recollections, television is framed as a crucial aspect of people's childhoods, especially the growing up period from a toddler to the adolescent years. People's narrative accounts of their childhood memories can be apprehended in terms of what Roger Silverstone (1991), drawing on the theory of 'object-relations' proposed by the British paediatrician and child psychologist, Donald Woods Winnicott, characterized television as a 'transitional object', and Sherry Turkle's (2007) notion of 'evocative object'. For Silverstone, television functions as a transitional object during those early years when a child begins to experience and learn her/his relationships with the others, thereby forging a sense of self. In Turkle's (2007: 8) account, evocative objects are associated with transitional times, reminding 'us of the blurry childhood line between self and the other'. While childhood serves as a marker of formative years of a person's life, it also influences generational and intergenerational memories. Indeed, the notion of television as an object—transitional as well as evocative—that mediates between people's memories of their childhood is useful to the extent that television functions as an object and an artifact. Overall, Silverstone's and Turkle's respective concepts refer to similar processes that underpin a child's relationship with herself and the external world. Therefore, instead of considering these as separate concepts, throughout the chapter I refer to them under the rubric of 'transitional-evocative object'.[2]

However, in several instances, television is perceived/characterized as more than an object, a 'mnemonic imaginative' audio-visual and symbolic resource that mediates people's individual and collective memories (Pickering and Keightley, 2012). For analytic purposes, I have organized these modalities of television memories as constituting the spatial and temporal dynamics of remembering. To illustrate and contextualize the spatial and temporal aspects of memories, I refer to the writings of Paddy Scannell (1998, 2004) on the 'ordinariness', and temporal organization of broadcasting in terms of programme schedules, standardized programme formats, and the viewing contexts of television in the domestic spaces of the household (Moores, 2007). For Silverstone (1993: 592), broadcasting is 'very much part of the seriality and spatiality of everyday life', where programme schedules and formats come to 'reproduce (or define) the structure of the household day itself significantly determined by the temporality of work in industrial societies'. Scannell offers a more detailed engagement with the temporalities of broadcasting, exploring how radio and television programmes serve as cultural and symbolic resources for individual listeners/viewers, and shared by a large collective audience within and across generations.[3] Scannell's main concern is not about how memories are constructed and produced; his work nonetheless offers crucial analytic insights to study people's spatial and temporal dimensions of remembering. Commenting on the beginnings of broadcasting's temporal arrangements in the 1930s Britain, Scannell (1998: 11) noted:

> ... working through the weeks and months of the year, programme output had a patterned regularity that grew stronger in the National Programme in the course of the thirties. The effects of this process are incremental. They

> accumulate in time as they are reproduced through time. In the course of the many years, over generations, broadcast output becomes sedimented in memory as traces both of a common past and of the biography of the individuals.

While broadcast television in the 1980s India largely remains unexamined (Asthana, 2014), a recent study (Punathambekar and Sundar, 2017) explored the temporal features of Doordarshan in the 1980s, examining how television realigned the time of everyday life through its programme schedules and through the textual time of programme genres. These multiple temporalities, they argue, offered the urban middle class new ways of experiencing time in the 1980s. Interestingly, the perceptive study by Punathambekar and Sundar (2017: 401) begins with a dismissive note on the same middle class audience of the 1980s, especially their memories of Doordarshan as largely nostalgic and sentimental:

> The 1980s are widely remembered as the 'time of television' in India. As even a casual glimpse of YouTube collections, Facebook pages, and blogs reveal, television programs from the 1980s offer a rich set of imaginative resources for remembering life in urban India as the time. Largely nostalgic in nature, these myriad references to the iconography, advertisements, and programs aired on Doordarshan, the state-run broadcast network, suggest as affective charge that is distinct and specific to the period's newly forged urban middle-class.

A third main theme of people's trigger for remembering television centred on programmes, especially various programme genres, were episodes and segments of the programmes, advertisements, jingles, signature tunes, programme openings and closings, presenters, television personalities and actors, and so on. Overall, people's recollections and reminiscences of television does not indicate a direct homology between television and their memories; rather, they are routed through a broad set of familial, social, cultural, political, and economic factors which shape their individual and collective memories.

In the following section, I analyse television memory, more specifically how people remember television in terms of the questions outlined above, and organize my discussion in terms of the three main themes. This section will focus on journalistic articles, online blogs, and YouTube collections. The digital media practices such as blogging, hyperlinking, tagging, vlogging, and incorporation of text, artwork, images, and so on, are producing new ways in which television memories are produced and shared across platforms. Although the online recollections and reflections do not constitute people's life stories, they may be considered as narratives of specific moments of their lives. The television memories on blogs and YouTube organized as a digital collage of forms such as diary narratives, clips of television programmes, personalities, advertisements, jingles, and so on, point to a subtle shift from *memory as representation*, involving the processes of recall and retention, to *memory as mediation*, characterized by appropriation and production of the past through media technologies (Urry, 1995; Hoskins, 2003; van Dijck, 2004).[4] While the term mediation points to the increasing interconnectedness between media and memory, a hermeneutic understanding of mediation refers to the constitution of narrative identity, and the relations between the self and the other. I deploy the idea of mediation in the dual sense.

FIGURATIONS OF NOSTALGIA AND MEMORIES ON BLOGS AND YOUTUBE

In 2009, India's state-run television, Doordarshan, celebrated its fifty-year anniversary by airing several old programmes. The commemoration of Doordarshan was widely covered in the print media in the form of news stories and featured articles that included interviews with advertising executives, and television and film personalities. In addition, people remembered Doordarshan on the Internet—hundreds of blogs, thousands of Facebook pages, Twitter, and YouTube collections.[5] The voluminous 'archives' of people's memories of Doordarshan on the Internet as well as in my interviews, deploy a range of Hindi/Urdu/Sanskrit/Persian/Telugu words for memory, nostalgia, remembering, and reminiscing such as *yaad*, *yaadashth*, *yaadein*, *gurthu*, *anusmaran*, *smrti*, *haniin*, *haafizah*, and so on. Such constellation of words and the vocabularies point to a more expansive semantics of meanings in people's usages that will be identified and explored in relation to the English usages as well as the elective affinities among the terms themselves in the following analysis.

Although the fifty-year anniversary in 2009 provided a context for remembering and reminiscing about Doordarshan, numerous blogs and YouTube collections predate by several years. The newspaper features on Doordarshan provided brief and evocative references to the history of state-run broadcaster in terms of specific moments such as the arrival of arrival of soap operas, sitcoms, mythological programs in the 1980s. Some of the nostalgic accounts of television viewing during the childhood years, although mixed with sentimental and biographical sketches, depicting a sense of wonder, irony, loss, nonetheless constitute generative recollections on their encounters with television.

For the generation of Indians whose childhood years coincided with the period of rapid growth of Doordarshan in the 1980s, television seems to have a 'holding power', marking a crucial link in their learning environments and relationships with the other. I begin with a few extracts from the news stories to point out how television functioned as a 'transitional-evocative object' in people's childhood memories, the role and significance of programmes, the familial contexts of viewing, and the spatiotemporal dynamics underpinning the mnemonic practices that have shaped their memories of the medium. A news story in the *Indian Express* newspaper begins with a query thus: 'Plasma may have replaced the old time black-and-white television and the numerous channels to surf may have increased big time but is it possible to forget the golden era of our very own Doordarshan?' (*Indian Express*, 2009). In this news story, most people remembered Doordarshan as being part of their childhood years, recounting how cartoons, advertising jingles, and television serials have stayed in their memories.

According to the sportsperson, Prasad Purandhare,

> The advertisements of Lijjat papad is still vivid in my memory and I remember imitating the voice (qarram qarram) while eating the papads. With hundreds of channels, we still have so much that we miss today; that one channels gave us more than we wanted in that era. I can still hum the Doordarshan signature tune to perfection. (*Indian Express*, 2009)

For Charu Deshmukh, a software developer,

> 'Jungle, jungle baat chali hai pata chala hai'—this is the first song that I learnt by heart, thanks to Doordarshan. I was and still am crazy about the cartoons that were aired during my childhood on Doordarshan. I still remember the animation song, 'Ek titli anek titliya' which combined fun and education. (*Indian Express*, 2009)

The *Indian Express* article ends with a eulogy to Doordarshan stating, 'Be it the advertisement of washing powder Nirma or serials like Khandaan, Yeh Jo Hai Zindagi or Hum Log, even the simple rotating circle which turned into the logo of Doordarshan with slow music playing in the background—it sure had us all glued to our television sets' (*Indian Express*, 2009).

An article in the newspaper *DNA India* featured interviews with several media professionals on their television memories. Anuradha Sengupta, feature editor at CNBC-TV18 noted:

> If you were a child like I was in the 80s, then Doordarshan was your window to the world … I am nostalgic about some things it compelled us to do. I still remember my grandfather expecting complete silence at 9:00 pm, because we had to watch the national news! … The regional, subtitled movies on Sunday afternoons brought to the fore different languages and cultures that make India. When was the last time you saw a film in another language other than Hindi or English? If Hum Log became an addiction, Malgudi Days gave us Swami and an incredible theme track by TS Vaidyanathan, if heard once, could never be forgotten. Doordarshan, with all its flaws, helped create the audio-visual context to who I am today. Pity, it didn't stay relevant to me and I still miss it and those simple times. (Chugh, 2009)

For Anand Krishnan, account director, MediaVest Worldwide, the shifts in the spatiotemporal dynamics of the 1980s are contextualized in terms of the arrival of Doordarshan as a media object, a cultural form, and a symbolic resource thus:

> There is something unique to about the generation of Indians born in the 70s or early 80s … Almost all of us were born into households that had no telephone, hadn't heard of a computer, and wouldn't have imagined in our wildest dreams about the phenomena called the Internet … largely born into households with no TV, graduating slowly into a black-and-white TV set and then to colour set, watching fictional shows on Doordarshan before slowly 'progressing' to watch shows based on 'reality' on newer, more aggressive channels … Most of us remember our routine Sunday mornings—watching Star Trek while having our morning tea and breakfast. Comedy was also served by way of Didi's Comedy Show or Yeh Jo Hai Zindagi … The advertisements became part of the daily entertainment. Enter the 90s and just like video killed the radio, the advent of satellite TV killed DD … certain innocence was lost as we embraced white cables and bade farewell to those roof top antennas. (Chugh, 2009)

The *Wall Street Journal*, India edition in 2011, two years after the fifty-years commemoration, reported that 'Doordarshan turned 52 this month, but the birthday celebrations for this creaky institution were muted rather than joyous: the broadcaster is no longer the nationwide sensation it was' (Mehta and Rana, 2011). In 2012, a news story in *The Hindu*, 'Sights and Sounds of Childhood Memories', reported on an event organized by a Bengaluru arts-based collective, Maraa that put together an audio-visual tribute to Doordarshan, 'One Screen, One Audience, One Channel', which included assemblage of programme segments, advertisements, jingles, signature tunes, clips of short animations and music, television newscasts, and so forth, from the 1980s. Ekta Mittal, a founding member of Maraa, noted, 'Even though we grew up in different cities, and come from different generations, we have the same childhood memories' (Verghese, 2012).

In addition to the journalistic articles and reports, the figurations and refashioning of Doordarshan memories become more vivid and detailed in the hundreds of blogs and YouTube collections on the Internet. The mnemonic modes of recollecting, remembering, and reminiscing are rendered in interactive formats, combining the affordances of writing, pictures, illustrations, audio, video, and so forth, into a collage of forms. For instance, people provide a catalogue of programmes aired on Doordarshan in the 1980s, identifying their 'favourite' programmes, uploading specific episodes and segments, the signature tunes, advertising, jingles, and so forth, writing brief summaries of the programmes along with their own commentaries, information on television personalities, and bits of trivia mixed with descriptions of their daily viewing contexts and practices. Although most people identified their blogs as nostalgic remembering, what can be discerned here are complex layers of memories. The mixing of auto-reminiscing, biographical sketches, and individual memories points to a dynamic constellation of communicative modalities, the interconnected nature of speech and writing. According to Edward Casey (1987: 119), people remember in multiple, plural ways, and the past invoked through the interplay of speech and writing is oriented 'in the form of intrapersonal self-address, as essentially *inter*personal tendency towards discourse-with-another, albeit another part of one's self'.

In the following extracts from blogs and YouTube collections, we discern people's individual memories of Doordarshan as biographical sketches of their childhoods, the influences of programmes and programme schedules on their daily/weekly viewing habits, and the spatial and temporal contexts of their televisual experiences. At an empirical level, the respective individual memories broadly exhibit similar characteristic features in terms of how and what of television memories, especially in terms of the surfacing of same themes and patterns of remembering, thereby pointing to their passage from individual to collective memories.

In his blog, 'Dust on My Shoes. Inside the Idiot Box of Memories', Neelesh Misra (2009), a Mumbai-based author and Bollywood script and lyrics writer, notes that Doordarshan was crucial to his growing up years in Lucknow and Nainital, shaping his childhood and individual identity like millions of others of his generation. The following extract from his blog captures the curiosity and wonder of a child's encounter with television:

> A massive click. I would switch on the thick cylindrical silver knob of the Uptron Urvashi TV set, encased in a wooden cabinet. Vertical vibgyor colour bands would show up, and then, suddenly, the rotating Doordarshan logo that seemed to us like two huge kajus hugging a rasgulla in the centre. Sublime pre-24x7 moment. The moment my brother and I would have waited for the whole day, killing time to prepare ourselves to open the rolling wooden shutter on the TV cabinet. (Misra, 2009)

The sense of anticipation and excitement in Misra's account of his childhood encounter with their first television set, and the description of Doordarshan's rotating logo in terms of *kaju*s and *rasgulla*[6] is suggestive of how television functions as a transitional-evocative object, mediating 'the blurry line between self and the other' (Turkle, 2007: 8). As we begin to explore the blog further, we notice that Misra's recollecting and reminiscing about Doordarshan, while anchored in his childhood, extends into his youth and adult years revealing how his mnemonic imagination of Doordarshan moves beyond the childhood liminal space of self and the other, pointing to an identity formation that can be grasped in terms of Ricoeur's idea of narrative identity, especially the interplay of *idem* and *ipse* identities.

Misra's account renders palpable how Doordarshan's programme genres and schedules reconfigured his and his family's everyday viewing practices; describing these in specific detail, he points to the televisual literary and cultural influences that shaped his adolescent life, and his subsequent work as a lyricist of Hindi commercial cinema. Referring to the rise of the multichannel television in the 1990s, and Doordarshan's decline, Misra invokes the nostalgic mode of lament, a sense of loss, and returns to his childhood: 'Doordarshan has remained to me what my small town is—the faraway, tiny island of memory that has so many personal stories wrapped around where I often take refuge when the past seems more comforting than the present' (Misra, 2009). Further, in a similar vein, he continues,

> I miss Doordarshan of my childhood. I miss my nani (grandmother). I miss the guavas she cut and sprinkled with the spicy 'buknu' powder ... I miss the trips to the messy chaotic lanes of Aminabad. I am a stranger to Doordarshan and those cobwebs of lanes now. But I intend to reclaim my memories someday. It was just an intermission. (Misra, 2009)

Annie Zaidi, an author, in her blog, 'Doordarshan, Nostalgia and the Lack of Answers', begins her recollections by referring to another blogger, Charu's comments on Doordarshan's generation of the 1980s; Zaidi says that she is indulging in nostalgia to think about Doordarshan and her childhood:

> Back to the time when television was Doordarshan. And vice versa. The logo slowly forms itself in my mind—the oval lines, the tangentially curvy edges, the Hindi alphabets forming themselves. The screen coming alive in the afternoon, but before that the sharp, whining sound of the vertical colourful lines in the screen, as I switched the television set on. And immediately turned the volume down to zero—I wasn't allowed more than an hour a day initially ... I remember watching regional movies—Tamil, Malayalam, Assamese, Punjabi—on Sunday afternoons. Some of these were award-winning. I also remember that once cable television came in, I didn't get a chance to watch such movies again. (Zaidi, 2005)

Figure 5.1 Doordarshan logo sequence

Source: Vinayak Razdan, available at http://8ate.blogspot.com/2009/09/50-years-of-doordarshan.html.

Zaidi's formative memories of Doordarshan, described in terms of the gestalt effect of television's rotating logo, the coloured lines on the screen, and the assembling of the Hindi alphabets cannot be reduced to the nostalgic mode of remembering, for it carries in itself generative and productive traces of her childhood encounter with television. Indeed, people's memories of Doordarshan, the specific encounters with television—as a box, a piece of furniture, an object—are situated in the spatial and temporal contexts of shared viewing, first in the neighbours' home, and later in their own homes. The recollecting and remembering of childhood televisual experiences point to a significant degree of overlap between and across people's individual and collective memories which can be discerned from similar programme preferences and viewing habits. The 'holding power' of Doordarshan as a 'transitional-evocative object' stems from the fact that for the generation of viewers their childhood years coincided with the expansion of television and the development of seriality and scheduling of programme genres on a daily and weekly basis.

The brief analysis of Neelesh Misra and Annie Zaidi's blogs revealed that the Doordarshan logo, montage, and signature tune was emblematic of their entry into the world of television. Indeed, for most people, Doordarshan's rotating logo and the signature tune has a special affective resonance serving as an index for their mnemonic uses of television. A spoof on Doordarshan's logo and signature tune in the 2011 Hindi/Urdu movie *Zindagi Na Milegi Dobara* (You Won't Get a Second Life) generated strong emotional responses on blogs, Twitter, Facebook pages, and in the mainstream press pointing out the movie's lack of sensitivity towards a 'revered' and 'sacred' institution that for millions of people evokes fond memories of the past, the childhood years, and new familial viewing contexts and experiences. Responding to the criticisms, the director of the movie, Zoya Akhtar noted,

> We grew up at a time when that tune was integral to our lives. When we'd out playing cricket, we could hear the Doordarshan tune from our windows and it signaled the end of our game. In the same way, it signals the end of the holidays for the three characters in ZNMD. (Jha, 2011)[7]

Although used as a framing device to mark the changes in the lives of the characters in the movie, for Akhtar too the logo and the signature tune carry a powerful, affective, and mnemonic charge.

Another indication of the importance of the Doordarshan logo can be gauged from the recent plans by Prasar Bharati, the governmental corporation that oversees Doordarshan, to change the logo which led to a resurgence of discussions in support of the old iconic logo. According to Indrani Sen, 'Indian viewers became nostalgic about the iconic logo and Twitter exploded with requests for not changing it' (Sen, 2017).[8] What reasons explain the 'holding power' of Doordarshan, especially the logo and the signature tune, on people? Is this just a question of brand loyalty and/or underlying sociocultural contexts? In the hundreds of blogs and YouTube collections, people invoked a sense of history, tradition, and collective memories that have become congealed in the Doordarshan logo and the signature tune.

The almost, sudden 'domestication' of television in the India in the 1980s, offered people for the first time new ways of watching and experiencing television, thereby realigning the contexts of family leisure and entertainment. Furthermore, what is significant about the first-person narratives and biographical accounts of television memories sketched on blogs and YouTube collections is the generation and production of 'informal knowledge' of audience/viewer experiences of television; the individual-collective memories of television available on the Internet can be considered as people's 'construction' of television history, thus offering substantial insights into the popular interpretations of the triad of television, memory, and history. Darian-Smith and Turnbull (2012), following John Hartley's work, suggest that it would be worthwhile to examine people's memories of television as constituting both a history of 'me' as the individual level, and a history of 'us' as the level of the group, family, or nation. The extracts from blogs and YouTube collections point to the similarities and overlaps between people's individual memories of television, the affective and emotional registers through which television is remembered, connecting the childhood years with televisual programmes and personalities, and the ways in which history of 'me' and 'us' is structured around the family and nation.

> But whenever you talk of Doordarshan one thing that flashes in my mind are the weekend programs on Sundays especially 'Sindbad the Sailor', 'Mogli', 'Alice in Wonderland', 'Malgudi Days' and of course my favorite 'Chandrakanta'. Doordarshan has got so many memories of mine and I am sure yours as well attached with it ... The way we cherish our memories with those serials I don't think we can get the same nostalgic feel with the serials and programs of the current lot, except a few. We all have to share our stories with our association with this good old friend Doordarshan. I would love to hear yours. Please feel free to share yours. (Sharma, 2009)

> A blog about recalling the 'Good times' we grew up watching as a child in the 70s through early 90s on Doordarshan national channel ... I am just glad to express my personal views and opinions along with our Blogger fans who send us amazing Fan mails about few Shows and Sitcoms aired on retro Doordarshan.[9]

> A nostalgia that cannot be reimbursed, Doordarshan, gave India its first taste of the picture tube and with it came a series of programs which paved the way to the television that we see today ... Doordarshan gave us a list of nostalgic songs which brings in a sense homesickness, some of them were, Mile Sur Mera Tumhara, Ek Anek, the title song of Malgudi Days, and the theme songs of Mahabharata and also Jungle Books—'jungle jungle baat chali hain', these are some songs which are irreplaceable. (Joyeeta, 2009)

> Good old days ... are here to stay forever ... jab main chota bacha tha ... badi sharart karta tha ... This is a little effort to keep alive the forgotten Doordarshan channel and all the memories we all have attached and associated with it. Now this is something which goes in the background of my mind every time ... The Title song ... of an old Doordarshan Serial ... Bharat Ek Khoj—Discovery of India ... Remember?? It goes like ... Sristi se pehle sach nahi tha ... Asatya bhi nahin ... antarisksh bhi nahin ... aaksh bhi nahin that ... chipa tha kahan ... kab. For those who don't know about Doordarshan: Click here. And click on the image to get a bigger view for a beautiful collage of DD serials and commercial made by me ... I remember I was a little kid and we used to live in a rented house, my father used to be a govt employee and my mother used to be a school teacher in a girl's high school. By that time, we did not have our own TV so we used to visit our neighbor to watch a few programmes. Here goes my exclusive collections of Doordarshan serials, commercials and sweet memories ... [referring to and linking the blog to an audio-visual collage of Doordarshan programs that he created]. (Samit, 2008)

A common thematic of the four blogs above pertains to how television programmes and specific genres constituted people's childhood years. The phenomenology of individual memories invoked the family and nation in terms of an overlap between a history of 'me' and 'us' organized by programme preferences and viewer experiences that become more pronounced in the following blogs. Concomitant with this, the Doordarshan era of the 1980s is distinguished from the current multichannel environment dominated by private television networks and an excess of programming.

> Remember the good old days of pre-satellite era? The doordarshan dominated era? The logo changing channels, what is it? We had only one channel,

> Doordarshan. Although boring most of the times; I miss some good non-commercial short films that Doordarshan used to telecast. Satellite TV channels these days are too commercialized and can't afford to waste even a second of air time for something that's good but non-profitable.[10]

> I was surfing through television channels lying on bed, and soon I noticed that I was doing nothing but going from 0 to 54 (that is the only number of channels I have on my television) ... I thought better it was to switch off the television and continue reading a book, long due—*One Hundred years of Solitude* [Gabriel Garcia Marquez novel]. My reading was short-lived as well; I thought of switching my television again, but then there is nothing to watch. Really? ... Has this all-time entertainer idiot-box turned into a dumb piece of scrap? I mean yes, there was once a time, when I used to run to watch particular program leaving back playing cricket or not worrying much about how crowded the train was. Ahhh! yes that was the time of Doordarshan—a single channel then (80s & 90s), which entertained, educated, informed, and served special feast of program on the weekends, especially Sunday ... I still cherish those memories of yesteryears—watching Doordarshan and its programs; memories which are shared by all people who were children when Ek-Anek used to be interruption their favorite programs. (Redij, 2008)

An interesting aspect of the blogs and YouTube collections pertained to the thousands of comments from a number of viewers who shared similar memories of Doordarshan in terms of snippets of childhood moments watching specific programmes, reminiscing about their families, places, and other 'fond moments' that constituted their televisual experiences, comparing Doordarshan programmes with the burgeoning programming on private networks, and so on. At a general level, while most comments pointed out that reading the specific blogs served as a 'trigger' for their own memories of Doordarshan, a characteristic feature of the comments sections was the creation of 'online affinity spaces' through which people shared information on Doordarshan ranging from programmes, televisual events, advertisements, cartoons, jingles, television actors, actresses, newsreaders, personalities, and so on.[11] There are feisty discussions that range from the popularity of Hindu television serials such as *Ramayan* (1987–88) and *Mahabharat* (1988–90) that appealed to people from different religious backgrounds to Smriti Irani's selection as a youth icon of Doordarshan. Apart from identifying their 'favorite' programmes and personalities, the online affinity spaces generated a rich repertoire of conversations and dialogues, a veritable informal 'archive' constituting a history of television based on people's memories and experiences.

> Just saw a Doordarshan special titled 'The Golden Trail, DD@50: Special Feature on the Golden Jubilee of Doordarshan', complete with rare footage and interviews, all celebrating the event. I was wallowing in the plain mushy nostalgia. The presentation was plain and simple, had it been one of those private channel affair things would have been equally typical – loud and jazzy and glossy and yet empty. Just this one time 'typical Doordarshan' was in fact strangely joyful. I would actually shell out money to buy stuff from Doordarshan archive. And I am sure many others would like to do that. People running Doordarshan should do something about it. Make the archive more accessible. There's even a view that projects funded by public money should be in the public domain. Maybe that's too much to ask in India. (Razdan, 2009)

The extract from Vivek Razdan's blog above points to the pleasures of watching Doordarshan in the 1980s, and contrasts the quality of Doordarshan's programmes with current programming on private television networks. For Razdan, Doordarshan was 'strangely joyful', and the private channels, 'loud, jazzy and glossy and yet empty'. The comparison between Doordarshan of the 1980s with the current private television programming is widely discussed in numerous blogs and YouTube collections. In addition, the online archiving of Doordarshan programmes and the construction of an accessible repository of programme materials shared across multiple platforms is another characteristic feature of blogs and YouTube collections. As the extract from Razdan's blog suggests, Doordarshan's archives are invaluable for public memory.[12]

Overall, people's recollections of their encounters with television during the 1980s centred on television's mediation of their childhoods, the realignment of their everyday habits and routines to television schedules and programmes, the emergence of new familial and social contexts of viewing, and their constitution as television 'audience'. All of these point to the entwinement of multiple temporalities: the everyday time of clocks, the lived time of the humans, and television's own temporalities (Scannell, 1996a). Indeed, a characteristic feature of people's television memories centres on the notion of *temporality*.

From a diversity of television programmes, people identified similar programmes as their 'favorite' ones. During the 1980s, the state-run television commissioned a number of leading 'art' directors to produce content for Doordarshan in the forms of single short films and multi-episode series and serials in a variety of genres. In addition, several programmes were commissioned from other countries and private corporations. Although Doordarshan's programming in the 1980s comprised of a wide repertoire of state-promoted ideological programmes that Rajagopal (1993) had categorized under the rubric of 'national programming', there was a large body of programmes that did not subscribe to the state-based ideologies.[13] A common motif in these television programmes is the rich repertoire of narrative forms and story traditions shared across languages and religions in India which offer an astonishing diversity of symbolic resources. To this end, the translation and adaptation of the rich repertoire of stories into the televisual medium in episodic, serial format, therefore 'resonate in memory in a double sense: they are both a cultural resource shared by millions, and yet are particular to the lives of individuals' (Scannell, 1996a: 18). Indeed, a characteristic feature of people's television memories centres on the notion of *narrative*.

The most remembered programmes included pro-development soap operas *Hum Log* (We People, 1984–85) and *Buniyaad* (Foundation, 1986); children's programmes *Jungle Book* (1989) *Disney Cartoons* (1987–90); mythological serials *Ramayan* (1986), *Mahabharat* (1988–90), *Vikram Aur Betaal* (Vikram and Betaal, 1985); music-based short videos *Ek Titli, Anek Tithliyan* (1984), *Mile Sur Mera Tumhara* (1988 onwards); film-based shows *Chitrahaar* (1985), *Phool Khile Hain Gulshan Gulshan* (1983 onwards); detective fictional series *Karamchand* (1985–89), *Byomkesh Bakshi* (1993–97), *Chandrakanta* (1994–96); situation comedies and dramas *Yeh Jo Hai Zindagi* (This Life As It Is, 1984–85), *Rajani* (1985), *Nukkad* (Street Corner, 1986–87), *Kachchi Dhoop* (Raw Sunshine, 1987), *Phir Wohi Talaash* (The Same Search Again, 1987), *Chunauti* (Challenge, 1987–88), *Oshin* (1988), *Mr. Yogi* (1988), *Waagle Ki Duniya* (Waagle's World, (1988–90), *Mungeri Lal Ke Haseen Sapne* (Colorful Dreams of Mungeri Lal, 1989–90), *Udaan* (Flight, 1989–91), *Flop Show* (1991); literary-based comic and drama series *Darpan* (Mirror, 1985), *Shrikant* (1985–86), *Malgudi Days* (1986), *Ek Kahani* (One Story, 1986), *Katha Sagar* (A Sea of Stories, 1986), *Rāg Darbāri* (1986–87), *Mailā Anchal* (Soiled Border, 1987–88), *Charitraheen* (Immoral, 1988), *Mirza Ghalib* (1988), *Mujrim Hazir* (Culprit Present, 1988), *Mulla Nasruddin* (1990), *Neem Ka Ped* (The Neem Tree, 1991), *Tenali Rama* (1990); and regional cinema in Indian languages.

RECUPERATING TRACES OF THE PAST: MEMORY, TELEVISION, AND HISTORY

To examine people's memories of Doordarshan in the 1980s, I conducted six in-depth interviews with men and women from Hyderabad. The overall goal was to identify broad representation of people from different class, caste, gender, religious, and geographical backgrounds. I selected people of a certain age range to ensure that their childhood years coincided with Doordarshan's growth and expansion beginning in the 1980s. When television sets arrived in the middle class homes, the exorbitant cost of the sets made it inaccessible for poor families. The memories of television from the 1980s on blogs and YouTube are of middle class individuals. To maintain salience with the blogs and YouTube, I conducted interviews with people from middle class backgrounds. However, I selected individuals from different caste, gender, and religious backgrounds. The interviews were conducted in people's homes and in public settings such as tea stalls and coffee shops. I followed a semi-structured interview pattern, beginning with open-ended exploration of the role and significance of television in their lives, particular memories of their encounters with the medium, to more detailed questions about specific programmes.[14]

As mentioned earlier, the study does not treat people's memories as objective and accurate accounts of the past; rather, memories are mediated by individual experiences, familial contexts and histories, and social, political, and economic factors. My concern is to explore the *how* and *what* of television memories, focusing on the interplay between phenomenological aspects of individual memories and sociological characteristics of collective memories. I also examine how 'the politics of memory' underpins people's remembering (and forgetting) of politics, events, places, and so on, in relation to television. Here I examine people's memories about Doordarshan's representations and coverage of sociopolitical issues such as the unrest and conflicts in the Northeast, Punjab, and Kashmir that marked the decade of the 1980s.

Although my analysis will concern itself with explicating the themes that emerged in people's memories—childhood, spatial and temporal dynamics, and programmes—I expand upon the two interlinked conceptual ideas of narrative and temporality that inform memory. To this end, I consider narrative as marking people's personal and social identities (narrative identity) and constituting television programmes (narrative forms). Ricoeur's (2003) philosophical explorations of memory and history enables me to examine the intersections between individual memory and collective memory, and the ways in which memory and history are linked together. Ricoeur's intersubjective approach to memory brings together two antagonistic discourses on memory —the sociology of collective memory and the phenomenology of individual memory—in terms of ordinary language, focusing on the semantics and pragmatics dimensions of mnemonic phenomena such as recollecting, remembering, and reminiscing to

> a phenomenology of memory, one less subject to what I venture to term as idealist prejudice, can draw from the competition presented to it by the

> sociology of memory as an incitement to develop in the direction of a direct phenomenology applied to social reality, which includes the participation of subjects capable of designating themselves as being, to different degrees of reflective consciousness, the authors of their acts. (Ricoeur, 2003: 128)

Furthermore, Ricoeur's intersubjective account of individual and collective memory is elaborated in terms of narrative, temporality, and identity.

In an earlier work, Ricoeur (1980: 169) noted that narrative and time presuppose each other, wherein

> narrativity and temporality are closely related—as closely as, in Wittgenstein's terms, a language game and a form of life. Indeed, I take temporality to be that structure of existence that reaches in language in narrativity and narrativity to be the language structure that has temporality as its ultimate referent. Their relationship therefore is reciprocal.

In subsequent writings, Ricoeur (1996) extended his theories of narrative and temporality to develop the concept of 'narrative identity'. For Ricoeur, narrative identity is elaborated in terms of two interlinked categories, *idem* and *ipse* constituting a person's identity at the individual and social levels. Whereas *idem*-identity is posited as the stable and permanent marker of the self (self-same), *ipse*-identity, understood as incorporating change in relation to the other, is the dynamic and interpretive component of selfhood which unfolds over time and is mediated through narration, myths, symbols, and signs, constituting one's life story. Narrative identity, therefore, bespeaks of the dialectic of *idem*, the 'what' of the self, and *ipse* the 'who' of the self. Furthermore, with regards to the relations between memory, history, and identity, Ricoeur (2003: 84–85) had argued that 'it is through narrative function that memory is incorporated in the formation of identity'. What this entails is that memories have a narrative structure through which individuals organize their experience. To this end, I explore how people's memories unfold over time, and study the narrative dimensions of their identity as they engage in the mnemonic practices of recollecting, remembering, and reminiscing about television.

The interviews are organized as six stories of the following individuals from different geographic regions of Hyderabad: Kishore Chandra, mid-forties, middle-class, upper-caste, Hindu, male, from Nallakunta; Danish Ahmed, mid-forties, middle-class, Muslim, male, from Tolichowki; Mohan Singh, mid-forties, middle-class, Sikh, male, from Kishan Bagh; Chitra Reddy, mid-forties, middle-class, upper-caste, Hindu, female, from Himayatnagar;

Qamar Mirza, mid-forties, middle-class, Muslim, female, from Barkatpura; and Satya Velu, working-class, lower-caste, Hindu, male, from Kachiguda. I begin with a few extracts of the interviews on their mnemonic uses of television.

All, except Satya, situated Doordarshan as significant in mediating their childhood years, remembering in specific detail the formative influences of television in their lives, the reorganization of daily routines to fit with the programme schedules, and in precipitating new viewing experiences and practices. Overall, their individual memories of Doordarshan vis-à-vis their childhoods suggest that television functioned as a 'transitional-evocative object', thereby pointing to similarities with people's memories on blogs and YouTube.

> ... my early memories of Doordarshan go back to the introduction of colour television in 1982 to coincide with the New Delhi Asian Games. I remember watching the opening ceremony at our neighbour's house ... I, and my older brother would watch glimpses of the various sporting events on and off. After the games, we convinced our father to buy a television set for us. It was an exciting moment ... acquire our own television ... we grew up around Doordarshan ... eagerly waiting for the programmes on Sunday mornings and weekday nights. Some of my favorite programmes were *Jungle Book* and *Disney's Cartoons*. Our family favorites were *Ramayan*, *Mahabharat*, *Yeh Jo Hai Zindagi*. (Kishore Chandra)

> I am fond of the 80s because I was a child during that time ... the childhood memories make me nostalgic about my family, the relationships we forged and the places we visited ... and this was also the time when Doordarshan came into our lives. I watched a few movies in neighbourhood homes. Abbu [father] bought us a television set sometime in 1984 or 1985. Watching programmes was like an event in itself. It was all so new to me as kid. Ammi [mother] would finish cooking and housework early so that we can watch programmes together. We all watched *Buniyaad*, *Ramayan*, and *The Sword of Tipu Sultan* with avid interest. As a kid, I enjoyed Sunday morning programmes for children, especially cartoons. Abbu and Ammi also regularly watched television news in Urdu along with some other entertainment programmes on the local, Hyderabad Doordarshan. (Danish Ahmed)

> Childhood memories of my first encounter with Doordarshan are hazy. I do remember that sometime in mid-eighties, I think, television viewing was a novel experience for me and my family ... apart from the entertainment and news, DD literally brought the world into our homes. I have some faint memories of watching *Hum Log* and *Rajani* serials. I do vividly remember the *Ramayan* and *Mahabarat* serials though since it was such a big family viewing experience. The television music animations and short videos, *Ek Titli* and

> *Mile Sur* still ring in my mind. I also remember the memorable Nirma, Surf, and other commercials. (Chitra Reddy)

> In our locality, owning a television set was a big deal, almost a public event for children and well as adults alike. I watched Hindi movies on Doordarshan in neighbour's home who would charge 25 paise for a movie. We all would sit on the floor and eagerly wait for the telecast to start. The neighbour, a grumpy old man and his wife, would sit of the chairs at the back of the room. These are some early memories of Doordarshan. Later we bought our own television set as television became very propular with so many programmes. I liked *Nukkad, Buniyaad, Ye Jo Hai Zindagi.* (Mohan Singh)

> I was around seven years old, I suppose when television slowly entered our home. I still remember our regular family listening of radio programmes such as 'Hawa Mahal', 'Fauji Bhaiyon Ke Liye' and 'Chaya Geet' on Vividh Bharati. My father was an avid enthusiast of Hindi–Urdu lyrics and song compositions. Even though we had Doordarshan, radio listening still remained a regular ritual at home. I have some nostalgic memories of the tussle between radio and television ... until Doordarshan gradually displaced our 'radio times'. The television weekdays and evenings were filled with so many popular serials, *Buniyaad, Nukkad, Ye Jo Hai Zindagi, Fauji* etc. My parents liked to watch *Phir Wahi Talaash* and *Mirza Ghalib*, and of course, *Neem Ka Ped* because of their enduring song compositions and storytelling. I liked Sunday morning programmes when I was a child. (Qamar Mirza)

Satya Velu's memories of Doordarshan connect his childhood years, assisting his mother with domestic work in middle class households. While the social relations of caste networks enable working class, lower caste families to work in middle class households, and are viewed as providing useful resources for livelihood, they are problematic in perpetuating caste hierarchies and exploitation as well. Satya sees the relationship in positive terms, pointing out that it provided him and his family emotional stability, and a sense of belonging. In a matter-of-fact way, Satya told me that his mother worked as a *pani manishi* (Telugu word for 'domestic worker').[15]

> Amma (mother) used to work as a 'pani manishi' in some three–four households in Kachiguda, and my nana (father) worked at a beedi factory. I and my sister would accompany amma to the households, helping out with some household chores and errands. I was about 9 years, my sister 8. My first memories of Doordarshan go back to this time in the households. On some occasions, we were allowed to watch Telugu movies, and *Ramayan* and *Mahabharat*. We bought our own television set in 1989 from a local dealer. By the time we

> were both teenagers attending government school, continuing to help amma with household work. It was a big fancy town a television set and watch in our home. (Satya Velu)

The above extracts from people's television memories of their encounters with Doordarshan, especially the recollections of their childhood years, the convivial experiences of watching television with neighbours and families are similar to those in the blogs and YouTube. Although these take the form of nostalgic, and in some instances, melancholic reflections on the past, they are largely cheerful accounts of the arrival of the medium in their homes. At first glance, these memories of Doordarshan seem unremarkable, trite, or even banal. However, as mnemonic fragments of biographic narratives they offer vivid accounts of the arrival of television in their homes, the particular communal, familial, and individual moments of watching television, reflections of their media worlds, kinship relations, and the effects of socioeconomic factors. In reminiscing about and reconstructing their childhood ipseities, these memories foreground the narrative and temporal dimensions of identity formation.

A significant, yet distinctive, aspect of television memories related to particular televisual events, places, and personalities. As I began to ask specific questions as to what they remember about the events, places, and personalities in relation to Doordarshan, the recollections moved beyond personal memories, and connected these to political forms and institutions; that is, towards a broader set of topics, moving from discussions of popular television newsreaders, actors, and actresses to how the 1980s witnessed a series of political and social strife, assassinations, civic unrest, and communal violence in India. These evocations of memories situated Doordarshan as a key institution in its coverage and reporting of the events such as the reports of Indira Gandhi's assassination and the subsequent 'live' coverage. The recollections of these televisual events were vivid, stark, and manifested as 'flashbulb' memories:

> Kishore Chandra: Doordarshan newsreaders had an interesting style of presentation. I enjoyed watching news in Hindi, particularly Shammi Narang and Salma Sultana. I never paid much attention to politics, but remember seeing Indira Gandhi and Rajiv Gandhi a lot in the news.
>
> Sanjay Asthana: Do you remember any major political events/situation covered by Doordarshan in the 1980s?
>
> Kishore Chandra: Indira Gandhi's assassination coverage broadcast on television in 1984 was a huge shock. The *mandir–masjid* dispute of Ayodhya

that went on for a few years, and the destruction of Babri Masjidin 1991. I remember the dome of the mosque being brought down on television. These were some disturbing aspects from the 1980s during my childhood and teenage years … and have stayed with me.

Chitra Reddy: I liked the English newscasts on DD. Rini Simon and Sunil Tandon were very good. I used to imitate Rini Simon's voice and diction as a child.

Sanjay Asthana: Do you remember any major political events/situation covered by Doordarshan in the 1980s?

Chitra Reddy: The situation in Punjab and Kashmir and Assam was getting bad. I was a teenager at that time, and have hazy memories of Indira Gandhi's assassination and the 'live' coverage on television. My father used to watch Prannoy Roy's *The World This Week* on Friday nights. The news here was more in-depth than Doordarshan's daily newscasts.

I met Danish Ahmed in an Irani restaurant in Tolichowki; sipping and relishing the famous chai, we started talking about the growth and expansion of Hyderabad city over the last two decades, rising real estate prices, influx of money from overseas, migration of people into the city from villages and towns, and the effects of economic liberalization policies since the early 1990s. I gradually shifted the conversation to the 1980s and Doordarshan, and asked him if he watched television news, and the coverage of politics and political events. Danish Ahmed pointed out that his parents regularly watched Hyderabad Doordarshan's broadcast of news in Urdu, and he would join them once in a while. With regards to the political events, he noted:

I remember the communal tensions in the old city of Hyderabad during the eighties. Although Tolichowki had majority of Muslims there were hundreds of Hindu homes and families in my neighbourhood. As a teenager, I would watch Doordarshan news in Urdu to see if everything was okay in Tolichowki and other parts of the city, I had several Hindu friends … we used to socialize, play cricket, watch movies, go to school. We all had harmonious relations, but communal tensions would disturb the peace. I always felt uneasy during these times. In late eighties, things gradually changed for the worse, when local political leaders began to sow seeds of discord among Hindus and Muslims. The mandir–masjid dispute led to communal riots. I never thought Doordarshan could instill communal feelings among the people. I still refuse to believe that Ramayan and Mahabharat led to communalization of politics. At home we watched *Ramayan*, *Mahabharat*, *Mirza Ghlaib*, *Nukkad*. My

> mother never missed an episode of *Ramayan*. She never saw it as a Hindu epic or through the lens of religion. I remember, however, that Doordarshan news was mostly biased because it was under the government control.

The mnemonic uses of Doordarshan suggest that people drew upon television's 'own' construction of history to remember and reminisce about political forms, institutions, and media events. This is evident in the particular ways in which class, caste, gender, religious, and geographic identities are imbricated with people's televisual memories, thus positing a complex dynamic between memory, history, and forgetting. For, as Ricoeur noted, the 'affective traces' of the past are the crucial connector of memory to history. It is in this context that Mohan Singh's recollections of Doordarshan in the 1980s—which I have noted shared similarities with others—become unsettling as he begins to reconstruct and negotiate his Sikh identity.[16]

For Mohan and his family, and the Sikh community at large, the political unrest in Punjab, the military intervention, and the subsequent violence and desecration of the Golden Temple in Amritsar by the militants and the military, assassination of Prime Minister Indira Gandhi, and the massacre of Sikhs in Delhi have shaped his memories and experiences of the 1980s.[17] Referring to Doordarshan, he noted that the coverage of these events were almost non-existent, and whatever was reported was biased. He remembers growing up in Kishan Bagh, a neighbourhood in the old city of Hyderabad, with a substantial Sikh population, and the local gurudwara that offered him and his family comfort and solace.[18] Speaking about the unrest in Punjab, he stated,

> ... my memories are hazy ... I do remember about the assault on the Golden Temple since Doordarshan did not mention it for several days ... the newspaper offered more details on what was going on in and around the Golden Temple, whereas television continued showing entertainment programmes with news blackout of the events in Punjab.

Mohan remembers the Doordarshan coverage of Indira Gandhi's assassination thus:

> ... the death of Prime Minister Indira Gandhi came as a major shock ... a pall of gloom descended in my home. What was equally shocking and disturbing unfolded as we were mourning the loss, watching Doordarshan's 'live' broadcast of cremation rituals. Sikhs in Delhi and elsewhere in northern India were being attacked; thousands of Sikhs were killed in the three to four days of

> mayhem that followed. I was a child, could not comprehend it fully, but was distraught, filled with anxiety and dread.

As we continued our conversation, I asked Mohan Singh if he and his family watched any of the documentaries and fictional series on Punjab aired on Doordarshan during the eighties. Remembering the programmes in relation to the traumatic events of 1984, he noted:

> I was around fifteen years old at the time, beginning to understand the situation in Punjab, and what it meant to be a Sikh. The serial, *Choli Daman* depicted the lives of ordinary families of Hindus and Sikhs, and how they coped with the grim realities of conflict and violence. In a sense, it was good that the events of 1984 were not directly mentioned in the serials. Nalini Singh's documentary, I don't remember the title though. I only watched a few episodes, my parents watched it all.

Mohan Singh's associative memories of Doordarshan, the televisual event, of places, politics, and the massacre of thousands of Sikhs as 'affective traces' of the past, render palpable the 'unsaid' of traumatic memories that linger on, existing at the intersections of memory, history, and forgetting. For Mohan Singh, forgetting abets epistemic violence, and that his Doordarshan memories also entail remembering the moments when he was in front of the television watching the mourning of a leader as the massacre of ordinary Sikhs in Delhi unfolded during the next few days. Doordarshan did not report on the largescale violence, hence he stated, *kyon bhooloun*? (why should I forget?). More crucially, however, the memories so reconceived point to an alternate history of television from the standpoint of viewers who experienced it. As Darian-Smith and Turnbull (2012) assert, people's own documentation of their individual memories of television, whether produced on the Internet—as blog and YouTube collections—or through oral interviews as 'archives' of viewers' television memories constitute an important counterpoint to the production of an 'official' history of television.

CONCLUDING REMARKS

Ricoeur's philosophical explorations of the connections between history and memory, I have argued and demonstrated, provide a deeper understanding of television —as a mediated 'symbolic form' (Thompson, 1995)—and opens up fresh insights into the play of power, narrative, affect, temporality on memory and history (Ricoeur, 2003; Hartley, 2008; Darian-Smith and Turnbull, 2012).

According to Ricoeur, if history is about the 'what was' of the past, memory is related to history in the sense that it entails a reconstruction of the past. The questions, therefore, for Ricoeur is not that history is an accurate representation of the 'what was' of the past, but rather, it is 'history as a mediating amalgam of trace and figurative language that brings us the meaning of the past' (Crowley, 2003: 7).

The analysis revealed the particular ways in which people appropriated and interpreted televisual memories by reconceiving moments and experiences of their past into narratives that suggest broad similarities across individual and collective memories. An interesting characteristic related to how remembering television meant remembering *with* television, reminiscing about histories of people, places, events, and so on. To this end, two main issues emerge from the interconnections between/across television, memory, and history. First, the significance of people's recollections and remembering about television offers an alternate history of the medium distinct from the 'official' and 'scholarly' historical accounts (Spigel, 1992; Hartley, 2008). Second, the internet and the emergence of digital media forms has created a transmedial and virtual environments for the storage, retrieval, and sharing of memories, thereby 'transform[ing] what was once "collective memory" into "connective memory"' (Hoskins, 2009: 149).[19]

Although the study broadly identified the influences of class, caste, gender, religion, and geographic identities on people's television memories, I have not pursued a detailed examination of their interlocking effects. The television memories on blogs and YouTube structured around middle class, upper-caste imagination of nation and family in terms of what John Hartley (2006) characterized as the mediation between a history of 'me' and a history of 'us'—borne out by similarities in programme preferences, viewing practices, and other aspects. For most people, watching Doordarshan in the 1980s connected them to their childhood years, the moments of the past 'reactivated' through their associations with family, neighbours, places, and events. While the memories invoked look similar to the Proustian Madeleine and Combray examples, they also differ in several ways. What is remembered is television as an object, cultural form, symbolic resource, an audiovisual world of unfolding characters, plots, narratives, stories, and so on, across temporal and spatial contexts. The happy memories of Doordarshan, therefore, dominant in people's imaginations are also similar to global instances of how the arrival of the medium has mediated people's life-worlds. What is significant, then, about Doordarshan memories? Scholarly literature in media and memory studies noted that the links between memory and media are not straightforward, but rather, people's individual memories are shaped by social and cultural forces (van Dijck, 2004). In the context of this study, Doordarshan memories from the 1980s are likewise shaped by the familial contexts and life-worlds, spatiotemporal dynamics, the intersections of social and cultural forces, and so on.

The retrospective 'unprompted' remembering and reminiscing about Doordarshan on blogs and YouTube collections, mostly invoked as happy memories, of fond moments of a time past, although filled with nostalgia and melancholy are produced as bittersweet moments. The 'prompted' memories in the interviews, however, elicited through detailed and specific questions reconceived 'as many-layered palimpsest of association in conjunction with a similarly many-layered palimpsest of places, upon which are written [our] history, traditions, experiences and ideas' (Donohoe, 2016: 1–2). The affective traces of the past that surfaced in people's remembering and forgetting about television, therefore, complicates our understanding of the relations between television, memory, and history.

In the context of South Asian and Indian history, scholarship has explored people's memories in terms of oral histories of refugees who fled the Partition of India in August 1947 which resulted in the creation of Pakistan, the largest displacement and movement of some fifteen million people along religious and ethnic lines within the newly created borders. People became refugees in their own lands, fleeing their homes, facing violence and death. It has been estimated that thousands of people lost their lives as a result of violence and communal riots. A recent initiative by Guneeta Singh Bhalla in creating an online archive of individual memories of people who lived through the violence, trauma, and pain of Partition where she characterizes the people as 'citizen historians' is an important project that seeks to bridge memory, history, and forgetting through the mediation of the internet.[20]

While this chapter explored a different, yet interrelated, aspect of how memory and history are mobilized by people in remembering television, it offers a similar perspective; that is, the importance of creating and sustaining people's archives of memories and histories of the past in a transmedial environment. Pointing out to the implications on individual as well as collective memories, Kansteiner (1999: 191) noted, '[W]e are only beginning to study the impact on memory caused by the first media revolution of the century, represented by film and television, while we are already in the middle of the second media revolution, which will force us to come to terms with the internet-based collective memories and new visual and discursive codes.'

NOTES

1. In fact, those who study television as a scholarly endeavour also produce 'informal knowledge'—that is, memories of the everyday experiences about television. For instance, one such scholar of Indian television noted, 'My first recollections of watching television as a child growing up in India are from my primary school days in the city of Bombay … Our Sunday mornings began with a mix of Indian, Hungarian, Japanese, and Disney cartoons. Following breakfast, we would lounge on the family couch all morning watching great Indian epics like *Ramayana*, folk mythologies like *Vikram aur Betal*, popular American shows like *I Love Lucy*, *Different Strokes*, *Star Trek*, and *National Geographic*, and German comedies and dramas like *The Didi Comedy Show* and *The Old Fox*. Our Sunday afternoons would consist of occasional English film and regional language films. Our Sunday evenings started with sporting events from around the world and ended with a blockbuster Hindi film. If that wasn't enough, there were always the song-and-dance sequences from Hindi films on weekdays. We were India's first television generation' (Parks and Kumar, 2006: 1).
2. The purpose is not to collapse Silverstone's 'transitional object' and Turkle's 'evocative object' into a singular theoretical construct; rather, my intent is to explore the specific ways in which television functions both as a transitional as well as an evocative object in people's mnemonic uses of television.
3. Scannell's (1996a; 1996b) phenomenological studies of broadcasting from 1930s–1990s in Britain present an interesting counterpoint to similarities and differences with India's history and development of broadcasting during the same period. Several similarities become obvious when we look at India's broadcast television in the 1980s, especially in terms of the creation of programme schedules, formats, and a variety of programme genres, marking the 'ordinariness' and temporal arrangements of broadcasting that Scannell has examined. The differences are stark, especially during 1930–1947, with India still under the British rule, and broadcasting serving as an instrument and apparatus of power and colonial sovereignty (see Chapter 2 for an elaboration).
4. With the increasing presence of digital media technologies and convergence, scholars have explored the characteristic features of 'old' and 'new' media in terms of 'remediation' and 'convergence culture' that has implications for history and memory. Garde-Hansen, Hoskins, and Reading (2009: 8) note that 'unlike history, which has been traditionally promoted and defended by the written word, memory has projected itself in multiple media and formats over the last few centuries: as script, audio, images, artefacts, sculpture, artwork and architecture to name a few. This is not to say that history is not currently embracing and engaging with other ways of distributing itself: film, television and websites for example, but rather that history is delivering itself technologies that befit memory-making. The shift away from the dominance of the logos toward more participatory systems of representation is one that lends itself particularly well to theories of memory within a culture of convergence of digital media'.

5. I did not study Facebook pages and Twitter posts; instead, I selected a representative sample of blogs and YouTube collections to pursue a focused analysis. A detailed exploration of the online 'archives' of people's memories of Doordarshan is outside the scope of my chapter.
6. The Hindi word *kaju* refers to cashews and *rasgulla* is an Indian dessert, a ball of cottage cheese cooked in syrup.
7. For example, here is one blog post on the issue along with the scene in question: http://cinephilia.travellingslacker.com/2011/07/zindagi-na-milegi-dobara-doordarshan/.
8. For background and context on the plans to change the logo, see http://www.hindustantimes.com/india-news/meet-the-nid-student-who-made-the-doordarshan-symbol-soon-to-be-history/story-owFIcYbSZe5OfmWIet7GiO.html; http://www.thehindu.com/news/national/dd-plans-to-change-its-logo-launches-design-contest/article19359270.ece.
9. See https://oldidiotbox.blogspot.com.
10. See http://www.ambimama.com/2006/03/30/childhood-memories-ek-aur-anek-doordarshan-videos/.
11. An online affinity space, according to James Paul Gee, is an informal place, spaces based on common endeavour and interests of people irrespective of people's sociocultural backgrounds where conversations occur, knowledge is exchanged, shared, and distributed. Some common online examples of affinity spaces include gaming environments, fan sites, chat rooms, and so on. I draw upon this idea of online affinity space to situate Doordarshan blogs and YouTube collections, especially the comments sections where common endeavours and interests take place. See Gee (2005) for a discussion of affinity spaces.
12. Razdan's blog itself is an interesting amalgam of Doordarshan materials, found objects, artifacts, materials, and trivia from popular culture. See http://8ate.blogspot.com/?view=mosaic.
13. The state-run television, Doordarshan sponsored several famous filmmakers of 'alternate' cinema to produce television programmes in the 1980s. Several famous directors such as Shyam Benegal, Mani Kaul, Govind Nihalani, Saeed Mirza, M. S. Sathyu, Kundan Shah, and Gulzar produced widely popular television serials and sitcoms. Despite this, however, Doordarshan has refused to air programmes of several filmmakers and documentary makers which raised socially relevant issues and were critical of the government and the postcolonial state. See Rajadhyaksha (1987) and Shahani (2002) for a discussion of Doordarshan blocking Anand Patwardhan's *Hamara Sheher* (Our City) and Mani Kaul's *Mati Manas* (The Mind of Clay) both of which were produced in 1985, and Kumar Shahani's experimental film, *Khayal Gatha* (The Saga of Khayal) produced in 1989.
14. Satya Velu and Chitra Reddi's mother tongue is Telugu, Kishore Chandra's Hindi, Danish Ahmed and Qamar Mirza's Urdu, and Mohan Singh's, Punjabi. However, they were all familiar with Hindi, Telugu, Urdu, and English languages, speaking with varying degrees of proficiency. At a more general level, all spoke in 'Deccani',

the common colloquial speech of Hyderabad that includes a mixture of Hindi, Urdu, and Telugu words and phrases. Most of the interviews were conducted in people's own mother tongues, shifting between/across languages wherever it became necessary.

15. In Hindi-Urdu, words such as *naukrani* (female servant) and *kaam karne waali* (female worker) are commonly used by middle class and upper caste families for domestic workers, mostly women, who wash dishes, cook, and clean the homes. However, these terms do not provide an adequate grasp of the social obligations, reproduction of structural inequalities, cultural taboos, and stigma that underpins such 'master–slave' relations. According to Shaziah Wasiuzzaman and Karen Wells (2010: 283), 'working-class families use children's domestic work with middle-class families as part of a web of resources to protect them from economic shocks and to enable them to afford to meet the cost of social obligations', and 'hiring domestic workers locks employers into relations of social obligations with their employees and families'. Further, they write, 'these webs of support are enabled precisely because the domestic workers are children and not adults; their status as children makes it possible for the labor contract to be mystified and reconfigured as a social relationship'.
16. In asking about specific details about the television events and coverage of news in the 1980s, the particular framing of my questions may have served as a 'prompt' for Mohan Singh's memories.
17. During the early 1980s, the political situation in the state of Punjab began to deteriorate from civic unrest to growing violence, particularly during the years of 1982–83. In June 1984, Prime Minister Indira Gandhi ordered the Army to enter the Golden Temple, the holiest Sikh shrine in Amritsar. In October 1984, Indira Gandhi was assassinated by her Sikh bodyguards to seek revenge for the assault on the Golden Temple. In November 1984, thousands of Sikhs were killed in Delhi and northern India. See Das (1985) and Devgun (2013) for an account of the events of 1984.
18. Kishan Bagh in the old city of Hyderabad is a historic place for Sikhs. In 1832, the ruler of the Deccan, Hyderabad, Asif Jah Nasir-ud-Dowlah, popularly referred to as the Fourth Nizam, requested a battalion of military from Maharaja Ranjeet Singh, ruler of Punjab, Kabul, and Kandhar to consolidate his army—and to quell any potential trouble from the *jagirdar*s. Around 1500 Lahori Sikh soldiers came to Hyderabad from Punjab, and were granted land (*jagir*) for their resettlement. The place came to be called as the 'Sikh Chawni' where Sikhs raised their families and worshipped in the Puratan Gurudwara Saheb Barambala built in 1832. The Chawni later came to be known as Kishan Bagh. For a history of the Gurudwara and Kishan Bagh, see http://www.gurudwarasahebbarambala.com.
19. Some recent efforts by state broadcasters with regards to television memories blends both the archiving and airing of old programmes ('nostalgic programming') and soliciting people to share and upload content; for instance, BBC MemoryShare, Spain's broadcaster TVE-50, European Union's Videoactive and EUSCREEN.

Television scholars from Australia have created an electronic resource for archiving of people's television memories. See Gutiérrez Lozano (2013) and Turnbull (2012). Hoskins (2009) refers to the 'mediatization' of memory in terms of two phases: the first one, associated with the institution of television, and a second, interconnected with television, yet distinctive due to the emergence of the web and digital technologies. See also Garde-Hansen, Hoskins, and Reading (2009) on how digital media is reshaping television memories.

20. See http://www.1947partitionarchive.org; in addition, for a brief background on the Partition Archives, see the National Public Radio Feature, https://www.npr.org/sections/parallels/2017/08/13/542803259/giving-voice-to-memories-from-1947-partition-and-the-birth-of-india-and-pakistan; see also Raj (2000) for an overview of partition memory studies in India.

Epilogue

This book explored the history and development of broadcasting in late colonial and postcolonial India through an examination of the intertwined genealogies of sovereignty, public, religion, and nation, and the spatiotemporal dynamics of radio and television. The colonial constructions of sovereignty, public, religion, and nation that underpinned the formative period of broadcasting continued to operate in the postcolonial careers of radio and television largely shaping the structural, institutional, and policy discourse. While the study of broadcasting's administrative structures and bureaucratic forms revealed particular configurations and power modalities, analyses of television's programme narratives and viewers' reception context pointed to incommensurability between the concepts and their explanations of sociocultural practices, with religion and the public in particular, as the most problematic. I argued that scholarly studies of India's state-run television glossed over the religious, the particular interplay between religion and secularism, and have not paid attention to how the colonial construction of broadcast public and the public–audience dialectic.

To overcome the incommensurability—and the conceptual conundrums—posed by colonial constructs, specifically religion and the public, I developed a theoretical approach drawing on Ricoeur's formulation of the 'double hermeneutic' and Foucault's late work on the 'hermeneutics of the self'. The analytic orientation enabled me to pursue concrete examination of modes of power and narrative dimensions that underpinned sovereignty, public, religion, and nation; more crucially, however, the heterodox theoretical approach opened up the possibility of exploring divergent meanings of religion and the public that existed in late colonial and postcolonial India, and the particular ways in which these operated in television narratives—at the aesthetic, cultural, and symbolic levels, in stories, plots, events, kinship relations, characters, and the life-worlds.

Instead of summarizing the chapters, I offer commentary on the Eurocentric/Western conceptions of history, modernity, and religion, especially since the presence of the universal categories in contemporary India continue to obfuscate, rather than illuminate and clarify historical, social, and cultural processes. In the following, I briefly explore some recent scholarship in television studies in India as well as the West, pointing to their possibilities and problems in reconceptualizing media and communication studies (MCS) in India. Next, I draw on few scholarly writings in philosophy, neo-Marxist critiques, postcolonial, South Asian, and religious studies that present strategies on how to engage and move beyond the Eurocentric/Western universals. Finally, I build these perspectives and outline programmatic arguments for their utility in conjunction with hermeneutics and philology as interpretive approaches for MCS in India.

I

In the last two decades major technological transformations precipitated by the digitization of information and communication, rise and consolidation of the Internet, and the increasing ubiquity of 'new' media have impacted network television broadcasting on the West, most notably the United States and Europe. A spate of scholarly studies has since declared that the broadcast television era is on its last legs, and the multichannel environment is best characterized as 'narrowcasting' (Gripsrud, 2004), an individualist medium rather than a collectivist one (Katz and Scannell, 2009), and television programme flows replaced by on-demand viewing driven by metadata protocols and algorithmic logic (Urrichio, 2004). Furthermore, the studies describe the changing configurations of television in the West as 'post-broadcast' which shaped my new media modalities and web-based architecture of 'interface, hyperlinks, and a database structure experienced via broadband rather than broadcasting' (Bennett and Strange, 2011; see also de Valck and Teurlings, 2013).

A common assumption in these studies pertains to the way in which the theoretical object of 'television' is framed as universal and a globalizing medium disregarding the complex interplay of national, regional, and local histories and genealogies of television in most parts of the world. Indeed, as G. Turner (2009) has persuasively argued, the nation remains a powerful vector for television in the non-West. And for Turner and Tay (2009: 3), the technological transformations are 'highly contingent with many national systems still dominated by broadcast media and national regulatory regimes, and others framed by subscription services and multichannel, transnational, and commercial environments ... the "old media" such as television are still the main game in most locations'. For instance, in India the last two decades witnessed the arrival of satellite television resulting in gradual diminution of state-run television, Doordarshan. The shift from state-run terrestrial television to private, satellite television networks—local, regional, transnational—led to the incorporation of hybridized and commodified production techniques, programme formats, and content that accommodates a mélange of regional–national–global forms, styles, and characteristics. India's state-run national network co-exists with the local, regional, and transnational television networks in a multilingual environment where programming is increasingly shaped by commercial cinema, geo-linguisitic and cultural factors, and particular articulations of national identity alongside transnational programme formats such as *Reality Television* and *Idol* (Athique, 2009; Thussu, 2005). Even though the commodification, corporatization, and commercialization of the television and economic globalization have disaggregated and altered particular components of sovereignty, television in India still operates within the nation, not beyond (Chatterjee, 1993). While the shifts can be considered a consequence of media globalization and technological transformations, it would be hasty to characterize the multichannel Indian television scenario as 'post-broadcast' just as yet or constituting something like a 'global television'.[1]

While explorations of national television systems and their specific histories and ontologies in the non-West remain crucial to comparative and cross-cultural accounts as a way to counter the universalist assumptions of television theory (as well as media and communication studies) in the West, they nonetheless are inadequate because the projects of 'de-westernizing media studies' (Curran and Park, 2000), internationalizing media studies (Thussu, 2009), and deconstructing television theory (Kumar, 2006) are posited on the notion of 'difference' which in itself is part of the universalism of the West that they seek to overcome (Roy, 2012).[2] Instead, a fundamental task on hand should be the decolonization of our epistemologies and knowledges, a formidable task for a media and communication scholar of the non-West. Instead of the usual refrain such as 'scholarship on television in South Asia continued to be neglected within Television Studies' (Punathambekar and Kumar, 2012: 483), we need to engage in a dual task: first, disaggregate the entrenched Eurocentric/Western categories that come with universalist biases and presuppositions, and, second, draw on the resources of our intellectual and cultural traditions and sociocultural experiences to study the histories of communication forms, radio and television broadcasting, the Internet, mobile telephony, other media technologies, and so forth.[3]

A crucial task, then, centres on developing heterodox, analytic 'constellations' that are not mere abstractions and decontextualized and disembodied figures of thought, but embedded in, and generative of, our sociocultural life-worlds and experiences, and intellectual and textual forms. In a programmatic manner, I offer some reflections on how we might pursue such a task by drawing on some recent writings that explore key ideas on theory, history, modernity, and religion in India.

II

Although earlier scholarly writings on colonialism and orientalism have examined the West's conquest, violence, and production of knowledge about the non-West, it was Dipesh Chakrabarty's (1992) work that explored how Eurocentrism operated as a universal category. Without going into the details of Chakrabarty's perceptive arguments, I briefly describe key summary points. According to Chakrabarty (1992: 1), for the academic discourse of history (and theory) produced in the West, 'Europe remains a sovereign, theoretical subject of all histories, including the ones we call "Indian", "Chinese", "Kenyan", and so on. There is a peculiar way in which all other histories tend to become variations of a master narrative that could be called "the history of Europe"'. Chakrabarty goes on to explore how the master narrative of Europe, under the sign of modernity and historical knowledge operated in India, manifesting as a 'lack', 'incompleteness', and 'inadequacy' during the British colonial rule, in anti-colonial nationalism, and even reappearing in nationalist and Marxist histories under the rubric of 'transition narrative' (this was evident in the discourse of broadcasting, see this book, Chapter 1).

According to Chakrabarty (1992: 21), since the universalist notions of citizenship, public, private, and nation-state are embedded within the dominant European discourse of history, one has no choice but to engage with modernity and its categories, unpacking their biases and presuppositions so as to 'write into the history of modernity the ambivalences, contradictions, the use of force, and the tragedies that attend it'. For Chakrabarty, this task is crucial and a fraught one for a scholar because such a critical history embodies a 'politics of despair', a necessary predicament for the project of 'Provincializing Europe'.

Chakrabarty's approach is one, among some others, that have been proposed as a way to counter the dominant Western/European narratives of history and theory. Vivek Dhareshwar (1995) suggested that Chakrabarty's approach does not provide enough intellectual resources to explain how critical history can account for the postcolonial present because for Chakrabarty the recuperation of the past generates a 'politics of despair'. According to Dhareshwar (1995: 318), since 'despair is disjoined from hope in Chakrabarty's critique of modernity', it leaves no room for theorizing the present, and, therefore, 'imprison[s] us even more deeply in a historicism that is unable to open itself to any future and thus unable to determine any historical present'. For Mithi Mukherjee (2010a: 457), the notion of 'difference' has operated as a central framing device in Chakrabarty's work where India's modernity as difference is posited as an excess in relation to the West. Hence, Chakrabarty does not see the possibility of an exteriority to the Western intellectual tradition ... and what began as a claim to provincialize Europe ended up as not much more than an exploration into how Western thought "may be renewed from and or the margins", that is, the non-West'. Mukherjee (2010a) demonstrates the possibility of an exteriority in her study of how Gandhi constructed a narrative of freedom outside the universalist Western discourse of political freedom, which is based on individual rights, private property, nation-state, and so on. Gandhi's notion of 'renunciative freedom', according to Mukherjee, was built on a different 'Indic' tradition of thought—Hindu, Buddhist, Jain—incorporating ideas of renunciation embodied in Sanskrit epistemologies and terms such as *moksha*, *nirvana*, and other ascetic practices.

In a similar vein, Akeel Bilgrami (2014) noted that Gandhi's counter to Western ideals of liberty and equality emerged from a position of exteriority as well: that is, from 'the spoken and spiritual traditions of the South'.[4] Indeed, in Gandhi's writings such as *Hind Swaraj*, and his movement of non-violent resistance, one encounters a different philosophical orientation to Western/Eurocentric universals, one that is grounded in indigenous traditions of thought.[5] According to Dhareshwar (2012: 259), Gandhi constructed a series of 'action-theoretic concepts' such as *yama*, *niyama*, *apagriha*, *ahimsa*, and so on, to counter the 'cognitive-evaluative frame' of the West. To this end, Dhareshwar (2012: 258) claims that '[O]ur problem is not simply that we no longer apply terms such as *atman*, *avidya*, *dharma* to reflect on our experience; the terms that we do indeed use—sovereignty, secularism, rights, civil society, political society, corruption—seem to insulate our experience from our reflection!'

In the introduction and subsequent chapters of this book, I outlined the aporias generated by some of the terms, particularly religion and the public, and examined their trajectories in broadcasting in late colonial and postcolonial

India. However, the question, how to respond to Eurocentric/ Western location of television studies (as well as media and communication studies) remained unanswered. To this end, I briefly discussed how the postcolonial approach of Chakrabarty built on the notion of 'difference' pointed to the limits of Eurocentric/Western universals. As Dhareshwar and Mukherjee argued, Chakrabarty's conceptual strategy of 'politics of despair' devolves into an endless critique of the universals without providing a theoretical opening. In the following, I explore some recent work that I believe provides a way out of the postcolonial ressentiment. In a recent piece, Prathama Banerjee, Aditya Nigam, and Rakesh Pandey (2016: 43) proposed a new approach to tackle the vexed predicament of theory/ history in India.[6] For them, while postcolonial scholars offer insights into the hegemony of universal categories, they could not provide resources to build 'autonomous theory' since they engage with the Eurocentric thought 'in criteria already prefigured in Western theoretical frameworks'. According to Banerjee, Nigam, and Pandey (2016: 42–43), there are three responses to the theory/history predicament in India:

> One, we espouse critiques as our mode of being, relentlessly showing up the limits of universal categories of thought. This is the mode of postcolonial theory. Two, we look towards practice as that which inflects Western theoretical concepts in our favour. That is, we believe that while we cannot do without Western concepts because they are the only modern concepts available, in practice, we deploy them in ways that affectively gives them new content and new contours. This approach is exemplified by Partha Chatterjee's narrative of democracy as practices and his concept of political society. Finally, we sometimes invoke an authentic indigenous mode. In its crude form, this becomes a kind of cultural nationalism. In more sophisticated versions, as in Ashis Nandy's writings, this becomes a demonstration of the pathology of modern/universal categories such as 'secularism', 'nationalism' and 'history', and of the positive powers of myth, spirituality, and poetry. We feel, however, that none of these really engages with any theoretical tradition other than the Western, which remains its reference point even in critique and disavowal. We gesture towards fourth way of relating to Western theory ... that we move from the position of a critic of Western theory to that of one which composes and assembles new theory from different sources and different histories.

Indeed, for Banerjee, Nigam, and Pandey, the fourth way, an egalitarian and a flexible approach, which they characterize as 'thinking across traditions' approach, allows them to generate multiple interpretations of sociocultural practices, human experiences, and connectedness. The reconfigurations of theory/history predicament along these lines, therefore, overcomes the either/or trap of a bland universalism and a naïve historicism. In addition, committing to theory as a movement between different levels and registers, acknowledges the fact that ideas and thoughts in history have always been on the move across regional, national, and continental borders. Furthermore, the 'thinking across traditions' approach thus points out that traditions are not to be considered as 'authentic' and hermetically sealed but rather in constant transaction and dialogue. To this end, Banerjee, Nigam, and Pandey discuss several studies to illustrate the thinking across traditions approach. I briefly summarize three studies they discuss as examples that offer conceptual and theoretical strategies for reconceptualizing media and communication studies in India.

The new media scholar, Laura Marks' (2010) genealogical study of Giles Deleuze's formulation of 'univocity' shows how the term carried within itself ideas from European thinkers, Gottfried Leibniz and Dans Scotus, who in turn drew upon the eleventh century Muslim philosopher, Ibn Sina from Bukhara, Iraq. For Marks, Deleuze's notion of univocity reveals its deep connections across traditions, pointing to their cross-transactions that emerge from the interplay between the Islamic concept of *tawhid* (the univocity of being), and the Islamic duality of *zahir* and *batin* that refers to enfold/unfold in Deleuze's usage. What is, indeed, important for Marks is not just the historical value in tracing concepts across traditions, but rather in 'disassembling' Delueze's concept of 'fold', and subsequent 'reassembling' of Islamic and European ideas in quite unexpected and original ways: examine the deep resonances between computer-generated art and Islamic art, their point of contact, and propagation of new forms.

A second example from Banerjee, Nigam, and Pandey (2016: 48) is about 'contemporizing tradition', that is, how diverse intellectual, nonmodern, and modern traditions are conceptualized as 'lived traditions' which become part of contemporary thought, responding to the plural ways in which we make sense of the present. They point to Gandhi, Ambedkar, and Tagore's engagement with Indian and Western philosophical traditions to 'construct a distinct third template for modern thought'. The third example, Sibaji Bandyopadhyay's (2015) literary hermeneutic exploration of *Gita* is a detailed tracing of how the term *adhikara* worked itself through numerous translations in its encounter with the notion of 'rights' formulated in colonial modernity. Bandyopadhyay deftly demonstrates that a word, a term, and an idea, instead of remaining fixed and frozen in texts, acquires new charge and meanings in its journey across different thought traditions. An approach such as Bandyopadhyay's has great utility in parsing out and pursuing detailed exposition of how particular terms—*darsan*, *ibadat*, *avidya*, *karma*, *satya*, *himsa*, and so on—sedimented in distinct traditions carry multiple meanings and histories than their linguistic nomenclature reveals.

Although the 'thinking across traditions' approach adumbrated by Banerjee, Nigam, and Pandey refers to studies of theoretical categories in thought traditions at the textual level, it can be extended to analyse narrative, symbolic, mediated forms, sociocultural practices, social action, and so on. By way of another example, I refer to the ethnographic study of Veena Das (2010: 241) among low-income neighbourhoods of Delhi. Das' work shows how terms, words, and concepts do not remain sedimented in traditions; instead, they become nomadic and travel in the everyday speech of Hindus and Muslims providing them resources 'to receive the claims of each other', and thus, 'ward off the violence that is always present as a possibility'. For Das (2010: 241), then, 'terms at hand such as *kaliyuga*, *rabb puja*, *ibadat*, *bhagwan*, *khuda*, which travel easily in speech of Hindus and Muslims are deployed in both formal and informal context, make it possible to imagine the practices of the other and to get on with the daily commerce of living together'. Furthermore, Das notes that these forms of speech should neither be considered as instances of 'syncreticism' nor 'secularism' as many scholars have noted.

My study of television narratives (Chapters 2 and 3) and viewers' memories of television (Chapter 5) similarly demonstrated the embeddedness of the religious and secular imaginaries, where the 'religious' (invoked as sacred and transcendental) became visible in people's habits, dispositions, and gestures in relation to practices of *darsan*, *ibadat*, *bhakti*, and so forth. Indeed, a significant feature was the ways in which words and their particular histories and semantic resonances indicated the presence of 'heteroreligious' and 'heterolinguistic' traditions. This was evident in the literary works of Premchand, Renu, and Shukla, their televisual adaptations, as well as in the television series, *Choli Daman* and *Gul Gulshan Gulfam*. This study did not pursue a detailed examination of the heteroreligious and heterolinguistic traditions in television narratives; however, it pointed to the translations of idioms, metaphors, and symbols across religious and linguistic boundaries marking people's cultural and social identities.

Scholars have argued that languages, dialects, and linguistic formations in precolonial India increasingly overlapped, bridging religious communities into diverse, multilingual formations across large swathes of India. According to Aijaz Ahmad (2000), the language traditions and cultural worlds through which people's identities were constituted up until the 1930s were not defined by their religious ascriptions, but rather by the fluid dynamics of linguistic usages, dialects, and speech forms. The colonial census operations, with their demarcation of clear boundaries between languages, and the creation of 'communal' identities devolved religion into languages and vice versa (Hindi for Hindus, Urdu for Muslims), the subsequent language debates in late colonial and early postcolonial period on 'Hindustani' as a common lingua franca of India, and the marginalization of Urdu as well as local, regional Hindi–Urdu dialects in favour of Sanskritized Hindi as the preferred language of radio and television collapsed the heteroreligious and heterolinguistic traditions into a monolithic, hegemonic one.

While the postcolonial mandate of 'Hindi' as the national language and the introduction of 'one person, one language' policy underpinned the discourse structures of broadcasting, several radio programmes and television narratives, however, pointed to the mixing of languages, idioms, and speech forms that continue to survive, albeit at the margins. The survival and persistence of heterolinguistic traditions can be attributed to the multiple semantic orders generated by the 'word' which exists at the intersections of language and speech. We can explain this by slightly modifying Ricoeur (1968: 121), who argued that the word as 'a trader between the system and the act, between the structure and the event', carries thick traces of 'theos' and histories across languages, and literary, cultural, and quotidian worlds.

In the context of India, the cultural affinities and cross-pollination between languages such as Sanskrit, Persian, Hindi, Urdu, and the several other regional and vernacular variations such as Braj Bhasha, Khari Boli, Avadhi, and so on, constituted a symbolic repertoire, a sort of a 'collective unconscious', or as Chris Bayly (1996: 193) noted, a 'north Indian ecumene', and Francesca Orsini (2012: 242) characterized as 'multilingualism' which

> is not a narrative of 'composite culture', where equally selective syncretic traditions are taken as definitive evidence that culture (selectively: music, Sufism, Sant Bhakti) acted as a great cohesive force in the Indo-Muslim polity. Both the single-language and the 'composite culture' narratives exclude large swathes of literary production, arbitrarily set language boundaries, construct chronologies that do not match, and answer questions of language and literary choices spuriously along an unproblematic continuum of script-language-religious identity and community.

Similarly, Virender Kalra's (2016: 74) study of music forms, *qawwali* and *kirtan*, in the Punjab region of colonial India and Pakistan indicated that these musical forms frequently overlapped, constituting a dense network of cultural and symbolic repertoire of compositions, idioms, practices, and so forth that travelled across religious and linguistic boundaries. Kalra's work calls into question the postcolonial Indian and Pakistani states' logic that posits a unidimensional view of religion and language. Furthermore, Kalra noted that 'literary analysis classifies these texts [*qawwali* and *kirtan* compositions] as Sufi, Bhakti, and Sikh and delineates separate linguistic and theological registers, but when these are inevitably performed, as this is the primary means of their circulation, they are not so neatly categorized'. Gopi Chand Narang (2014) noted that the qawwali genre should be considered 'first and foremost as exquisite manifestation of music and culture born from the interaction of Hinduism and Islam', and the Urdu *ghazal* as 'embedded within the Persian couplets or the *doha*s of Braj Bhasha ... and the collective memory of the people of the subcontinent'. For Narang, the *qawwali* and *ghazal* genres dissolve the separation between religious–secular and can be viewed 'as part of the subcontinental secular music' (Narang, 2014).[7]

Abdul Jamil Khan (2006), among others, explored the multilingual transactions across Sanskrit, Persian, Hindi, Urdu, and other vernacular languages in the writings of poets, bhakti and Sufi saints, social reformers, progressive writers, and so forth. Perhaps, the most vivid illustrations of how words, metaphors, idioms, and symbols travel across languages accreting meanings is the domain of popular Hindi/Urdu films of the 1940s–60s. Indeed, the lyricists, scriptwriters, song composers, and producers working across linguistic registers and cultural and religious boundaries exemplified a pluralist-humanist ethos that stood in sharp contrast to the Sanskritized Hindi of radio and television (Lelyveld, 1993; Jinghan 2011). David Lunn (2015) noted that a certain 'filmi Hindustani' resonated with cinema audiences because it was situated within the speech forms and linguistic repertoire of ordinary people.[8]

III

In this section, I draw on earlier discussions to explore possibilities for reconceptualizing media and communication studies (henceforth, MCS) in India. I propose that in order to move beyond the history/theory problematic and the Eurocentric and Western biases of MCS, we need to integrate the thinking across traditions approach with Ricoeur's philosophic hermeneutics and Foucault's late work on 'the hermeneutics of the self'. Despite the European provenance of his hermeneutics, Ricoeur (2007c: 28–29) too had argued in favour of thinking across traditions, pointing to the generative possibilities of transactions and translations across traditions thus:

> Entire cultures have been born from these frontier crossings that were at the same time far-reaching linguistic transgressions ... Buddhism passed from Sanskrit to Chinese ... Cicero literally created a learned Latin by translating Greek philosophical idioms. Without the impact of Arabic and Hebrew transmitters, what would the knowledge of Greek philosophy be for Latin-influenced West?

For Ricoeur, concepts and ideas are not simply transferred between languages and different linguistic-cultural formations. Rather, the act of translation across traditions remakes the ideas and concepts so as to make them speak to new sociocultural realities; thus, 'the metaphorics that give rise to concepts works beneath our abstractions like a kind of silent hermeneutics'. In addition, hermeneutics and thinking across traditions approach have analytic affinities in the sense that both involve 'close readings' of intellectual and thought traditions, literary, cultural, political textual forms, social practices, and so forth, at once alert to the plurality of meanings and multiple interpretations. Furthermore, hermeneutics as a textual method for the exegesis of meanings existed in the precolonial non-West, albeit under a different name: philology. Overall, hermeneutics shares deep kinship and filiation with philology, another approach that is concerned with textual and linguistic interpretations. For these reasons, hermeneutics and philology have been considered as constituting a 'global knowledge practice' across traditions.

The common origins of hermeneutics and philology as methods for the exegesis of religious texts and traditions, literary and linguistic formations accord a holistic understanding of the sacred and the secular immanent to particular traditions and cultures.[9] Both cut across different epochs: premodern, modern, precolonial, colonial, postcolonial, acquiring new resonances in particular conjunctures. And in their modern avatars, hermeneutics and philology have not only withstood the assaults from 'high theory' since the 1960s, but have returned with renewed conceptual energy (Weinsheimer, 1995; Pollock, 2009; Felski, 2015). For these reasons, they offer theoretical resources to enter and engage with traditions from within their universe of discourse, reworking and re-animating aspects of the traditions that speak to the present, or in the words of Banerjee, Nigam, and Pandey, 'contemporizing traditions'.

Within the field of postcolonial studies, however, hermeneutics and philology remain at the margins even though Edward Said (2004) in his last writings distanced himself from post-structuralism and deconstruction that had informed much of his earlier scholarly work and returned to what he termed as 'philological hermeneutics'. Said (2004: 92) stated that

> in order to be able to understand a humanistic text, one must try to do so as if one is the author of that text, living the author's reality, undergoing the kind of life experiences intrinsic to the author's life, and so forth, all by that combination of erudition and sympathy that is the hallmark of philological hermeneutics.

For Said, then, 'the return to philology' meant an active and patient reading of literature and linguistic-cultural formations with their constellations of words, elaborating their democratic and humanistic potentialities while simultaneously examining their hegemonic underpinnings. Indeed, the humanism of Said resonates with Ricoeur's work not because of his espousal of a positive hermeneutics but rather in the way in which Said seeks to overcome the aporia generated by deconstruction and postmodern approaches that devolve into 'undecidability' of meanings. Suarez Muller (2013: 66) argued that Said seeks to resolve his allegiance to deconstruction by developing the method of philological hermeneutics which is, then, 'explicitly contrasted with "deconstructive Derridean readings" that always end in some kind of "undecidability". In deconstruction theory, one always comes home empty-handed'.

Although Said mentioned the Islamic concept of *ijtihad* as an example of positive hermeneutics, his work has largely drawn on the European philological tradition inaugurated by Giambattista Vico, Erich Auerbach, and Leo Spitzer to study Euro-American literature without a detailed exploration of Middle Eastern literary cultural traditions. The leading Indologist and Sanskrit scholar, Sheldon Pollock (2009) argued that despite the enormous influence of Said on a generation of scholars, philology as a scholarly endeavour has largely remained neglected.[10] For Pollock, this stems from Said's own theoretical oeuvre that moved from an embrace of anti-humanist methods of deconstruction and postmodernism to the humanism of philological hermeneutics.

What is important for Pollock is the value in learning languages such as Sanskrit, Arabic, Persian, and so forth, that enables a scholar to apply philological methods of study to literary cultures and linguistic-cultural formations across traditions. Furthermore, Pollock (2009: 960) noted that the method of philology is not of a European provenance and '[d]espite the astonishing assumption in almost all writing about philology that it is the discipline of studying classical European antiquity, philology is and has always been a global knowledge practice, albeit no such global account of its history has ever been written'. In addition, 'as scholars have begun to argue, this fertile seed of modern philology may in fact lie in non-Western premodernity'.

A glaring weakness in postcolonial studies scholarship is the absence of an engagement with South Asian premodern sociocultural practices, intellectual thought traditions, and the diversity of literary forms. As Pollock (2006, 2011) rightly pointed out, this calls into question the mode of postcolonial critiques of colonialism and modernity.[11] The postcolonial studies' neglect of South Asian multilingual and vernacular knowledges, and the linguistic formations, and its exclusive focus on transnationalism, diasporic identities, mobility, hybridity, liminality, in-betweenness, and so on, as categories of thought mediating the colonial, postcolonial, modern, and postmodern conjunctures (Loomba, 1998; Shankar, 2012). While a major strain of postcolonial inquiry is grounded in literary theory, it is ironic that that examination of vernacular literatures of India have remained unexamined. Also, an understanding of Dalit literature and the vernacular configurations of caste have remained outside the ambit of postcolonial studies (Gajarawala, 2011). Several key scholarly insights on languages, literature, and people's everyday speech have emerged from fields that have explicitly engaged with hermeneutics and philological methods (Pollock, 2011; Orsini, 2012).

To overcome the weaknesses of postcolonial studies, Shankar (2017: 1) has outlined a philological approach under the rubric of 'postcolonial philology' that he defined as a 'mode of tracing within the context of the modern colonial encounter and its aftermath the movement of words through texts and more broadly, discourse in general'. Shankar's perspective is grounded in a multilingual exploration of linguistic-symbolic practices, tracking how words travel and accrete meanings across languages and traditions. For Shankar (2017: 2), therefore, 'postcolonial philology is able to plug gaps in postcolonial studies—for example, to provide critical engagement in a manner rarely done before with multilingual and vernacular richness that was and is the contact zone of colonialism and its aftermath'.[12]

I posit that the first task of reconceptualizing MCS in India would have to be how to overcome the Eurocentric/ Western universals that underpin media and communication, including television theory. Instead of pointing to the limits of the universal categories, which exemplifies the mode of postcolonial studies, MCS in India needs to work out 'autonomous' theories that are drawn from, and speak to, sociocultural practices, and political and economic realities in India. The task entails a substantive engagement with the history/theory problematic and the West/non-West binary since MCS draws extensive conceptual insights from the social sciences and humanities.[13] It is here we could incorporate the thinking across traditions approach to 'dissemble' and 'reassemble' theoretical ideas, insights, and idioms from diverse intellectual traditions.[14] In conjunction with the thinking across traditions, hermeneutics and philology enable us to reopen the monolithic constructions of history, modernity, religion, and language, and examine the genealogies of political categories such as sovereignty, public, and secularism from a position of exteriority even as we study their co-imbrications.

I would argue that alongside the thinking across traditions approach we need to outline a *thinking within traditions* perspective to study traditions from inside their universe of discourse so as to disaggregate their narrative modes and forms. As noted in my earlier discussions, hermeneutics and philology offer rich theoretical resources to pursue such a task. However, both hermeneutics and philology are rather weak in accounting for the power dimensions that inhere within traditions.

MCS in India should undertake detailed explorations of communicative media prior to the arrival of printing in India, so as to trace the broad historical contours and genealogies of diverse media forms—oral, performative, print-based illustrated manuscripts, scripts, graphics, typography, and so forth. This would enable us to test Pollock's (2006: 78) argument that 'the effects of print often seem to be exaggerated in scholarship, at least from the perspective of a student of South Asia. Here the true watershed in the history of communicative media was the invention, not of print-capitalism, but of script-mercantilism'.[15]

Thus, a reconceptualized MCS in India could begin to explore the pluralistic literary, musical, and popular cultural forms and traditions that existed at the margins of radio and television, the particular ways in which oral, performative, and popular practices intersected with broadcast narratives, the imbrications of premodern and precolonial, with modern, colonial, and postmodern categories; examine the histories of oral 'Indic' traditions in premodern India, specifically the dual modes of transmission in terms of *sruti* (hearing) and *smrti* (memorizing) that have constituted several genres of literatures ranging from *gatha* (song), *akhyana* (dramatic narrative), *carita* (biography), *itihasa* (history), and so forth (Pollock, 2006; Thapar, 2013, Orsini and Schofield, 2015). Several narrative genres continue to exist in print cultures and graphic forms, and unlike in the West, the history of the media in South Asia does not follow a linear, teleological, 'stagist' path (Chakrabarty, 2000; Pollock, 2006). Rather, various media forms have coexisted in a multilingual environment nourished by Hindu, Buddhist, Jain, and Islamic thought traditions.

In contemporary India, media and political discourse has sought to link particular ideological aspects of tradition with neoliberal capitalism to produce a complex set of exclusionary logics: for instance, the attempts to remake 'Hinduism' as 'Hindutva'. In addition, the commodification and corporatization of media and television, whether television is accessed via broadcast or broadband, and the increasing presence of the Internet and mobile media forms have resulted in the diminution of journalistic integrity and dissenting voices. To counter these hegemonies, we ought to follow Said (2004: 73–4) when he argued for a 'a close scrutiny of language and rhetorical strategies employed by media, advertising, and political discourse in the form of prepackaged information and soundbites designed to obfuscate rather than illuminate the citizens'.

NOTES

1. The pervasive presence of low-cost mobile phones and inexpensive internet access in urban cities and towns in India, for instance, have led to the inter- and cross-media practices influencing the ways in which television is produced, distributed, and watched. Several internet-based over-the-top (OTT) platforms such as US-based Netflix, Chinese-based Vivo Hotstar, Voot, and platforms hosted by television networks themselves, alongside apps, are increasingly producing and sharing content online, thus linking broadcast with broadband (See Pant, 2016 for a discussion on the ongoing shifts)
2. Recent initiatives such as 'internationalizing media studies' and 'global communication' undertaken either in the form of scholarly publications of professional programmes do not question the universalist claims embedded in Western theory. Despite the acknowledgment and protestations about Euro- and US-centric dominance of media and communication studies, scholarship has not examined the persistence of universal categories. Instead, a primary impetus has been an 'additive logic', that is, increasing the output of non-Western studies of media as a way to seek balance. The terms 'international' and 'global' remain entrenched, settled binaries, unable to offer alternate frames of analyses. Although recent formulations such as 'transcultural communication' have been proposed to overcome the dichotomies and unwieldiness of terms such as 'international' and 'global', they too operate within the logic of 'difference'.
3. A few studies have demonstrated that technologies are integrated and 'domesticated' in India in ways that do not follow their planned trajectories. For instance, a whole

domain of technological market has opened up in India in the 1980s with regards to audio-cassette culture (Alvarado, 1988), computers, computer peripherals, and software in the late 1990s (Sundaram, 2010); and the domestication of everyday technologies such as sewing machines, rice mills, and typewriters in late colonial India (Arnold, 2013).

4. See https://www.youtube.com/watch?v=Pv9m6L_mptU.
5. For an excellent account of Gandhi's Hinduism and how it shaped his politics, see Bilgrami (2011).
6. The predicament centres on the 'application' of Western categories to Indian realities. Banerjee, Nigam, and Pandey refer to the 'mode of production debate' in the 1970s when Indian historians and economists 'applied' Marxist categories to explain agricultural practices, and the 'secularism debates' of the 1990s when social theorists deployed the term to interpret the rise of the Hindu Right, Muslim militancy, and religious conflicts.
7. See http://gopichandnarang.com/articles-the-indo.php.
8. Lunn (2015: 6) examined several films from the 1940s to show how language scripts and linguistic features employed in film texts. For instance, S. U. Sunny's *Mela* (Fair, 1948) juxtaposes several scripts, in particular Kashmiri, mixing Sanskrit, Persian, and Arabic to produce a 'mixed Hindustani register and largely eschews higher registers and styles'. Lunn noted that 'the paradigm is one of accessibility, and the context is one wherein characters converse in a shared language; this is a language that is the property of no one individual or community, is understood by all, and that easily accommodates Sanskritic or Perso-Arabic terms as and when they seem appropriate. Thus, the dialogue of *Mela* in many ways exemplifies the feasibility of unmarked Hindustani as the language of cinema' (For discussion of 1950s film songs in relation to AIR's 'classical' music, see Jinghan, 2001; see also, Appadurai, 2013: 202–03).
9. For Ricoeur (2007b: 55), 'Hermeneutics was born with the attempt to raise exegesis and philology to the level of *kunstlehre*, that is a technology that is not restricted to a mere collection of unconnected operations'. In Boyd Blundell's (2010: 34, original emphasis) view, hermeneutics constituted two separate branches, 'the philology of classical texts and the exegesis of sacred texts'. Hermeneutics sought to become a *science* by bringing the two branches under a 'general rubric of *understanding*, subjecting all texts to the same rules of interpretations'.
10. Timothy Brennan's work is an exception. See Brennan (2004, 2014, 2015) for a splendid discussion of Saidian legacies and the significance of philology.
11. Pollock's criticism is directed against the social theorists and thinkers of modernity for their neglect and assumptions about premodernity even as they are involved in theorizing modernity. Similarly, in the context of colonial and postcolonial studies, Pollock (2011: 5) noted that 'it is indeed astonishing, then, that while colonial criticism depends on precolonial knowledge, so little of that knowledge has been produced for early modern South Asia, the period prior to 1800, just before the British colonial power changed the rules of the knowledge game'.

12. Shankar's (2012) examined vernacular knowledge, languages, and literary contexts, particularly Tamil by drawing on philological approach. More recently, Shankar (2017) examined the multiple, contradictory meanings of English words such as 'thuggee', 'pariah', and 'pundit' that have been derived from Tamil, Hindi, and other languages of India. The genealogies of the words, their linguistic interchange across semiotic and semantic registers, and symbolic resonances carry congeries of meanings and interpretations that show incommensurable gaps. More crucially, perhaps, how power and discourse underpin these genealogies. For insightful observations on the forthcoming Hindi–Urdu popular cinema, *Thugs of Hindostan* (released in November 2018), see https://sshankar.net/tag/thuggee.
13. Immanuel Wallerstein (1996, 1997) pointed to five ways in which social sciences perpetuate Eurocentrism—historiography, universalism, civilizational assumptions, orientalism, theory of progress— which have reappeared in much of MCS literature.
14. This should not just be a research/theoretical strategy, but crucial to teaching and pedagogic practices. For instance, in my course on visual and graphic history, I avoid the universalist and Eurocentric biases of MCS—especially as they manifest in history of visual communication and graphic design—by emphasizing history in the plural, tracing the contours of multiple, overlapping histories of graphic and media forms in oral, illustrated, literary traditions; the evolution of writing and typographic cultures, photographic, broadcast, digital media, and so forth, both *across and within traditions*, detailing the peregrination of graphic ideas, movements, religious and secular thought and idioms, artefacts, object, technologies, and people. An illustrative example I use in my teaching pertains to print-making and woodcuts. In most influential accounts, Albrecht Dürer's 'Rhinocéros', a woodcut print of 1515, is viewed as precipitating the beginnings of print culture disregarding the fact that Chinese had pursued woodcut printing much earlier. The story of how Dürer envisioned his woodcut Rhinocéros makes a fascinating reading, especially since the rhino was not seen in Europe for 1000 years, and the news of 'Babu' the one-horned rhino gifted to Alfonso d'Albuquerque, the first governor of Portuguese Empire in India by Sultan Muzaffar Shah II of Gujarat, created a stir in Europe. The rhino set sail on a ship but died in a shipwreck before reaching European land. Dürer never saw the animal and made the woodcut based on people's accounts. The story of the one-horned India rhino, like much else in visual and graphic history, narrates the colonial and precolonial world as passive and inert, and maps the emergence of print forms, technologies, and cultures as intrinsic of Europe. See Ivins (1969), Feiman (2012), and Orosz (2016).
15. Pollock (2006: 78) stated that 'prior to the arrival of printing with missionary and colonial expansion, the history of literary culture in South Asia was shaped by two momentous events: (1) the invention of the Indian writing system in the third century BCE, setting the stage for the creation of the Sanskrit cosmopolitan culture-power formation, and (2) the vernacular revolution of the early centuries of the second millennium CE, associated with the newly consolidated regional kingdoms. These two events are more closely associated than might be assumed'. According

to Pollock, the vernacular revolution was to a large extent promoted by the royal court. The 'court-centered view' of vernacularization of Pollock has been critiqued by Orsini (2012) for its narrow definition of literature as *kavya* and *sahitya* neglecting the oral and performative traditions constituting the 'literature of the people'. For Orsini (2012: 236), 'Pollock's Sanskrit theorists disdained orality and literature in non-cosmopolitan languages and consigned songs to a different order of discourse (*gita*).' The oral poets such as Kabir, Surdas, and Mira Bai remain outside the ambit of Pollock's conception of literature. However, Pollock (2006: 85) acknowledged the resistance of oral poets against the Brahminical vernacularization: 'thus the "Militant Saivas", with their *vacanas* (sayings) in late twelfth-century Karnataka, Narasimha Maheta with his *prabhatiyas* (spiritual aubades) in fifteenth-century Gujarat, or Kabir with his *pads* (songs) about the same time in Avadh, rejected the values, and the very fact, of manuscript culture.'

Bibliography

Abbott, Porter (2002) *The Cambridge Introduction to Narrative*. UK: Cambridge University Press.

Agrawal, Purushottam (2012) 'Modernity and Public Sphere in Vernacular'. *Journal of Contemporary Thought* 35(Summer): 39–51.

Ahmad, Aijaz (1995) 'The Politics of Literary Postcoloniality'. *Race & Class* 36(3): 1–20.

——— (2000) 'In the Mirror of Urdu: Recompositions of Nation and Community, 1947–65'. In *Lineages of the Present: Ideology and Politics in Contemporary South Asia*, edited by Aijaz Ahmad, 103–28. New York: Verso.

——— (2005) 'The Making of India'. *Social Scientist* 33(11–12): 3–19.

Alam, Muzaffar (2003) 'The Culture and Politics of Persian in Precolonial Hindustan'. In *Literary Cultures in History: Reconstructions from South Asia*, edited by Sheldon Pollock Berkeley: University of California Press, 131–98.

Altman, Rick (1986) 'Television/Sound', in *Studies in Entertainment: Critical Approaches to Mass Culture*, edited by Tania Modleski. Bloomington: Indiana University Press. (39–54).

Amin, Shahid (2004) 'On Representing the Musalman'. *Sarai Reader* 04, Crisis/Media: 92–97.

Anderson, Benedict (1983) *Imagined Communities: Reflections on the Origin and Spread of Nationalism*. London: Verso.

Anderson, Steve (2000) 'Loafing in the Garden of Knowledge: History TV and Popular Memory'. *Film & History: An Interdisciplinary Journal of Film and Television Studies* 30(1): 14–23.

Andrew, Dudley (1993) 'History and Timelessness in Films and Theory'. In *Meanings in Texts and Actions: Questioning Paul Ricoeur*, edited by David Klemm and William Schweiker, 115–32. Charlottesville and London: University Press of Virginia.

——— (2000) 'Tracing Ricoeur'. *Diacritics* 30(2): 43–69.

Anidjar, Gil (2006) 'Secularism'. *Critical Inquiry* 33(1): 52–74.

Anjaria, Ulka (2006) 'Satire, Literary Realism and the Indian State: *Six Acres and a Third* and *Raag Darbari*'. *Economic and Political Weekly* 41(46) (Nov. 18-24): 4795–800.

Anon (2006) 'Childhood Memories, Ek Aur Anek, Doordarshan', available at http://www.ambimama.com/2006/03/30/childhood-memories-ek-aur-anek-doordarshan-videos/ (accessed on 27 October 2017).

Appadurai, Arjun (1996) *Modernity at Large: Cultural Dimensions of Globalization*. Minneapolis: University of Minnesota Press.

——— (2013) *The Future as Cultural Fact: Essays on the Global Condition*. New York: Verso.

Appadurai, Arjun and Carol Breckenridge (1996) *Consuming Modernity: Public Culture in Contemporary India*. Delhi, Bombay, Calcutta, Madras: Oxford University Press.

Arnold, David (2015) *Everyday Technology: Machines and the Making of India's Modernity*. Chicago and London: The University of Chicago Press.

Asad, Talal (1993) *Genealogies of Religion: Discipline and Reasons of Power in Christianity and Islam*. Baltimore: Johns Hopkins University Press.

——— (2003) *Formations of the Secular: Christianity, Islam, Modernity*. Stanford: Stanford University Press.

Assmann, Jan (2010) 'Communicative and Cultural Memory'. In *A Companion to Cultural Memory Studies*, edited by Astrid Erll and Ansgar Nünning, 109–118. Berlin: De Gruyter.

Asthana, Sanjay (2012) *Youth Media Imaginaries from around the World*. New York: Peter Lang.

——— (2014) 'Television, Narrative Identity, and Social Imaginaries: A Hermeneutic Approach'. In *Channeling Cultures: Television Studies from India*, edited by Biswarup Sen and Abhijit Roy. New Delhi, London: Oxford University Press.

Asthana, Sanjay and Nishan Havandjian (2017) *Palestinian Youth Media and the Pedagogies of Estrangement*. New York: Palgrave.

Athique, Adrian (2009) 'From Monopoly to Polypony: India in the Era of Television'. In *Television Studies after TV*, edited by Graeme Turner and Jinna Tay, 159–67. London: Routledge.

Awaasthi, Kavita (2016) 'Gul Gulshan Gulfam: Parikshit Sahni Recalls His Kashmir days'. *The Hindustan Times*, June 30, available at http://www.hindustantimes.com/tv/gul-gulshan-gulfam-parikshit sahnishin-recalls-his-kashmir-days/story-MmJot12KWOiLGohEXybUXK.html.

Awasthy, G. C. (1965) *Broadcasting in India*. New Delhi: Allied Publishers.

Bajpai, Rochana (2000) 'Constituent Assembly Debates and Minority Rights'. *Economic & Political Weekly* 35(21/22) (27 May–2 June 2000): 1837–45.

Bandyopadhyay, Sibaji (2013) *Three Essays on Mahabharata: Exercises in Literary Hermeneutics*. Delhi: Orient Blackswan.

Banerjee, Prathama, Aditya Nigam and Rakesh Pandey (2016) 'The Work of Theory: Thinking Across Traditions'. *Economic & Political Weekly* 37: 42–50.

Barfield, Ray (2008) *A Word from Our Viewers: Reflections from Early Television Audience*. Westport, Connecticut and London: Praeger.

Barnett, Chris et al. (2008) 'The Elusive Subjects of Neoliberalism: Beyond the Analytics of Governmentality'. *Cultural Studies* 22(5): 624–53.

Barrett, Clive (2004) 'Neither Poison nor Cure: Space, Scale and Public Life in Media Today'. In *MediaSpace: Place, Scale, and Culture in a Media Age*, edited by Nick Couldry and Anna McCarthy, 58–74. London and New York: Routledge.

Barthes, Roland (1977) *Image-Music-Text: Essays Selected and Translated by Stephen Heath*. New York: Hill and Wang.

Bassett, Caroline (2007) *The Arc and the Machine: Narrative and New Media*. Manchester and New York: Manchester University Press.

Basu, Kaushik and Sanjay Subrahmanyam (eds) (1996) *Unravelling the Nation: Sectarian Conflict and India's Secular Identity*. New Delhi: Penguin Books.

Bayly, Christopher (1993) 'Informing Empire and Nation: Publicity, Propaganda, and the Press, 1880–1920'. In *Information, Media and Power through the Ages*, edited by Hiram Morgan, 179–208. Dublin: University College Dublin Press.

——— (1996) *Empire and Communications: Intelligence Gathering and Social Communication in India, 1780–1870*. Cambridge: Cambridge University Press.

——— (2004) *The Birth of the Modern World, 1740–1914*. Oxford: Blackwell.

Behl, Aditya (2003) 'The Magic of Doe: Desire and Narrative in a Hindavi Sufi Romance, circa 1503'. In *India's Islamic Traditions, 711–1750*, edited by Richard Eaton. New Delhi: Oxford University Press.

Bell, Ducan (2007) *The Idea of Great Britain: Empire and the Future of World Order, 1860–1900*. Princeton: Princeton University Press.

Bennett, James and Nikki Strange (eds) (2011) *Television as a Digital Media*. Durham: Duke University Press.

Bennett, Tony (1992) 'Putting Policy into Cultural Studies'. In *Cultural Studies*, edited by Larry Grossberg, Cary Nelson and Paula Treichler, 23–37. New York: Routledge.

Berger, John. 1972. *Ways of Seeing*. London: British Broadcasting Corporation.

Bernstein, Richard J (2013) 'Ricoeur's Freud'. *Études Ricoeuriennes/Ricoeur Studies* 4(1): 130–39.

Bhandari, Vivek (2006) 'Civil Society and the Predicament of Multiple Publics'. *Comparative Studies of South Asia, Africa and the Middle East* 26(1): 36–50.

Bhargava, Rajeev (ed.) (1998) *Secularism and its Critics*. Delhi, Calcutta, Chennai, Mumbai: Oxford University Press.

——— (2017) 'The Mimetic, the Mythic and the Theoretic'. *The Hindu*, 23 July, available at https://www.thehindu.com/opinion/columns/the-mimetic-the-mythic-and-the-theoretic/article19332593.ece.

Bilgrami, Akeel (1992) 'What Is a Muslim: Fundamental Commitment and Cultural Identity'. *Critical Inquiry* 18(4): 821–42.

——— (1998) 'Secularism, Modernity, and Nationalism'. In *Secularism and its Critics*, edited by Rajeev Bhargava, 345–379. New Delhi: Oxford University Press.

——— (2011) 'Gandhi's Religion and Its Relation to His Politics'. In *The Cambridge Companion to Gandhi*, edited by Judith Brown and Anthony Parel, 93–116. Cambridge: Cambridge University Press.

——— (2014) 'Gandhi and the Mentality of Modernity', available at https://www.youtube.com/watch?v=Pv9m6L_mptU (accessed on 15 January 2018).

Bilimoria, Purushottama (2003) 'What Is the "Subaltern" of the Comparative Philosophy of Religion?' *Philosophy East & West* 53(3): 340–66.

——— (2004) 'Toward Revisioning Ricoeur's Hermenutics of Suspicion in Other Spaces and Cultures'. In *Space, Time, and Culture*, edited by David Carr and Cheung Chan- Fai, 89–109. Dordrecht, Netherlands: Springer.

——— (2008) 'Being and Text: Dialogic Fecundation of Western Hermeneutics and Hindu Mīmāmsāin the Critical Era'. In *Hermeneutics and Hindu Thought: Towards a Fusion of Horizons*, edited by R.D. Sharma and Arvind Sharma, 45–79. Germany: Springer.

Birla, Ritu (2015) 'Jurisprudence of Emergence: Neo-Liberalism and the Public as Market in India'. *South Asia: Journal of South Asian Studies* 38(3): 466–80.

Blundell, Boyd (2010) *Paul Ricoeur between Theology and Philosophy: Detour and Return*. Bloomington: Indiana University Press.

Boer, Roland (2014) *In the Vale of Tears: On Marxism and Theology, V.* Boston, Leiden: Brill.

Bommes, Michael and Patrick Wright (1982) 'The Charms of Residence: The Public and the Past'. In *Making Histories: Studies in History-writing and Politics*, edited by Richard Johnson, Gregor McLennan, Bill Schwarz and David Sutton, 253–69. London: Anchor.

Bordwell, David (1985) *Narration in the Fiction Film*. Madison: University of Wisconsin Press.

——— (1989) 'Historical Poetics of Cinema'. In *The Cinematic Text: Methods and Approaches*, edited by Barton Palmer, 369–98. New York: AMS Press.

Bose, Sumantra (1997) '"Hindu Nationalism" and the Crisis of the Indian State: A Theoretical Perspective'. In *Nationalism, Democracy and Development: State and Politics in India*, edited by Sugata Bose and Ayesha Jalal, 104–64. Delhi, Calcutta, Madras and Mumbai: Oxford University Press.

Bourdon, Jerome (2003) 'Some Sense of Time: Remembering Television'. *History and Memory* 15(2): 5–35.

Boym, Svetlana (2001) *The Future of Nostalgia*. New York: Basic Books.

Braman, Sandra (1995) 'Horizons of the State: Information Policy and Power'. *Journal of Communication* 45(4): 4–23.

Brayne, Frank Lughard (1929) *The Remaking of Village India*. London: Oxford University Press.

Brennan, Timothy (1997) *At Home in the World: Cosmopolitanism Now*. Cambridge, Massachusetts: Cambridge University Press.

——— (2004) 'Places of Mind, Occupied Lands: Edward Said and Philology'. *The Arab World Geographer* 7(1–2): 47–64.

——— (2014) 'Philology', available at https://stateofthediscipline.acla.org/entry/philology (accessed on 14 January 2018).

——— (2015) 'The Legacies of Vico: Philology, the Internet, the Posthuman'. In *L'immaginario Politico*, edited by S. Albertazzi, F. Bertonni, E. Piga, L. Raimondi and G. Tinelli. *Between* 10, available at http://www.Betweenjournal.it/ (accessed on 14 January 2018).

Buonanno, Milli (2008) *The Age of Television: Experiences and Theories*. Chicago: University of Chicago Press.

Butcher, Melissa (2003) *Transnational Television, Cultural Identity and Change: When STAR Came to India*. New Delhi, Thousand Oaks, London: Sage Publications.

Butsch, Richard (2000) *The Making of American Audiences: From Stage to Television, 1750–1990*. Cambridge: Cambridge University Press.

——— (2007) *The Citizen Audience: Crowds, Publics, and Individuals*. New York: Routledge.

Carey, James (1989) *Communication as Culture: Essays on Media and Society*. London and New York: Routledge.

Carr, David (2004) 'Times Zones: Phenomenological Reflections on Cultural Time'. In *Space, Time, and Culture*, edited by David Carr and Cheung Chan-Fai, 3–14. Dordrecht, Netherlands: Springer.

Caruth, Cathy (1996) *Unclaimed Experience: Trauma, Narrative and History*. Baltimore, MD and London: Johns Hopkins University Press.

Casanova, Jose (1994) *Public Religions in the Modern World*. Chicago: University of Chicago Press.

Casey, Edward (1987) *Remembering: A Phenomenological Study* (Second Edition). Bloomington: Indiana University Press.

Castells, Manuel (1989) *The Informational City: Information Technology, Economic Restructuring, and the Urban-Regional Process*. Oxford: Oxford University Press.

Castree, Noel (2009) 'The Spatiotemporality of Capitalism'. *Time & Society* 18(1): 26–61.

Caughie, John (2000) *Television Drama: Realism, Modernism, and British Culture*. Oxford: Oxford University Press.

Cavagna, Mattia and Constantino Maeder (eds) (2014) *Philology and Performing Arts: A Challenge*. Belgium: Universitairres De Louvain.

Cavell, Stanley (1982) 'The Fact of Television'. *Daedalus* 111(4): 75–96.

Chakrabarty, Dipesh (1992) 'Postcoloniality and the Artifice of History: Who Speaks for "Indian" Pasts?' *Representations* 37: 1–26.

——— (2000) *Provincializing Europe: Postcolonial Thought and Historical Difference*. Princeton and Oxford: Princeton University Press.

——— (2002a) *Habitations of Modernity: Essays in the Wake of Subaltern Studies*. Chicago: The University of Chicago Press.

——— (2002b) 'Presence of Europe. Interviewed by Saurabh Dube'. *South Atlantic Quarterly* 101(4): 859–68.

——— (2004) 'Where Is the Now?' *Critical Inquiry* 30(2): 458–62.

——— (2007) 'In the Name of Politics: Democracy and the Power of the Multitude in India'. In *From Colonial to the Postcolonial: India and Pakistan in Transition*, edited by Dipesh Chakrabarty, Rochana Majumdar and Andrew Sartori, 31–54. Delhi: Oxford University Press.

Chakravarty, Uma (1998) 'Saffroning the Past: Of Myths, Histories and Right-Wing Agendas'. *Economic & Political Weekly* 33(5), 31 January: 225–32.

Chakravartty, Paula (2004) 'Telecom, National Development and the Indian State: A Postcolonial Critique'. *Media, Culture & Society* 26(2): 227–249.

Chakravartty, Paula and Katherine Sarikakis (2006) *Media Policy and Globalization*. Edinburgh: Edinburgh University Press.

Chander, Ramesh and Kiran Karnik (1976) *Planning for Satellite Broadcasting: The Indian Instructional Television Experiment*. Paris: UNESCO.

Chandoke, Neera (1999) *Beyond Secularism: The Rights of Religious Minorities*. New Delhi: Oxford University Press.

Chandra, Sudhir (1982) 'Premchand and Indian Nationalism'. *Modern Asian Studies* 16 (4): 601–21.

Chatterjee, Partha (1993) *The Nation and Its Fragments: Colonial and Postcolonial Histories*. New Jersey: Princeton University Press.

——— (1998) 'Beyond the Nation? Or Within?' *Social Text 56* 16(3): 57–69.

——— (2004) *The Politics of the Governed: Reflections on Popular Politics in Most of the World*. New York: Columbia University Press.

——— (2011) *Lineages of Political Society: Studies in Postcolonial Democracy*. New York: Columbia University Press.

Chatterjee, P. C. (1991) *Broadcasting in India*. New Delhi: Sage Publications.

Chatterjee, Saibal (2004) 'Gulzar's Vision of Timeless Classics'. *The Tribune*, 15 August, available at https://www.tribuneindia.com/2004/20040815/spectrum/main6.htm.

Chatman, Seymour (1978) *Story and Discourse: Narrative Structure in Fiction and Film*. Ithaca and London: Cornell University Press.

Chowdhury, Deep Kanta Lahiri (2004) 'Sinews of Panic and Nerves of Empire: The Imagined State's Entanglement with Information Panic, India c. 1880-1912'. *Modern Asian Studies* 38(4): 965–1002.

——— (2010) *Telegraphic Imperialism: Crisis and Panic in the Indian Empire*. Basingstoke: Palgrave Macmillan.

Chugh, Anoop (2009) 'DD – Days That Were'. *DNA*, 1 October, available at http://www.dnaindia.com/money/report_dd-days-that-were_1294090-all.

Cinephilia (2011) 'Zindagi Na Milegi Dobara and Doordarshan: A Tasteless Remembrance of the Golden Age and Some Nostalgia', available at http://cinephilia.travellingslacker.com/2011/07/zindagi-na-milegi-dobara-doordarshan/.

Cohn, Bernard (1996) *Colonialism and Its Forms of Knowledge: The British in India*. Princeton: Princeton University Press.

Connerty, J. P. (1990) 'History's Many Cunning Passages: Paul Ricoeur's Time and Narrative'. *Poetics Today* 11(2): 383–403.

Connolly, William (1999) *Why I Am Not a Secularist*. Minneapolis, London: University of Minnesota Press.

——— (2006) 'Europe: A Minor Tradition'. In *Powers of the Secular Modern: Talal Asad and His Interlocutors*, edited by David Scott and Charles Hirschkind, 75–92. Stanford: Stanford University Press.

Corbett, Krystlyn (1996) 'The Rise of Private Property Rights in the Broadcast Spectrum'. *Duke Law Journal* 46(3): 611–50.

Corner, John (1992) 'Presumption as Theory: "Realism" in Television Studies'. *Screen* 33(1): 97–102.

Crossman, Brenda and Ratna Kapur (1999) *Secularism's Last Sigh? Hindutva and the (Mis) Rule of Law*. New Delhi, London, New York: Oxford University Press.

Crowley, Patrick (2003) 'Paul Ricoeur: The Concept of Narrative Identity, the Trace of Autobiography'. *Paragraph* 26(3): 1–12.

Cunningham, Stuart and Toby Miller (1994) *Contemporary Australian Television*. Kensington: New South Wales University Press.

Curran, James and Myung-Jin Park (2000) 'Introduction: Beyond Globalization Theory'. In *De-Westernizing Media Studies*, edited by James Curran Myung-Jin Park, 1–24. New York: Routledge.

Darian-Smith, Kate and Sue Turnbull (2012) 'Remembering and Misremembering Television'. In *Remembering Television: Histories, Technologies, Memories*, edited by Kate Darian-Smith and Sue Turnbull, 1–16. UK: Cambridge Scholars Publishing.

Das, Biswajit (2006) 'Mediating Modernity: Colonial Discourse and Radio Broadcasting, c. 1924-1947'. In *Media and Mediation*, edited by Bernard Bel, Jan Brouer and Biswajit Das, 229–54. New Delhi: Sage Publications.

Das, Veena (1985) 'Anthropological Knowledge and Collective Violence: The Riots in Delhi, November 1984'. *Anthropology Today* 1(3): 4–6.

——— (1995) 'On Soap Opera: What Kind of an Anthropological Object Is It?' In *Worlds Apart: Modernity through the Prism of the Local*, edited by Daniel Miller, 169–189. New York: Routledge.

——— (2010) 'Moral and Spiritual Striving in the Everyday: To Be a Muslim in Contemporary India'. In *Ethical Life in South Asia*, edited by Anand Pandian and Daud Ali, 232–253. Bloomington and Indianapolis: Indiana University Press.

Dass, Manshita (2016) *Outside the Lettered City: Cinema, Modernity & the Public Sphere in Late Colonial India*. New York: Oxford University Press.

Dawar, Jagdish Lal (1996) 'Representations of Popular Culture in Premchand's Works'. *Social Scientist* 24 (4–5): 109–29.

Dayan, Daniel (2001) 'The Peculiar Public of Television'. *Media, Culture & Society* 23(6): 743–65.

Derrida, Jacques (ed) (2001) *Acts of Religion*. Translated by Gil Anidjar. London and New York: Routledge.

——— (2010) 'The Word: Giving, Naming, Calling'. In *Reading Derrida and Ricoeur: Improbable Encounters between Deconstruction and Hermeneutics*, edited by Pirovolakis Eftichis. Albany, New York: State University of New York Press.

Deshpande, Satish (1993) 'Imagined Economies: Styles of Nation-Building in Twentieth Century India'. *Journal of Arts and Ideas* 25(26): 5–35.

——— (1998) 'Hegemonic Spatial Strategies: The Nation-Space and the Hindu Communalism in Twentieth-Century India'. *Public Culture* 10(2): 249–83.

Desoulieres, Alain (1999) 'A Study of Kamal Ahmad Rizvi's Urdu TV Drama Alif Nun'. *Annual of Urdu Studies* 14: 55–84.

Deutsch, Karl (1960) *Nationalism and Social Communication: An Inquiry into the Foundations of Nationality*. Cambridge: MIT Press.

De Valck, Marijke and Jan Teurlings (eds) (2013) *After the Break: Television Theory Today*. Amsterdam: Amsterdam University Press.

Devgun, Shruti (2013) 'From the "Cervices in the Dominant Memories": Virtual Commemoration and the 1984 Anti-Sikh Violence'. *Identities: Global Studies in Culture and Power* 20(2): 207–33.

Dhareshwar, Vivek (1993) 'Caste and the Secular Self'. *Journal of Arts and Ideas* 25(26): 115–26.

——— (1995) '"Our Time": History, Sovereignty and Politics'. *Economic and Political Weekly* 30(6): 317–24.

——— (1999) 'Politics and History after Sovereignty'. In *Multiculturalism, Liberalism and Democracy*, edited by Rajeev Bhargava, Amiya Kumar Bagchi and R. Sudarshan, 401–02. New Delhi: Oxford University Press.

——— (2010) 'Politics, Experience and Cognitive Enslavement: Gandhi's Hind Swaraj'. *Economic & Political Weekly* XLV(12): 51–58.

——— (2012) 'Framing the Predicament of Indian Thought: Gandhi, the Gita, and Ethical Action'. *Asian Philosophy* 22(3): 257–74.

Dharwadker, Aparna (2008) 'Mohan Rakesh, Modernism, and the Postcolonial Present'. *South Central Review* 25(1): 136–62.

Dhawan, B. D. (1974) *Economics of Television in India*. New Delhi: S. Chand and Co.

Dhoest, Alexander (2007) 'Nostalgic Memories, Qualitative Reception Analysis of Flemish TV Fiction, 1953–1989'. *Communication* 32(1): 31–50.

Dienst, Richard (1992) 'Image/Machine/Image: On the Use and Abuse of Marx and Metaphor in Television Theory'. In *Classical Hollywood Narrative: The Paradigm Wars*, edited by Jane Gaines, 313–39. Durham and London: Duke University Press.

Digital Dictionaries of South Asia, available at http://dsal.uchicago.edu/dictionaries/platts/ (accessed on 15 February 2018).

Dillon, Martin (1995) 'Sovereignty and Governmentality: From the Problematics of the "New World Order" to the Ethical Problematic of the World Order'. *Alternatives* 20: 323–68.

Dingwaney Needham, Anuradha and Rajeswari Sunder Rajan (eds) (2007) *The Crisis of Secularism in India*. Durham and London: Duke University Press.

Doane, Mary Anne (1990) 'Information, Crisis and Catastrophe'. In *Logics of Television: Essays in Cultural Criticism*, edited by Patricia Mellencamp, 251–64. London: British Film Institute.

Donald, Merlin (2014) 'The Digital Era: Challenges for the Modern Mind'. *Cadmus* 2(2): 68–79.

Donohoe, Janet (2016) *Remembering Places: A Phenomenological Study of the Relationship between Memory and Place*. Kentucky: Lexington Books.

Duara, Prasenjit (1993) 'Bifurcating Linear History: Nation and Histories in China and India'. *Positions* 1(3): 779–804.

Dubrow, Jennifer (2017) 'Serial Fiction: Urdu Print Culture and the Novel in Colonial South Asia'. *The Indian Economic and Social History Review* 54(4): 423–22.

Dwyer, Rachel (2006) *Filming the Gods: Religion and Indian Cinema*. New York: Routledge.

Edensor, Tim (2006) 'Reconsidering National Temporalities: Institutional Times, Everyday Routines, Serial Spaces and Synchronicities'. *European Journal of Social Theory* 9(4): 2–28.

Edney, Mathew (1997) *Mapping an Empire: The Geographical Construction of British India, 1765–1843*. Chicago and London: The University of Chicago Press.

Elangovan, Arvind (2016) 'Provincial Autonomy, Sir Benegal Narsing Rau and an Improbable Imagination of Constitutionalism in India, 1935–38'. *Comparative Studies of South Asia, Africa, and the Middle East* 36(1): 66–82.

Erll, Astrid and Ann Rigney (eds) (2009) *Mediation, Remediation and the Dynamics of Cultural Memory*. Berlin: Walter de Guyter.

Facts n Fiction (2008) 'Down the Memory Lane – The Times of Doordarshan', 29 December, available at https://amolsviews.blogspot.com/2008/12/times-of-dd-down-memory-lane.html (accessed on 12 September 2017).

Feiman, Jesse (2012) 'The Matrix of Meaning in Dürer's Rhinoceros'. *Art in Print* 2(4): 22–6.

Felski, Rita (2015) *The Limits of Critique*. Chicago: University of Chicago Press.

Fernandes, Leela (2000) 'Nationalizing the "Global": Media Images, Cultural Politics and the Middle Class in India'. *Media, Culture & Society* 22(5): 611–28.

Ferguson, James and Akhil Gupta (2002) 'Spatializing States: Toward an Ethnography of Neo-Liberal Governmentality'. *American Ethnologist* 29(4): 981–1002.

Feuer, Jane (1986) 'Narrative Form in American Network Television'. In *High Theory/Low Culture: Analyzing Popular Television and Film*, edited by Colin MacCabe, 101–114. New York: Palgrave Macmillan.

Fielden, Lionel (1940) *Report on the Progress of Broadcasting in India*. Delhi: Manager of Publications.

Fiske, John (1987). *Television Culture*. London and New York: Routledge.

Flew, Terry (1997) 'Citizenship, Participation and Media Policy Formation'. *Communication and Social Policy* 4(4): 87–102.

Fliethmann, Axel (2007) 'Word and Image: Framing Philology'. *Thesis Eleven* 89(1): 43–57.

Fornäs, Johann (2012) 'Post-Anti-Hermeneutics: Reclaiming Culture, Meaning and Interpretation'. In *Hunting High and Low: Skriftfest til Jostein Gripsrud på 60-årsdagen*, edited by Jan Fredrik Hovden and Karl Knapskog, 490–518. Oslo: Scandinavian Academic Press.

Foster, Hal (ed.) (1988) *Vision and Visuality: Discussions in Contemporary Culture*. New York: The New Press.

Foucault, Michel (1988) 'Technologies of the Self'. In *Technologies of the Self: A Seminar with Michel Foucault*, edited by Luther Martin, Huck Gutman and Patrick Hutton, 16–49. Cambridge, Massachusetts: MIT Press.

Freitag, Sandria (1989) *Collective Action and Community: Public Arenas and the Emergence of Communalism in North India*. Berkeley: University of California Press.

——— (1991) 'Introduction: "The Public" and Its Meanings in Colonial South Asia'. *South Asia: Journal of South Asian Studies* XIV(1): 1–13.

——— (2001) 'Visions of Nation: Theorizing the Nexus between Creation, Consumption, and Participation in the Public Sphere'. In *Pleasure and the Nation: The History, Politics, and Consumption of Public Culture in India*, edited by Rachel Dwyer and Christopher Pinney, 35–75. New York: Oxford University Press.

——— (2006) *The Hermeneutics of the Subject: Lectures at the Collège de France, 1981–1982*. New York: Picador.

Gajarawala, Toral Jatin (2011) 'Some Time between Revisionist Revolutionary: Unreading History in Dalit Literature'. *PMLA* 126(3): 575–91.

Gaonkar, Dilip Parameshwar (2002) 'Toward New Imaginaries: An Introduction'. *Public Culture* 14(1): 1–19.

Garcia, Leovino Ma (1997) 'The Meaning of Being Human in Ricoeur's Philosophy of the Will'. *Budhi: A Journal of Ideas and Culture* 1(3): 81–154.

Garde-Hansen, J., A. Hoskins and A. Reading (eds) (2009) *Save As … Digital Memories*. New York: Palgrave Macmillan.

Gardner, Philip (2010) *Hermeneutics, History, and Memory*. New York and London: Routledge.

Garnham, Nicholas (1978) *Structures of Broadcasting*. London: British Film Institute.

Gee, James Paul (2005) 'Semiotic Social Spaces and Affinity Spaces'. In *Beyond Communities of Practice: Language Power and Social Context*, edited by David Barton and Karin Tusting, 214–232. Cambridge, Cambridge University Press.

Ghosh, Bisnupriya (2004) 'On Grafting the Vernacular: The Consequences of Postcolonial Spectrology'. *Boundary 2* 31(2): 197–218.

Ghosh, Paramita (2017) 'Meet the Man behind the Iconic Doordarshan Logo that will Soon become History'. *Hindustan Times*, 9 August, available at http://www.hindustantimes.com/india-news/meet-the-nid-student-who-made-the-doordarshan-symbol-soon-to-be-history/story-owFIcYbSZe5OfmWIet7GiO.html.

Gilmartin, David (2015) 'Rethinking the Public through the Lens of Sovereignty'. *South Asia* 38(3): 371–86.

Gilmartin, David and Bruce Lawrence (2000) *Beyond Turk and Hindu: Rethinking Religious Identities in Islamicate South Asia*. Miami: University Press of Florida.

Gitlin, Todd (1979) 'Prime Time Ideology: The Hegemonic Process in Television Entertainment'. *Social Problems* 26(3): 251–66.

Goetz, Rose (2004) 'Paul Ricoeur et Michel Foucault'. *Le Portique* [En ligne], 13(14): 1–6.

Göle, Nilüfer (2002) 'Islam in Public: New Visibilities and New Imaginaries'. *Public Culture* 14(1): 173–90.

Gopal, Madan (1964) *Munshi Premchand: A Literary Biography*. New Delhi: Asia House.

Goswami, Manu (2004) *Producing India: From Colonial Economy to National Space*. Chicago and London: The University of Chicago Press.

Government of India (1939) *Report on the Progress of Broadcasting in India*. Delhi: Office of the Controller of Broadcasting, Manager of Publications.

Gripsrud, Jostein (2004) 'Broadcast Television: The Changes of Its Survival in the Digital Age'. In *Television after TV: Essays on a Medium in Transition*, edited by Lynn Spigel and Jan Olsson. Durham: Duke University Press.

Gripsrud, Jostein (ed.) (2010) *Relocating Television: Television in the Digital Context*. London and New York: Routledge.

Gülşah Çapan, Zeynep (2017) 'Enacting the International/ Reproducing Eurocentrism'. *Contexto Internacional* 39(3): 655–72.

Gupta, Charu (2002) *Sexuality, Obscenity, Community: Women, Muslims, and the Hindu Public in Colonial India*. New York: Palgrave.

Gupta, Nilanjana (1998) *Switching Channels: Ideologies of Television in India*. New Delhi: Oxford University Press.

Gupta, Parthasarathi (2002) *Power, Politics and the People: Studies in British Imperialism and Indian Nationalism*. New Delhi: Permanent Black.

Halbwachs, Maurice (1992) *On Collective Memory*, translated by Lewis A. Coser. Chicago: University of Chicago Press.

Hall, Stuart (1973) 'The Determination of News Photographs'. In *The Manufacture of News: A Reader*, edited by Stanley Cohen and Jock Young, 226–47. Beverly Hills, California: Sage.

——— (1977) 'Culture, the Media and "Ideological Effect"'. In *Mass Communication and Society*, edited by James Curran, Michael Gurevitch and Janet Woollacott. London: Hodder Arnold.

——— (1986) 'The Problem of Ideology – Marxism without Guarantees'. *Journal of Communication Inquiry* 10(2), 28–44.

——— (1991) 'The Local and the Global: Globalization and Ethnicity'. In *Culture, Globalization and the World-System: Contemporary Conditions for the Representation of Identity*, edited by Anthony D King, 19–40. Minneapolis: University of Minnesota Press.

——— (1993) 'Culture, Community, Nation'. *Cultural Studies* 7 (3): 349–63.

Hall, Stuart, Ian Connell and Lidia Curti (1981) 'The "Unity" of Current Affairs Television'. In *Popular Film and Television*, edited by Tony Bennett et al., 215–37. London: BFI.

Hallisey, Charles (2010) 'Between Intuition and Judgment: Moral Creativity in Theravada Buddhist Ethics'. In *Ethical Life in South Asia*, edited by Anand Pandian and Daud Ali, 141–52. Bloomington and Indianapolis: Indiana University Press.

Hansen, Kathryn (1981) 'Renu's Regionalism: Language and Form'. *Journal of Asian Studies* XL(2): 273–94.

Hansen, T. B. (2008) 'Sovereigns beyond the State: On Legality and Authority in Urban India'. In *Sovereign Bodies: Citizens, Migrants, and States in the Postcolonial World*, edited by Thomas Blom Hansen and Finn Stepputat, 169–91. Princeton: Princeton University Press.

Hardinge, H. R. (1934) 'Broadcasting for Rural India'. *The Asiatic Review* XXX(104): 619–23.

Hartley, John (ed) (2006) *TV50*. Melbourne: Australian Centre for the Moving Image.
——— (2008) *Television Truths: Forms of Knowledge in Popular Culture*. Oxford: Blackwell, 2008.
Harvey, David (1989) *The Condition of Postmodernity: An Enquiry into the Origins of Cultural Change*. Cambridge, Massachusetts and Oxford, UK: Blackwell.
——— (1996) 'Cities or Urbanization?' *City* 1: 38–61.
Hasan, Zoya (1994) *Forging Identities: Gender, Communities and the State in India*. Boulder, Oxford, San Francisco: Westview Press.
Hay, James (2001) 'Locating the Televisual'. *Television & New Media* 2(3): 205–34.
Headrick, Daniel (2010) 'A Double-Edged Sword: Communications and Imperial Control in British India'. *Historical Social Research* 35(1): 51–65.
Heath, Stephen (1990) 'Representing Television'. In *Logics of Television: Essays in Cultural Criticism*, edited by Patricia Mellencamp, 267–302. London: British Film Institute.
Held, David (1995) *Democracy and the Global Order*. Cambridge: Polity Press.
Hill, Andrew (2010) 'The BBC Empire Service: The Voice, The Discourse of the Master and Ventriloquism'. *South Asian Diaspora* 2(1): 25–38.
Hodgson, Michael (1977) *The Venture of Islam, Volume 1: The Classical Age of Islam*. Chicago and London: University of Chicago Press.
Holdsworth, Amy (2010) 'Televisual Memory'. *Screen* 51(2): 129–142.
Holton, Robert (1998) *Globalization and the Nation-State*. London: Macmillan.
Hoskins, Andrew (2003) 'Signs of the Holocaust: Exhibiting Memory in a Mediated Age'. *Media, Culture & Society* 25(1): 7–22.
——— (2009) 'Flashbulb Memories, Psychology and Media Studies: Fertile Ground for Interdisciplinarity'. *Memory Studies* 2(2): 147–50.
Hughes, Stephen (2002) 'The "Music Boom" in Tamil South India: Gramophone, Radio and the Making of Mass Culture'. *Historical Journal of Film, Radio and Television* 22(4): 446–69.
Indian Express (2009) 'Life Begins at 50', available at http://archive.indianexpress.com/news/life-begins-at-50/517996/0.
Innis, Harold (1990) *Empire and Communications*. Oxford: Oxford University Press.
Ivins, William (1969) *Prints and Visual Communication*. Massachusetts: MIT Press.
Jakobsen, Janet and Ann Pellegrini (2000) 'World Secularisms at the Millennium'. *Social Text 64* 18(3): 1–27.
Jain, Kajri (1995) 'Of the Everyday and the "National Pencil": Calendars in Postcolonial India'. *Journal of Arts and Ideas* 27(28): 57–89.
——— (2003) 'More Than Meets the Eye: The Circulation of Images and the Embodiment of Value'. In *Beyond Appearances? Visual Practices and Ideologies in Modern India*, edited by Sumathi Ramaswamy, 33–70. New Delhi: Sage.
Jameson, Fredric (1981) *Political Unconscious: Narrative as a Socially Symbolic Act*. New York, Ithaca: Cornell University Press.
——— (1998) 'Notes of Globalization as a Philosophical Issue'. In *The Cultures of Globalization*, edited by Fredric Jameson and Miyosh Masao. Durham, NC: Duke University Press.

——— (2009) 'Ricoeur's Project'. In *Valences of Dialectic*, edited by Fredric Jameson, 475–532. New York: Verso.

Jeffrey, Robin (2006) 'The Mahatma Didn't Like the Movies and Why It Matters: Indian Broadcasting Policy, 1920s–1990s'. *Global Media and Communication* 2(2): 204–24.

Jha, Subhash K. (2011) 'ZNMD Spoofs Doordarshan'. *Mid-Day*, 24 July, available at http://www.mid-day.com/articles/znmd-spoofs-doordarshan/129211.

Jinghan, Shikha (2011) 'Re-embodying the "Classical": The Bombay Film Song in the 1950s'. *BioScope: South Asian Screen Studies* 2(2): 157–179.

Johnson, Victoria (2008) *Heartland TV: Prime Time Television and the Struggle for U.S. Identity*. New York: New York University Press.

Joshi, P. C. (1984) *An Indian Personality for Television, Report of the Working Group on Software for Doordarshan*. New Delhi: Publications Division, Ministry of Information and Broadcasting, Government of India.

Joyeeta (2009) 'A Tribute to Classic Doordarshan Entertainment'. *Old Idiot-Box*, available at https://oldidiotbox.blogspot.com (accessed on 26 July 2017).

Kalpagam, Udita (2014) *Rule by Numbers: Colonial Governmentality in India*. Kentucky: Lexington Books.

Kalra, Virender (2016) *Sacred and Secular Musics: A Postcolonial Approach*. London: Bloomsbury.

Kansteiner, Wulf (2002) 'Finding Meaning in Memory: A Methodological Critique of Collective Memory Studies'. *History and Theory* 41(2): 179–97.

Kapur, Geeta (1987) 'Mythic Material in Indian Cinema'. *Journal of Arts and Ideas* 14(15): 79–108.

——— (2000) *When Was Modernism: Essays on Contemporary Cultural Practice in India*. New Delhi: Tulika.

Kapur, Geeta, and Ashish Rajadhyaksha (2001) 'Bombay/Mumbai: 1992–2001'. In *Century City: Art and Culture in Modern Metropolis*, edited by Iowana Blazwick, 12–21. London: Tate.

Katz, Elihu and Paddy Scannell (eds) (2009) 'The End of Television? Its Impact on the World (So Far)'. *The Annals of the American Academy of Political and Social Science* 625(1): 6–18.

Kaul, Arun Pt (Producer) (1996) *Kashmir File*. New Delhi: Vyeth Television.

Kaviraj, Sudipta (1993) 'The Imaginary Institution of India'. In *Subaltern Studies VII: Writings on South Asian History and Society*, edited by Partha Chatterjee and Gyanendra Pandey, 1–39. New Delhi: Oxford University Press.

——— (1998) 'The Culture of Representative Democracy'. In *Wages of Freedom: Fifty Years of the Indian Nation-State*, edited by Partha Chatterjee. Delhi: Oxford University Press, 171–75.

Kearney, Richard (1989) 'Paul Ricoeur and the Hermeneutic Imagination'. In *The Narrative Path: The Later Works of Paul Ricoeur*, edited by Peter Kemp and David Rasmussen, 3–18. London, Cambridge: MIT Press.

——— (2004) *Paul Ricoeur: The Owl of Minerva*. Hampshire, England: Ashgate.

——— (2009) 'Returning to God after God: Levinas, Derrida, Ricoeur'. *Research in Phenomenology* 39: 167–83.

——— (2011) 'What Is Diacritical Hermeneutics?' *Journal of Applied Hermeneutics*, 10 December, available at https://jah.journalhosting.ucalgary.ca/jah/index.php/jah/article/view/6/7 (accessed on 22 November 2017).

Keightley, Emily (2011) 'From Dynasty to Songs of Praise: Television as Cultural Resource for Gendered Remembering'. *European Journal of Cultural Studies* 14(4): 395–410.

Kermabon, Jacques and Kumar Shahani (1991) *Cinema and Television: Fifty Years of Reflection in France*. Hyderabad and New Delhi: Orient Longman.

Kent, Elisa and Tazim Kassam (eds) (2013) *Lines in the Water: Religious Boundaries in South Asia*. Syracuse: Syracuse University Press.

Kesavan, Mukul (1994) 'Urdu, Awadh and the Tawaif: The Islamicate Roots of Hindi Cinema'. In *Forging Identities: Gender, Communities and the State*, edited by Zoya Hasan, 244–257. Delhi: Kali for Women.

Khan, Abdul Jamil (2006) *Urdu/Hindi: An Artificial Divide*. UK: Agora Publishing

Khan, Pasha (2015) 'A Handbook for Storytellers: The Ṭirāz al-akhbār and the Qissa Genre'. In *Tellings and Texts: Music, Literature and Performance in North India*, edited by Francesca Orsini and B. Schofield, 185–207. Cambridge, UK: Open Book Publishers.

Khilnani, Sunil (1997) *The Idea of India*. New York: Farrar Straus Giroux.

Khubchandani, Lachman (2003) 'Defining Mother Tongue Education in Plurilingual Contexts'. *Language Policy* 2(3): 239–54.

——— (2012) 'Language Plurality in South Asia: A Search for Alternative Models in Knowledge Construction'. *Applied Linguistics Review* 3(2): 315–31.

King, Richard (1999) *Orientalism and Religion: Postcolonial Theory, India and 'The Mythic' East*. London: Routledge.

Kishen, Prem, and Sunil Mehta (Producers) (1990) *Gul Gulshan Gulfam*. Bombay: Cine Vista.

Kortti, Jukka, and Tuuli Anna Mähönen (2009) 'Reminiscing Television: Media Ethnography, Oral History and Finnish Third Generation Media History'. *European Journal of Communication* 24(1): 49–67.

Krishna, Daya (1988) 'Comparative Philosophy: What It Is and What It Ought to Be'. In *Interpreting across Boundaries: New Essays in Comparative Philosophy*, edited by Gerald James Larson and Eliot Deutsch, 71–83. Princeton: Princeton University Press.

Krishna, Sankaran (1999) *Postcolonial Insecurities: India, Sri Lanka, and the Question of Nationhood*. Minneapolis, London: University of Minnesota Press.

Kuhn, Annette (1995) *Family Secrets: Acts of Memory and Imagination*. London: Verso.

——— (ed) (2013) *Little Madnesses: Winnicott, Transitional Phenomena and Cultural Experience*. London: I.B.Tauris

Kumar, Priya (2008) *Limiting Secularism: The Ethics of Coexistence in Indian Literature and Film*. Minneapolis: University of Minnesota Press.

Kumar, Sanjay (2012) 'The Fault Lines of Hindi and Urdu'. *Frontline* 29(15), 28 July–10 August, available at https://www.frontline.in/static/html/fl2915/stories/20120810291509100.htm (accessed on 11 October 2017).

Kumar, Shanti (2006) *Gandhi Meets Primetime: Globalization and Nationalism in Indian Television*. Urbana and Chicago: University of Illinois Press.

Kumar, Keval (2006) 'Remembering Violence: Media Events, Childhood and the Global'. In *News in Public Memory: An International Study of Media Memories across Generations*, edited by Ingrid Volkmer, 95–118. New York: Peter Lang.

Laughier, Sandra (2015) 'The Ethics of Care as a Politics of the Ordinary'. *New Literary History* 46(2): 217–40.

Lazarus, Neil (1999) *Nationalism and Cultural Practice in the Postcolonial World*. Cambridge, UK: Cambridge University Press.

Lefebvre, Henri (1974) *The Production of Space*. Oxford, UK, Cambridge, USA: Blackwell Publishing.

Legg, Stephen (2007) *Spaces of Colonialism: Delhi's Urban Governmentalities*. Malden, Massachusetts: Blackwell.

——— (2016) 'Dyarchy: Democracy, Autocracy, and Scalar Sovereignty of Interwar India'. *Comparative Studies of South Asia, Africa, and the Middle East* 36(1): 44–64.

Leichter, David J. (2012) 'Collective Identity and Collective Memory in the Philosophy of Paul Ricoeur'. *Études Ricoeuriennes/Ricoeur Studies* 3(1): 114–31.

Lelyveld, David (1990) 'Transmitters and Culture: The Colonial Roots of Indian Broadcasting'. *South Asia Research* 10(1): 41–52.

——— (1993) 'Colonial Knowledge and the Fate of Hindustani'. *Comparative Studies in History and Society* 35(4): 665–82.

——— (1994) 'Upon the Subdominant: Administering Music on All India Radio'. *Social Text* 39: 111–27.

Lewis, David, Dennis Rodgers and Michael Woolcock (2006) 'The Fiction of Development: Literary Representation as a Source of Authoritative Knowledge'. *The Journal of Development Studies*, 44(2): 198–216.

Livingstone, Sonia (ed) (2005) 'On the Relations between Audience and Public'. In *Audiences and Publics: When Cultural Engagement Matters for the Public Sphere*, edited by Sonia Livingstone, 17–42. Bristol, UK: Intellect Books.

Lodziak, Conrad (1986) *The Power of Television: A Critical Appraisal*. New York: St. Martin's Press.

Longhurst, Brian (1987) 'Realism, Naturalism and Television Soap Opera'. *Theory, Culture and Society* 4(4): 633–49.

Loomba, Ania (1998) *Colonialism/Postcolonialism*. New York: Routledge.

Losonczi, Peter and Walter Van Herek (eds) (2011) *Secularism, Religion, and Politics: India and Europe*. London, New York and New Delhi: Routledge.

Lozano, Juan Francisco Gutiérrez (2013) 'Television Memory after the End of Television History'. In *After the Break: Television Theory Today*, edited by Marijke de valck and Jan Teurlings, 131–44. Amsterdam: Amsterdam University Press.

Lunn, David (2015) 'The Eloquent Language: Hindustani in 1940s Indian Cinema'. *BioScope* 6(1): 1–26.

Luthra, H. R. (1986) *Indian Broadcasting*. New Delhi: Publications Division, Ministry of Information and Broadcasting, Govt. of India.

Madan, Triloki Nath (1997) 'Secularism in Its Place'. In *Politics in India*, edited by Sudipta Kaviraj, 297–320. Delhi, Calcutta, Chennai, Mumbai: Oxford University Press.

Mahajan, Gurpreet and Surinder Singh Jodhka (2010) *Religion, Community and Development: Changing Contours of Politics and Policy in India*. London, New York, and New Delhi: Routledge.

Majid, Anouar (2000) *Unveiling Traditions: Postcolonial Islam in a Polycentric World*. Durham and London: Duke University Press.

Manuel, Peter (1988) *Cassette Culture: Popular Music Technology in North India*. Chicago and London: University of Chicago Press.

Mani, Lata (2009) *SacredSecular: Contemplative Cultural Critique*. London and New York: Routledge.

Mankekar, Purnima (1999) *Screening Culture, Viewing Politics: An Ethnography of Television, and Nation in Postcolonial India*. Durham, NC: Duke University Press.

Marcelo, Goncalo (2010) 'From Conflict to Conciliation and Back Again: Some Notes on Ricoeur's Dialectic'. *Revista Filosófica de Coimbra* (19)38: 341–66.

Marks, Laura (2010) *Enfoldment and Infinity: As Islamic Genealogy of New Media Art*. Cambridge: MIT Press.

Massey, Doreen (1994) *Space, Place and Gender*. Cambridge: Polity Press.

Mathieu, David (2015) 'Audience Research beyond the Hermeneutics of Suspicion'. *International Journal of Media & Cultural Politics* 11(2): 251–58.

Mathur, Jagdish Chandra and Paul Neurath (1959) *An Indian Experiment in Farm Radio Forums*. Paris: UNESCO, available at http://unesdoc.unesco.org/images/0004/000432/043238eb.pdf (accessed on 29 October 2018).

Mathur, Kuckoo (Producer) (1989) *Choli Daman*. Bombay: Mathur Video Vision.

Mathur, Kuldip (1992) 'The State and the Use of Coercive Power in India'. *Asian Survey* XXXII(4): 337–349.

May, Peter and Nigel Thrift (eds) (2001) *TimeSpace: Geographies of Temporality*. London and New York: Routledge.

Mazzarella, Willam (2012) '"Reality Must Improve": The Perversity of Expertise and the Belatedness of Indian Developmental Television'. *Global Media and Communication*, 8(3): 215–41.

Mazzarella, William, and Raminder Kaur (2009) *Censorship in South Asia: Cultural Regulation from Sedition to Seduction*. Bloomington: Indiana University Press.

Mc Arthur, Colin (1978) *Television and History*. London: BFI.

McChesney, Robert (1990) 'The Battle for the US Airwaves, 1928–1935'. *Journal of Communication* 40(4): 29–57.

McDowell, Stephen (1997) 'Globalization and Policy Choice: Television and Audiovisual Services Policies in India'. *Media, Culture & Society* 19(2): 151–72.

McNay, Lois (1999) 'Gender and Narrative Identity'. *Journal of Political Ideologies* 4(3): 315–36.

——— (2009) 'Self as Enterprise: Dilemmas of Control and Resistance in Foucault's The Birth of Biopolitics'. *Theory, Culture & Society* 26(2): 55–77.

Mehta, Nikita and Preetika Rana (2011) 'Doordarshan: A Long Lost Memory?' *The Wall Street Journal*, 22 September, available at https://blogs.wsj.com/indiarealtime/2011/09/22/doordarshan-a-long-lost-memory/.

Mehta, Uday Singh (1999) *Liberalism and Empire: A Study in Nineteenth Century British Liberal Thought*. Chicago: University of Chicago Press.

Meinhoff, Ulrike Hanna (2005) 'Appendix: Audiences and Publics: Comparing Semantic Fields across Different Languages. In *Audiences and Publics: When Cultural Engagement Matters for the Public Sphere, Changing Media, Changing Europe*, edited by Sonia Livingstone. Bristol, UK: Intellect.

Michel, Johan (2015) *Ricoeur and the Post-Structuralists: Bourdieu, Derrida, Deleuze, Foucault, Castoriadis*, translated by Scott Davidson. Lanham, MD: Rowman and Littlefield.

Mill, John Stuart (1858) *Memorandum of the Improvements in the Administration of India During the Last Thirty Years: And the Petition of the East-India Company to Parliament*. London: W.M.H Allen & Company.

Ministry of Information and Broadcasting (1990) *Prasar Bharati Act* (Broadcasting Corporation of India). New Delhi: Government of India.

Mishra, Pankaj (1995) *Butter Chicken in Ludhiana*: *Travels in Small Town India*. New Delhi: Penguin.

Misra, Neelesh (2009) 'Inside the Idiot Box of Memory', *Writer at Large*, available at http://rovingwriter.blogspot.com/2009/01/inside-idiot-box-of-memory.html.

Mitra, Ananda (1994) *Television and Popular Culture in India: A Study of the Mahabharat*. New Delhi: Sage Publications.

Mody, Bella (1979) 'Programming for SITE'. *Journal of Communication* 29: 90–7.

Moran, A. and Kean M. (2003) *Television across Asia: TV Industries, Program Formats and Globalization*. London: Routledge.

Mohammadi, Ali (2010) *International Communication and Globalization*. New York: Sage Publications.

Moores, Shaun (2007) *Media/Theory: Thinking About Media and Communication*. London and New York: Routledge.

Morris, Nancy and Silvio Ricardo Waisboard (eds) (2001) *Media and Globalization: Why the State Matters*. Lanham, Maryland: Rowman & Littlefield.

Mufti, Amir (2010) 'Orientalism and the Institution of World Literatures'. *Critical Inquiry* 36(3): 458–93.

Mukherjee, Mithi (2010a) 'Transcending Identity: Gandhi, Nonviolence, and the Pursuit of a "Different" Freedom in Modern India'. *The American Historical Review* 115(2): 453–73.

——— (2010b) *India in the Shadow of Empire: A Legal and Political History, 1774–1950*. New Delhi: Oxford University Press.

Muldoon, Andrew (2009) 'Politics, Intelligence and Elections in Late Colonial India: Congress and the Raj in 1937'. *Journal of the Canadian Historical Association* 20(2): 160–88.

Muller, Simone and Heid Tworek (2015) 'The Telegraph and the Bank: On the Interdependence of Global Communication and Capitalism, 1866–1914'. *Journal of Global History* 10(2): 259–83.

Nair, Rukmini Bhaya (2001) 'Singing a Nation into Being'. *Seminar* (497): 95–106.

Naqash, Rayan (2017) 'Why Tourists Still Look for "Gul Gulshan Gulfam" When They Visit the Dal Lake in Srinagar'. *Scroll*, June 14, available at https://thereel.scroll.in/840511/here-is-why-tourists-still-look-for-gul-gulshan-gulfam-when-they-visit-the-dal-lake-in-srinagar.

Nandy, Ashis (1997) 'A Critique of Modernist Secularism'. In *Politics in India*, edited by Sudipta Kaviraj, 340–57. Delhi, Calcutta, Chennai, Mumbai: Oxford University Press.

——— (1999a) 'Coping with the Politics of Faiths and Cultures: Between Secular State and Ecumenical Traditions in India'. In *Ethnic Futures: The State and Identity Politics in Asia*, edited by Joanna Pfaff-Czarnecka, Darini Rajasingham-Senanayake, Ashis Nandy and Edmund Terence Gomez, 135–66. New Delhi, Thousand Oaks, London: Sage Publications.

——— (1999b) 'The Twilight of Certitudes: Secularism, Hindu Nationalism and Other Masks of Deculturation'. In *Tradition, Pluralism and Identity: In Honour of T. N. Madan*, edited by Veena Das, Dipankar Gupta and Patricia Uberoi, 401–19. New Delhi, Thousand Oaks, London: Sage Publications.

——— (2001) 'A Report on the Present State of Gods and Goddesses in South Asia'. *Postcolonial Studies* 4(2): 123–34.

Narang, Gopichand (2014) 'The Indo-Islamic Cultural Fusion and the Institution of the Qawwali', 25 March, available at http://gopichandnarang.com/articles-the-indo.php (accessed on 7 December 2017).

Naregal, Veena (2002) *Language, Politics, Elites and the Public Sphere: Western India under Colonialism*. London: Anthem.

Nayar, Sheila J. (2012) *The Sacred and the Cinema: Reconfiguring the 'Genuinely' Religious Film*. New York: Continuum.

Neurath, Paul (1962) 'Radio Farm Forum as a Tool of Change in Indian Villages'. *Economic Development and Cultural Change* 10(3): 278–83.

Newcomb, Horace and Hirsch Paul (1983) 'Television as a Cultural Forum: Implications for Research'. *Quarterly Review of Film Studies* 8(3): 45–55.

Newman, Michael Z (2006) 'From Beats to Arcs: Toward a Poetics of Television Narrative', *The Velvet Light Trap* 58(Fall): 16–28.

Nijhawan, Shobna (2012) *Women and Girls in the Hindi Public Sphere: Periodical Literature in Colonial North India*. Oxford: Oxford University Press.

Nijman, Jan (2007) 'Paul Ricoeur and International Law: Beyond "The End of Subject"'. Towards a Reconceptualization of International Law'. *Leiden Journal of International Law* 20: 25–64.

Ninan, Sevanti (1998) 'History of Indian Broadcasting Reform'. In *Broadcasting Reform in India*, edited by Monroe Price and Stefaan Verhulst, 23–37. New Delhi: Oxford University Press.

Nishat, Jameela (2000) 'Dakhini Urdu as a Vehicle of Social Interaction'. In *Deccan Heritage*, edited by Harsh Gupta, Aloka Parasher-Sen and D. Balasubramanian, 201–220. Hyderabad: Orient Longman.

Nixon, Jon (2006) 'Towards a Hermeneutics of Hope: The Legacy of Edward W. Said'. *Discourse: Studies in the Cultural Politics of Education* 27(3): 341–56.

Nora, Pierre (1984) *Les lieux de mémoire* (Realms of Memory). Paris: Gallimard.

Nordenstreng, Karle and Herbert Schiller (eds) (1979) *National Sovereignty and International Communication*. Norwood, NJ: Ablex Publishing.

——— (eds) (1993) *Beyond National Sovereignty: International Communication in the 1990s*. Norwood, NJ: Ablex Publishing.

Novetzke, Christian (2007) 'Bhakti and Its Public'. *International Journal of Hindu Studies* 11(3): 255–72.

Oberoi, Harjeet (1994) *The Construction of Religious Boundaries: Culture, Identity, and Diversity in the Sikh Tradition*. Chicago: University of Chicago Press.

Ong, Aiwa (2006) 'Neoliberalism as a Mobile Technology'. *Transactions of the Institute of British Geographers* 32(10): 3–8.

Orosz, István (2016) 'A Rhino Remembered: On the 500th Anniversary of a Shipwreck'. *Hungarian Review* VII(3): 85–102.

Orsini, Francesca (2009) *Print and Pleasure: Popular Literature and Entertaining Fictions in Colonial North India*. New Delhi: Permanent Black.

——— (ed) (2010) *Before the Divide: Hindi and Urdu Literary Culture*. Orient Blackswan: Hyderabad.

——— (2012) 'How to Do Multilingual Literary History? Lessons from Fifteenth- and Sixteenth-Century North India'. *The Indian Economic and Social History Review* 49(2): 225–46.

——— (2015) *The Hindi Public Sphere, 1920–1940: Language and Literature in the Age of Nationalism*. New Delhi: Oxford University Press.

Orsini, Francesca and Bernard Schofield (eds) (2015) *Tellings and Texts: Music, Literature and Performance in North India*. Cambridge, UK: Open Book Publishers.

O'Sullivan, Tim (1991) 'Television Memories and Cultures of Viewing, 1950–65'. In *Popular Television in Britain: Studies in Cultural History*, edited by John Corner, 159–81. London: British Film Institute.

Ott, Brian (2007) *The Small Screen: How Television Equips Us to Live in the Information Age*. Malden, MA: Blackwell Publishing.

Pant, Ritika (2016) 'Broadcast to Broadband: Televisual Experiences in the Age of the Internet', available at http://sarai.net/broadcast-to-broadband-televisual-experiences-in-the-age-of-the-digital/ (accessed on 14 January 2017).

Parks, Lisa and Shanti Kumar (eds) (2006) *Planet TV: A Global Television Reader*. New York: New York University Press.

Paswan, Ram Vilas (1996) *National Media Policy: A Working Paper*. New Delhi: Government of India.

Patnode, Randall (2003) '"What These People Need Is Radio": New Technology, the Press, and Otherness in 1920s America'. *Technology and Culture* 44(2): 285–305.

Peacock, Steven and Jason Jacobs (eds) (2013) *Television Aesthetics and Style*. London and New York: Bloomsbury Academic.

Pendakur, Manjunath (1991) 'A Political Economy of Television: State, Class and Corporate Confluence in India'. In *Transnational Communications: Wiring the Third World*, edited by Gerald Sussman and John A. Lent, 234–62. New Delhi, Newbury Park and London: Sage.

Peters, John Durham (2008) 'The History as a Communication Problem'. In *Explorations in Communication and History*, edited by Barbie Zelizer, 19–34. London and New York: Routledge.

Phelan, Sean (2016) 'Reinvigorating Ideology Critique: Between Trust and Suspicion'. *Media, Culture & Society*, 38(2): 274–83.

Pickering, Michael and Emily Keightley (2006) 'The Modalities of Nostalgia'. *Current Sociology* 54(6): 919–41.

——— (2012) *The Mnemonic Imagination: Remembering as Creative Practice*. New York: Palgrave.

Pickering, Michael, and Graeme Murdoch (2008) 'The Birth of Distance: Communications and the Changing Conceptions of Elsewhere'. In *Narrating Media History*, edited by Mark Bailey, 171–83. London: Routledge.

Pinch, William (1999) 'Same Difference in India and Europe'. *History and Theory* 38(3): 389–407.

Pinkerton, Alisdair (2008) 'Radio and the Raj: Broadcasting in British India (1920-1940)'. *Journal of the Royal Asiatic Society* 18(2): 1–30.

Pinney, Christopher (2001) 'Indian Magical Realism: Notes on Popular Visual Culture'. In *Subaltern Studies XI: Community, Gender and Violence*, edited by Partha Chatterjee and Pradeep Jeganathan. New York: Columbia University Press.

Poduval, Satish (1999) 'The Possible Histories of Indian Television'. *Journal of Arts and Ideas* 32–33: 108–18.

Pollock, Sheldon (2006) 'Literary Culture and Manuscript Culture in Precolonial India'. In *History of the Book and Literary Cultures*, edited by Simon Eliot, Andrew Nash and Ian Willison. London, 77–94: British Library.

——— (2009) 'Future Philology? The Fate of a Soft Science in a Hard World'. *Critical Inquiry* 35(4): 931–61.

——— (2011) 'Introduction'. In *Forms of Knowledge in Early Modern Asia: Explorations in the Intellectual Histories of India and Tibet, 1500–1800*, edited by Sheldon Pollock, 1–18. Durham and London: Duke University Press.

Prakash, Gyan (2000) *Another Reason: Science and Imagination of Modern India*. Delhi: Oxford University Press.

Prasad, Leela (2010) 'Ethical Subjects: Time, Timing, and Tellability'. In *Ethical Life in South Asia*, edited by Anand Pandian and Daud Ali, 174–90. Bloomington and Indianapolis: Indiana University Press.

Prasad, Madhava (1998) 'The State in/of Cinema'. In *Wages of Freedom: Fifty Years of the Indian Nation-State*, edited by Partha Chatterjee, 123–46. Delhi, Calcutta, Chennai, and Mumbai: Oxford University Press.

——— (1999) 'Television and National Culture'. *Journal of Arts & Ideas* 32–33: 119–21.

Premchand, Munshi (1936) *Godān*. Delhi: Rupa & Company.

Price, Monroe (2002) *Media and Sovereignty: The Global Information Revolution and Its Challenge to State Power*. Cambridge, USA: MIT Press.

Price, Monroe and Stephaan Verhulst (eds) (1998) *Broadcasting Reform in India: Media Law from a Global Perspective*. Delhi, Calcutta, Chennai and Mumbai: Oxford University Press.

Punathambekar, Aswin and Parvati Sundar (2017) 'The Time of Television: Broadcasting, Daily Life, and the New Indian Middle Class'. *Communication, Culture & Critique* 10(3): 401–21.

Punathambekar, Aswin and Shanti Kumar (2012) 'Introduction: Television at Large'. *South Asian History and Culture* 3(4): 483–90.

Radstone, Susannah (ed.) (2000) *Memory and Methodology*. Oxford and New York: Berg.

——— (2005) 'Reconceiving Binaries: The Limits of Memory'. *History Workshop Journal* 59: 134–50.

Raj, Dhooleka Sarhadi (2000) 'Ignorance, Forgetting, and Family Nostalgia: Partition, the Nation State, and Refugees in Delhi'. *Social Analysis* 44(2): 30–55.

Rajadhyaksha, Ashish (1987) 'The Utter Mediocrity of Doordarshan'. *The Indian Post*. May 15.

——— (1990) 'Beaming Messages to the Nation'. *Journal of Arts and Ideas* 19: 132–50.

——— (1999) 'The Judgement: Re-Forming the "Public"'. *Journal of Arts and Ideas* 32–33: 34–52.

——— (2011) *The Last Cultural Mile: An Inquiry into Technology and Governance in India*. Bangalore: CIS-RAW.

Rajagopal, Arvind (1993) 'The Rise of National Programming: The Case of Indian Television'. *Media, Culture and Society* 15(1): 91–111.

——— (1998) 'Advertising, Politics and the Sentimental Education of the Indian Consumer'. *Visual Anthropology Review* 14(2): 14–31.

——— (2001) *Politics after Television: Hindu Nationalism and the Reshaping of the Public in India*. Cambridge, UK, New York: Cambridge University Press.

——— (ed.) (2009) *The Indian Public Sphere: Readings in Media History*. Cambridge: Cambridge University Press.

Rantanen, Terhi (2005) *The Media and Globalization*. Thousand Oaks: Sage.

Rao, Anupama (1995) 'Televisions, Maharastrian Social Reform and Literary Imagination: Bombay Doordarshan's *Paulakhuna*'. *Economic & Political Weekly* 30(10): 521–26.

Razdan, Vinayak (2016) 'Remembering a Kashmiri Night: When We Were at Chattbal'. *Economic & Political Weekly* 51(17): 1–6.

Renu, Phanishwarnath (1954) *Mailā Anchal*. Delhi: Rajkamal Prakashan.

Ricoeur, Paul (1965) *Freud and Philosophy: An Essay on Interpretation*. New Haven and London: Yale University Press.

——— (1968) 'Structure, Word, Event'. *Philosophy Today* 12(2): 114–29.
——— (1979) 'Ideology and Utopia as Cultural Imagination'. In *Being Human in a Technological Age*, edited by Donald Borchert and David Stewart, 107–25. Athens, Ohio: Ohio University Press.
——— (1980) 'Narrative Time'. *Critical Inquiry* 7(1): 169–90.
——— (1981) *Hermeneutics and the Human Sciences: Essays on Language, Action and Interpretation*, translated by John B. Thompson. Cambridge: Cambridge University Press.
——— (1984, 1986, 1988) *Time and Narrative* (Vols 1, 2, and 3). Chicago, London: University of Chicago Press.
——— (1991) 'The Human Experience of Time'. In *A Ricouer Reader: Reflection and Imagination*, edited by Mario J. Valdes, 321–43. Toronto and Buffalo: University of Toronto Press.
——— (1995) *Figuring the Sacred: Religion, Narrative, and Imagination*. Minneapolis: Augsburg Fortress Publishing.
——— (1996) *Oneself as Another*, translated by Kathleen Blamey. Chicago, London: University of Chicago Press.
——— (1998) *Critique and Conviction: Conversations with Francois Azouvi and Marc de Launay*. New York: Columbia University Press.
——— (2003) *Memory, History, Forgetting*, translated by David Pellauer and Kathleen Blamey. Chicago: University of Chicago Press.
——— (2004) 'The Creativity of Language (An interview)'. In *Paul Ricoeur: The Owl of Minerva*, edited by Richard Kearney, 127–44. Hampshire, England: Ashgate.
——— (2007a) *The Conflict of Interpretations: Essays in Hermeneutics* (First published in French in 1969, and in English, 1974). Evanston, Illinois: Northwestern University Press.
——— (2007b) *From Text to Action: Essays in Hermeneutics II*, translated by Kathleen Blamey and John Thompson (First published in French in 1986, and in English,1991). Evanston, Illinois: Northwestern University Press.
——— (2007c) *Reflections on the Just*, translated by David Pellaeur. Chicago and London: The University of Chicago Press.
Robbins, Bruce. 1999. *Feeling Global: Internationalism in Distress*. New York: New York University Press.
Rosen, Philip (1993) 'Traces of the Past: From Historicity Film'. In *Meanings in Texts and Actions: Questioning Paul Ricoeur*, edited by David Klemm and William Schweiker, 67–89. Charlottesville and London: University Press of Virginia.
Roy, Abhijit (2005) 'The Apparatus and Its Constituencies: On India's Encounters with Television'. *Journal of the Moving Image* 5: 1–31.
——— (2008) 'Bringing up TV: Popular Culture and Development Modern in India'. *South Asian Popular Culture* 6(1): 29–43.
——— (2012) 'A Reflexive Turn in Television Studies? Conjectures from South Asia'. *South Asian History and Culture* 3(4): 636–48.

Roy, Srirupa (2001) 'Nation and Institution: Commemorating the Fiftieth Anniversary of Indian Independence'. *Interventions: International Journal of Postcolonial Studies* 3(2): 246–61.

——— (2002) 'Moving Pictures: The Postcolonial State and Visual Representation of India'. *Contributions to Indian Sociology* 36(1/2): 233–47.

Roy, Supriya (2007) *Beyond Belief: India and the Politics of Postcolonial Nationalism.* Durham: Duke University Press.

Ruggie, James (1993) 'Territoriality and Beyond: Problematizing Modernity in International Relations'. *International Organization* 47(1): 139–74.

Runions, Erin (2010) '"Effects of Grace": Detranscendentalizing'. In *Planetary Loves: Spivak, Postcoloniality, and Theology*, edited by Stephen D. Moore and Mayra Rivera, 225–37. New York: Fordham University Press.

Sackley, Nicole (2011) 'The Village as Cold War Site: Experts, Development, and the History of Rural Reconstruction'. *Journal of Global History*, 6(3): 481–504

Said, Edward (2004). 'The Return of Philology'. In Edward Said, *Humanism and Democratic Criticism*, 57–84. New York: Columbia University Press.

Samit (2008) 'Doordarshan Days Sweet Memories will Always Linger on'. *Creative Heaven*, available at http://creativesamits.blogspot.com/2008/05/doordarshan-days-sweet-memories-will_22.html (accessed on 6 April 2018).

Sangari, Kumkum (2009) 'Conjunction and Flow: The Gendered Temporalities of (Media) Disaster 1'. *Journal of e-Media Studies* 2(1): 1–7.

Sanjay, B. P. (1989) 'The Role of Institutional Relationships in Communication Technology Transfer: A Case Study of the Indian National Satellite System INSAT'. PhD dissertation, Simon Fraser University.

Sankaran, Chitra (1991) 'Patterns of Story-telling in R. K. Narayan's *The Guide*'. *The Journal of Commonwealth Literature* 26(1): 127–50.

Sawant, P. (1995) Ministry Of Information and Broadcasting vs Cricket Association of Bengal & ANR. *Indian Kanoon*, 9 February, available at https://indiankanoon.org/doc/539407/, 88 (accessed on 12 March 2018).

Scannell, Paddy (1996a) 'Radio Times: The Temporal Arrangements of Broadcasting in the Modern World'. Paper Presented at the International Television Studies Conference. London, England, July 10–12.

——— (1996b) *Radio, Television and Modern Life: A Phenomenological Approach.* Oxford, UK; Cambridge, USA: Blackwell.

——— (1998) 'Media-Language-World'. In *Approaches to Media Discourse*, edited by Andrew Bell and Garrett, 251–67. Oxford: Wiley Blackwell.

——— (2004) 'Broadcasting Historiography and Historicality'. *Screen* 45(2): 130–41.

Schlesinger, Philip (1991) *Media, State and Nation: Political Violence and Collective Identities.* London, Newbury Park and New Delhi: Sage.

Scott-Baumann, Alison (2009) *Ricoeur and the Hermeneutics of Suspicion.* London and New York: Bloomsbury Academic.

Scott, Barton and Brannon Ingram (2015) 'What Is a Public? Notes from South Asia'. *South Asia: Journal of South Asian Studies* 38(3): 357–70.

Scott, David and Charles Hirschkind (eds) (2006). *Powers of the Secular Modern: Talal Asad and His Interlocutors*. Stanford: Stanford University Press.

Sen, Indrani (2017) 'Rebranding Doordarshan'. *MX Media*, 7 August, available at http://www.mxmindia.com/2017/08/rebranding-doordarshan/.

Sengupta, Nitish (1996) *Report on the High-Powered Committee on Prasar Bharati*. New Delhi: Ministry of Information & Broadcasting Government of India.

Seth, Sanjay (1995) *Marxist Theory and Nationalist Politics: The Case of Colonial India*. New Delhi, Thousand Oaks, London: Sage.

——— (2004) 'Smashing Statues, Dancing Sivas: Two Tales of Indian Icons'. *Humanities Research* XI(I): 42–53.

Shackle, Christopher and Rupert Snell (eds) (1992) *The Indian Narrative: Perspectives and Patterns*. Wiesbaden: O. Harrassowitz.

Shah, Kushal Talaksi (1937) *Provincial Autonomy: Under the Government of India Act, 1935*. Bombay: Vora.

Shahani, Kumar (2002) 'Musings of a Marxist'. *The Hindu*, May 12.

Shankar, Subramanian (2012) *Flesh and Fish Blood: Postcolonialism, Translation, and the Vernacular*. Berkeley: University of California Press.

——— (2017) 'What Is Postcolonial Philology? Multilingual Locals and

Significant Geographies, SOAS', available at mulosige.soas.ac.uk/what-is-postcolonial-philology/.

Sharma, Sunil (2002) 'Amir Khusraw and the Genre of Historical Narratives in Verse'. *Comparative Studies of South Asia, Africa and the Middle East* 22(1): 112–18.

Sharma, Tanu (2009) 'Doordarsha Turns 50!!!, A Slice of My Life', 16 September, available at http://tanushriguchhait.blogspot.com/2009/09/doordarshan-turns-50.html (accessed on 10 November 2017).

Shingi, Prakash and Bela Mody (1976) 'The Communication Effect Gap: A Field Experiment on Television and Agricultural Ignorance in India. *Communication Research* 3(2): 171–190.

Shome, Raka (2003) 'Space Matters: The Power and Practice of Space'. *Communication Theory* 13(1): 39–56.

——— (2016) 'When Postcolonial Studies Meets Media Studies'. *Critical Studies in Media Communication* 33(3): 245–63.

Shukla, Srilal (1968) *Rāg Darbārī*. New Delhi: Rajkamal Prakashan.

Silverstone, Roger (1993) 'Television, Ontological Security and the Transitional Object'. *Media, Culture & Society* 15(4): 573–98.

——— (1994) *Television and Everyday Life*. London and New York: Routledge.

Singh, Bhrigupati (2014) 'How Concepts Make the World Look Different: Affirmative and Negative Genealogies of Thought.' In *Anthropologists Engage Philosophy*, edited by Veena Das, Arthur Kleinman and Michael Jackson. Durham: Duke university Press.

Singh, Bhrigupati and Ashok Bhargava (2002) 'Review of and Commentary on Three of Anand Patwardhan's Films'. *Critical Asian Studies* 34(4): 623–36.

Singh, Nalini (Producer) (1983) *Punjab 1983*. New Delhi: Nalini Singh Productions.

Singh, Pritam (1984) 'AIR and Doordarshan Coverage of Punjab after Army Action'. *Economic and Political Weekly* 19(36): 1569–71.

Sinha, Nitin (2012) *Communication and Colonialism in Eastern India: Bihar, 1760s–1880s*. New Delhi: Anthem Press.

Sinha, Nikhil and Sanjay Asthana (2004) 'Television in Postcolonial India', in *Encyclopedia of Television*, edited by Horace Newcomb, 1173–77. New York: Routledge.

Sinha, Subir (2008) 'Lineages of the Developmentalist State: Transnationality and Village India, 1900–1965'. *Comparative Studies in Society and History* 50(1): 57–90.

Sobchack, Vivian (2009) 'Vivian Sobchack in Conversation with Scott Bukatman'. *Journal of E-Media Studies* 2(1): 1–11.

Somers, Margaret (1994) 'The Narrative Constitution of Identity: A Relational and Network Approach'. *Theory and Society* 23(5): 605–49.

Snell, Rupert (1990) 'Rural Travesties: Shrilal Shukla's *Rāg Darbārī*'. *The Journal of Commonwealth Literature* XXV(1): 156–79.

Spigel, Lynn (1992) *Make Room for TV: Television and the Family Ideal in Postwar America*. Chicago: University of Chicago Press.

Spivak, Gayatri Chakravorty (2004) 'Terror: A Speech after 9/11'. *Boundary* 2(31): 98–112.

Sprinker, Michael (1989) 'Marxism and Nationalism: Ideology and Class Struggle in Premchand's *Godan*'. *Social Text* 23: 59–82.

Srivatsan, R. (2000) *Conditions of Visibility*: *Writings on Photography in Contemporary India*. Mumbai, Calcutta, Delhi: Popular Prakashan.

Stadler, Harald (1990) 'Film as Experience: Phenomenological Concepts in Cinema and Television Studies'. *Quarterly Review of Film and Video* 12(3): 37–50.

Straubhaar, Joseph (2007) *World Television: Form Global to Local*. New York: Sage.

Strickland, C. F. (1934) 'Broadcasting in the Indian Village: Address to the East India Association'. *The Asiatic Review* XXX(101): 1–26.

Sturman, Rachel (2012) *The Government of Social Life in Colonial India: Liberalism, Religious Law, and Women's Rights*. Cambridge, UK: Cambridge University Press.

Suarez Muller, Fernando (2013) 'Towards Synthesis of Humanism in a Cosmopolitan Age: The Late Philosophy of Edward Said'. *Literature & Theology* 28(4): 476–90.

Sundaram, Ravi. (1999) 'The Bazaar and the City: History and the Contemporary in Urban Electronic Culture'. Paper presented to the conference 'Architecture and Globalization' at the Bauhaus University, Weimar, October.

——— (2010) *Pirate Modernity: Delhi's Media Urbanism*. Oxford, New York: Routledge.

Thakur, Manish (2014a). 'Understanding Ruralities: Contemporary Debates'. CAS Working Paper Series, 14–1, Centre for the Study of Social Systems, Jawaharlal Nehru University, New Delhi.

——— (2014b) *Indian Village: A Conceptual History*. New Delhi: Rawat.

Thapar, Romila (2013) *The Past Before Us: Historical Traditions of Early North India*. Harvard: Harvard University Press.

Tharu, Susie and Tejaswini Niranjana (1994) 'Problems for a Contemporary Theory of Gender'. *Social Scientist* 22(3–4): 93–117.

The Hindu (2017) 'DD Plans to Change Its Logo, Launches Design Contest', 25 July, available at http://www.thehindu.com/news/national/dd-plans-to-change-its-logo-launches-design-contest/article19359270.ece.

Thompson, John B. (ed) (1981) *Paul Ricoeur: Hermeneutics and the Human Sciences*. New York: Cambridge University Press.

Thompson, Kristin (2003) *Storytelling in Film and Television*. Cambridge, Massachusetts, and London: Harvard University Press.

Thorburn, David (1987) 'Television as an Aesthetic Medium'. *Critical Studies in Mass Communication* 4(2): 161–73.

Thussu, Daya Kishan (2002) 'Managing the Media in an Era off Round-the-Clock News: Notes from India's First Tele-War'. *Journalism Studies* 3(2): 203–12.

——— (2005) 'The Transnationalization of Television: The Indian Experience'. In *Transnational Television Worldwide: Towards a New Media Order*, edited by Jean Chalaby, 156–72. London: IB Tauris.

——— (ed) (2009) *Internationalizing Media Studies*. London and New York: Routledge.

Tichi, Cecelia (1992) *Electronic Hearth: Creating an American Television Culture*. London: Oxford University Press.

Turkle, Sherry (2007) *Evocative Objects: Things We Think With*. Massachusetts: The MIT Press.

Turnbull, Sue (2012) 'A Gap in the Record'. In *Remembering Television: Histories, Technologies, Memories*, edited by Kate Darian-Smith and Sue Turnbull, 17–29. UK: Cambridge Scholars Publishing.

Turner, Graeme (2009) 'Television and the Nation: Does it Matter Anymore'. In *Television Studies after TV: Understanding Television in the Post-Broadcast Era*, edited by Graeme Turner and Jinna Tay, 54–64. London and New York: Routledge.

Turner, Graeme and Jinna Tay (2009) 'Introduction.' In *Television Studies after TV: Understanding Television in the Post-Broadcast Era*, edited by Graeme Turner and Jinna Tay, 1–6. New York: Routledge.

Uberoi, Patricia (2002) '"Unity in Diversity?" Dilemmas of Nationhood in Indian Calendar Art'. *Contributions to Indian Sociology* 36(1/2): 191–232.

Upadhyaya, Prakash Chandra (1992) 'The Politics of Indian Secularism'. *Modern Asian Studies* 26(4): 815–53.

Urrichio, William (2004) 'Television's Next Generation: Technology/Interface/Flow'. In *Television after TV: Essays on a Medium in Transition*, edited by Lynn Spigel and Jan Olsson, 232–61. Durham and London: Duke University Press.

Urry, John (1995) *Consuming Places*. London and New York: Routledge.

Valdes, Mario J. (ed.) (1991) *A Ricoeur Reader: Reflection and Imagination*. Toronto and Buffalo: University of Toronto Press.

Vanaik, Achin (1997) *Furies of Indian Communalism: Religion, Modernity and Secularization* London: Verso.

Van Dijck, José (2004) 'Mediated Memories: Personal Cultural Memory as Object of Cultural Analysis'. *Continuum: Journal of Media & Cultural Studies* 18(2): 261–77.

——— (2007) *Mediated Memories in the Digital Age*. Stanford, CA. Stanford University Press.

Verghese, Nischita (2012) 'Sights and Sounds of Childhood Memories'. *The Hindu*, 22 August, available at http://www.thehindu.com/news/cities/bangalore/article3807311.ece?css=print.

Vlacos, Sophie (2014) *Ricoeur, Literature and Imagination*. London and New York: Bloomsbury Academic.

Verghese, Boobli George (1978) *Akash Bharati, National Broadcast Trust: Report of the Working Group on Autonomy for Akashvani and Doordarshan*. New Delhi: Ministry of Information and Broadcasting, Government of India.

Vilchis, Marco Antonio Miramón (2013) 'Michel Foucault y Paul Ricoeur: Dos Enfoques Del Discurso'. *La Colmena: Revista de la Universidad Autonoma del Estado de Mexico* 78: 53–57.

Walder, Dennis (2010) *Postcolonial Nostalgias: Writing, Representation and Memory*. New York: Routledge.

Wallace, Mark (1995) 'Introduction'. In *Figuring the Sacred: Religion, Narrative, and Imagination*, edited by Paul Ricoeur, 1–22. Minneapolis: Fortress Press.

Wallerstein, Immanuel (1996) *Open the Social Sciences: Report on the Gulbenkian Commission on the Restructuring of the Social Sciences*. Stanford: Stanford University Press.

——— (1997) 'Eurocentrism and Its Avatars: The Dilemmas of Social Science'. *Sociological Bulletin* 46(1): 21–39.

Wassiuzzaman, Shaziah and Karen Wells (2010) 'Assembling Webs of Support: Child Domestic Workers in India'. *Children & Society* 24(4): 282–92.

Weidmann, Amanda (2006) *Singing the Classical, Voicing the Modern: The Postcolonial Politics of Music in South India*. Durham and London: Duke University Press.

Weinsheimer, Joel (1995) 'Foreword'. In *Introduction to Literary Hermeneutics*, edited by Peter Szondi. Cambridge: Cambridge University Press.

Weintraub, Jeff and Krishan Kumar (eds) (1997) *Public and Private in Thought and Practice: Perspectives on a Grand Dichotomy*. Chicago: University of Chicago Press.

Wenzlhuemer, Roland (2013) *Connecting the Nineteenth-Century World: The Telegraph and Globalization*. Cambridge, UK: Cambridge University Press.

West, Cornel (1982) 'Fredric Jameson's Marxist Hermeneutics'. *Boundary 2* 11(1): 177–200.

Wharf, Barney (2008) *Time-Space Compression: Historical Geographies*. London: Routledge.

White, Hayden (1980) 'The Value of Narrativity in the Representation of Reality'. *Critical Inquiry* 7(1): 5–27.

White, Mimi (1999) 'Television Liveness: History, Banality, Attractions, Spectator. *Journal of Film and Television* 20(1): 39–56.

Williamson, Judith (1978) *Decoding Advertisements: Ideology and Meaning in Advertising*. London, New York: Marion Boyars.

Williams, Raymond (1977) 'A Lecture on Realism'. *Screen* 18(1): 61–74.

——— (1992 [1973]). *Television: Technology and Cultural Form*. Hanover and London: Weselyan University Press.

Winseck, Dwayne and Robert Pike (2007) *Communication and Empire: Media, Markets, and Globalization, 1860–1930*. Durham, North Carolina: Duke University Press.

Worth, Aaron (2014) *Imperial Media: Colonial Networks and Information Technologies in British Literary Imagination, 1857–1918*. Columbus, OH: The Ohio University Press.

Zaidi, Annie (2005) 'Doordarshan, Nostalgia and the Lack of Answers'. *Known Turf*, 4 August, available at http://knownturf.blogspot.com/2005/08/doordarshan-nostalgia-and-lack-of.html.

Zerubavel, Eviatar (1982) 'The Standardization of Time: A Sociocultural Perspective'. *American Journal of Sociology* 88(1): 1–23.

——— (2003) *Time Maps: Collective Memory and the Social Shape of the Past*. Chicago: University of Chicago Press.

Zivin, Joselyn (1998) 'The Imagined Reign of the Iron Lecturer: Village Broadcasting in Colonial India'. *Modern Asian Studies* 32(3): 717–738.

Index

actions, human and social, 9, 10, 11, 65, 70, 74, 75, 77, 79, 80n9, 90, 166
adhikara, 165
affective traces, 151–152, 154
affinity spaces, 142
ahimsa, 163
Ahmad, Aijaz, 15, 102, 113, 167
akhbarat, 31
Anderson, Benedict, 27, 76, 88–89, 104n12, 109, 113, 128
Anjaria, 74, 177
apagriha, 163
anusmaran, 133
Appadurai, Arjun, 113, 125n1, 174n8
Asad, Talal, 6, 13, 102n3
Asthana, Sanjay, 103, n6, 132, 149, 150, 178
Avadhi, 167
audiences, 2, 15–17, 35, 37, 39–41, 46–55, 59, 62n20, 66, 80n5, 103n9, 114, 119, 128, 131–132, 135, 140, 143, 159, 168

baithaks, 41
Bandyopadhyaya, Sibaji, 165–166, 178
Banerjee, Prathama, 164–166, 169, 174n6
Bayly, Chris, 20n2, 30–31, 60n5, n6, 62n20, 167
Bernstein, Richard, 12
bhakti, 62n20, 95, 102, 166, 168
Bhargava, Rajeev, 8, 14, 23n18, 105n20
Bilgrami, Akeel, 8, 163, 174n5
Bilimoria, Purushottama, 12, 22n12, n14, n17
blogs, blogging, 132–133, 136, 139–143, 145, 147, 149, 153–154, 156n5, n13
Bourdon, Jerome, 18, 128–129
Braj Bhasa, 167–168
Braman, Sandra, 26
broadband, 160, 173, 173n1
broadcasting, 1–6, 9–10, 14, 16, 18–19, 19n1, 24–62, 66, 78, 80n7, 103n6, n8, 131, 155n3, 159–160, 162–163, 167
broadcasting circles, 39, 43–44
Buonanno, Milli, 5, 16
Butsch, Richard, 47, 53–54

Carey, James, 4–5, 20n2, 30
Casey, Edward, 136
Chakrabarty, Dipesh, 76, 79n3, 83–84, 88–89, 102n2, 162–164, 173
Chatterjee, Partha, 8–9, 27, 61n7, 88, 113, 121, 161, 164
Choli Daman, 17, 88, 92–93, 96, 152, 166
*choupal*s, 41
Cohn, Bernard, 29, 60n5, 62n21
collective memory, 129–130, 145–146, 153, 168
Colonial Office, 35
colonial state, 2, 6, 8, 30, 35–37, 52, 60n4
communal violence, 7, 94, 149
community development, 28, 41, 43–44, 46, 61n12

composite culture, 96, 117, 167
Connolly, William, 83, 95, 102n3
consensus narrative, 15, 93

Dalits, 13, 103n4, 171
Darian-Smith, Kate, 127–128, 140, 152
Das, Veena, 6, 12, 15, 67, 86, 103n4, 157n19, 166
dastan, 6, 82n17
dawk, 31
deconstruction, 170, 183
Deleuze, Giles, 165, 192
Derrida, Jacques, 13, 22n15, 81n10
Deshpande, Satish, 27–28, 57, 110, 116, 124
de-territorialization, 112, 117, 119
de-westernizing media, 161, 183
Dhareshwar, Vivek, 122, 163–164
discourse, 2, 5–6, 8–9, 11, 15, 19, 24–26, 28–31, 34–35, 39, 41, 43–47, 51–59, 60n5, 61n12, 62n18, 69, 71–72, 77–78, 79n2, 80n9, 81n15, 84–86, 90–93, 101–102, 103n8, 108–112, 114, 116–117, 125, 125n4, 136, 145, 159, 162–163, 167, 169, 171–173, 175n12, 176
Doordarshan, 14–15, 17–18, 44, 46, 54, 56–57, 62n16, 63–82, 84, 86, 92, 103n4, 104n9, n11, 110–111, 115, 127–158, 161

East India Company, 20n4, 29–30, 61n11
economic liberalization, 1, 24, 108, 150
embedded imaginaries, 3, 6, 8–9, 13, 16, 78, 84, 91–93, 102
embodied, 6, 35, 45, 61n13, 64, 66, 74, 77, 88, 129, 162–163
Euro-American, 5, 170
Eurocentric, 11, 164, 171n14
Eurocentric/Western universals, 18, 160–161, 163–164, 168, 171
evocative object, 18, 130–131, 155n2

Ferguson, James, 26, 43
Fernandes, Leela, 107–108
Flew, Terry, 26
Foucault, Michel, 3, 9–11, 15, 21n10, 25–28, 30–31, 60n3, n5, 159, 169

Gajarawala, Toran Jatin, 171
Gandhi, Mahatma, 21n8, 163, 165, 174n5
gatha, 6, 73, 75, 172
genealogies, 1–2, 16, 19, 53, 61n11, 159–160, 165, 172, 175n12
Ghosh, Bisnupriya, 65, 79n3
Gilmartin, David, 2, 62n21
globalization, 18–19, 24–26, 28–29, 54, 59, 60n2, 64, 79n5, 107–109, 111–112, 114–115, 119, 124, 161
Godān, 17, 47, 63, 65, 70–74, 76–77, 81n14
Golden Temple, 120, 151, 157n19
Goswami, Manu, 25, 27–30, 35, 57, 60n4, 61n8
governmentality, 9–11, 14–15, 25–27, 31, 35–36, 43, 53, 60n1, n3
Goyder, C. W., 39, 41
Gul Gulshan Gulfam, 17, 88, 93, 96, 166
Gulzar, 17, 63, 77, 82n18, 87, 104n9, 156n15
Gupta, Akhil, 26, 43, 81n15
gurthu, 133

haafizah, 133
Hall, Stuart, 105n15, 112, 116–117
haniin, 133
Hardinge, H.R., 36–38, 48, 66
Hartley, John, 140, 152–153
Harvey, David, 3, 19n1
hermeneutic of restoration, 11
hermeneutic of suspicion, 11–12
hermeneutics, 3–4, 10–13, 15–16, 19, 21n10, n12, 22n13, 47, 60n6, 64, 68–70, 72, 74, 78, 79n1, 84, 88–92, 95, 102, 103n5, 104n14, 105n16, 133, 159–160, 165, 168–172, 174n9
hermeneutics of the self/subject, 3, 10, 15, 21n10, 159, 169
heterolinguistic traditions, 166–167
Hindi–Urdu, 20, 86, 104n9, 116, 125n3, 148, 157n17, 167, 175n12

Hindu majoritarianism, 13
Hindustani, 49, 51–52, 167–168, 174n8
hybridity, 108, 171
hyperlinking, 132

ibadat, 95, 102, 166
idem and *ipse*, 137, 146
ideological, 1, 11–12, 14–17, 22n13, 29, 39–40, 46–47, 54, 59, 67–68, 71, 79, 79n1, 80n9, 84, 87–88, 90–91, 105n15, n16, 108, 111, 117, 124, 127–128, 143, 173
ideology, 6, 31, 40, 61n8, 62n19, 65, 67, 74, 90, 105n16, 113, 116–117, 129
imagined community, 76, 88, 104n12, 113
Indian ecumene, 167
Indian Village Welfare Association, 36
informal knowledge, 127, 140, 155n1
Innis, Harold, 24, 31
internationalizing media, 161, 173n2, 201

Jain, Kajri, 113–114, 121
Jameson, Fredric, 22n13, 65, 70, 79n2 112
Judeo-Christian, 13, 22n17
juridical, 2, 52–53, 58, 61n7, 62n21

Kansteiner, Wulf, 129–130, 154
Kant, Immanuel, 12–13, 22n16
Kapur, Geeta, 8, 68, 79n1, 113
Kashmir, 17, 54, 84, 87-88, 91, 93-94, 96, 98-101
Kashmir File, 17, 88, 93, 96–99, 101
katha, 6, 73, 75
Kaviraj, Sudipta, 8–9, 20n7, 51
Kearney, Richard, 11–12, 22n15, 68, 104n14, 105n16
Keskar, B. V., 50-51
Khari Boli, 167
Kheda Television, 36, 45–46
Khilnani, Sunil, 112, 118
Kirke, H.L, 38-39
kirtans, 168
Krishi Darshan, 44
Kumar, Shanti, 19, 24, 155n1, 161

lambardars, 37, 41
Lefebvre, Henri, 3, 25–26, 28, 59n1
Loomba, Ania, 171

Madan, Triloki Nath, 20n7
Mailā Anchal, 17, 47, 63, 65, 70–77, 144
Mangal Pandey, 20n3
Mani, Lata, 20n6
Mankekar, Purnima, 19, 20n5, 86–87, 104n10
Marks, Laura, 165
Mazzarella, William, 2, 45–46, 192
media and communication studies, 4, 5, 22n12, 53, 160–161, 164–165, 168, 173n2
Mehta, Uday Singh, 61n10
memory, 18, 94–95, 100, 112, 115, 127–158, 166, 168, 172
methodological nationalism, 25
Mill, John Stuart, 20n4, 34, 40, 61n10
Mishra, Pankaj, 112
mnemonic traditions, 129
Mukherjee, Mithi, 163–164
multilingual formations, 166
multiple temporalities, 4, 6, 64, 70, 73–74, 76, 85, 90, 102, 132, 143
Muslim extremism, 13

Nandy, Ashis, 8, 12–13, 164
narrative identity, 9, 17, 63–82, 84, 91, 128, 130, 133, 137, 145–146
narrative, 3, 6, 9–11, 13, 15–17, 20n3, 62n20, 63–78, 79n1–n2, 80n9, 81n12, n15, 82, 84–102, 102n1, 103n4–n5, 105n16–n17, 107, 111, 119–124, 127–130, 133, 137, 140, 144–146, 149, 152–153, 159, 162–164, 166–167, 172
nation, 1–2, 4, 8, 14–19, 21n8, 24, 27, 35–36, 46, 51–52, 54–55, 57–59, 62n19, 67, 71, 75–76, 85–89, 91–93, 96, 98–101, 103n7, 104n12, 106–113, 115–118, 123–125, 125n1, n4, 140–141, 153, 159–163

nation building, 27, 35–36, 50, 86, 103n7, 109
national–global, xii, 17, 107–108, 114, 119, 161
national integration, 14, 17, 44, 51, 55, 85, 87–88, 103n7, n9, 111, 115, 117, 120–121
nationalism, 17–19, 24–29, 37, 42, 50–51, 59, 60n4, 61n8, 63, 71–72, 74, 81n14, 87, 92, 107–110, 112, 114–115, 118–119, 122, 124–125, 162, 164
neoliberal, 2, 52–53, 55, 59, 64, 111, 173
Nigam, Aditya, 164–166, 169, 174n6
nostalgia, 18, 100, 113, 127–158

Orsini, Franscesca, 6, 15, 62n20, 82n17, 167, 171–172, 176

pandit, Kashmiri, 98–99
patriotism, 17–18, 107–126
Persian, 6, 82n17, 133, 167-168, 170, 174n8
phenomenology, 4, 19n1, 22n15, 68, 76, 89–90, 92, 141, 145–146, 155n3
phenomenology of memory, 145–146
philology, 160, 169–172, 174n9, n10
Pinney, Christopher, 113, 185, 196
Plymouth Report, 35
Poduval, Satish, 45
politics of despair, 162–164
Pollock, Sheldon, 169–173, 174n11, 175–176n15
post-broadcast, 160–161, 201
postcolonial, 1–6, 8–12, 14–15, 17, 21n12, 24–29, 31–32, 35–36, 38–44, 46–47, 49–53, 55, 59, 60n7, 63–66, 70–71, 74, 77–79, 81n12, 83–84, 86–88, 95–96, 98, 102, 103n4, n7, n13, 106n23, 107, 109–110, 113–114, 116, 125n1, n4, 156n15, 159–160, 163–164, 167–171, 174n11
postcolonial philology, 171, 199
post-critical faith, 12–13, 22n15
post-national, 107, 112–113, 117–118, 125n1
poststructuralist, 11–12
power, 3, 5, 8–11, 15–16, 19n2, 21n11, 24–62, 68, 70–71, 84, 86, 94, 100, 105n15, 108–109, 113, 119, 123, 134, 139–140, 152, 155n3, 159, 164, 172, 174n11, 175n12
power-geometries, 37, 44
Prakash, Gyan, 10, 27
Prasad, Madhava, 55, 67
Prasar Bharati Act, 36, 52, 56, 139, 192
Price, Monroe, 25–26
proselytization, 13
psychoanalytic, 10–11, 64, 68–69, 81n11
public, 1–2, 4, 10, 14–19, 24, 28, 35–37, 40–41, 47–55, 58–59, 62n20–n21, 63, 78, 86–87, 91–92, 94–95, 101–102, 103n8, 108, 110–111, 113, 125n1, 128, 130, 143, 145, 148, 159, 162–163, 172
Punathambekar, Aswin, 132, 161

qawwali, 168, 194
qissa, 6, 73, 75, 82n17

radio, 1–6, 14–17, 19, 19n1, 24, 32–33, 35–45, 47–54, 56–57, 61n9, n10, n13, n15, 62n18, 65–66, 82n16, 103n8, 110, 131, 135, 148, 159, 162, 167–168, 172
Rāg Darbārī, 17, 47, 63, 65, 70–77, 81n15, 86–87, 144
Rajadhyaksha, Ashish, 45–46, 53, 58, 113, 156n15
Rajagopal, Arvind, 2, 19, 86–87, 103n8, 107–108, 126n7, 143–144
religion, 1–2, 4, 6–9, 12–19, 20n5, 21n8, 22n13–n17, 40, 51, 62n21, 78, 83–88, 91–102, 102n1–n2, 103n8, 117, 128, 144, 151, 153, 159–160, 162–163, 167–168, 172
religious institutions, 7–8

reminiscence, 132
re-territorialization, 117, 119
Ricoeur, Paul, 3, 9–13, 15, 21n10, n12, 22n13, n15, n16, 64–65, 68–74, 76, 78, 79n2, 80n10, 81n11, n12, 84, 88–91, 104n14, 105n16, 128, 130, 137, 145–146, 151–153, 159, 167–170, 174
Roy, Abhijit, 54, 67–68, 80n6, 161
Roy, Supriya, 115, 125n4
RRF, 35, 37, 41, 43–44, 46, 61n9, n15
rural reconstruction, 41, 46

Said, Edward, 60n5, 84, 170, 173
Sanskrit, xi, 6, 51, 57, 73, 75, 82n17, 97, 133, 163, 167–170, 174n8, 175n15, 176
Sanskritized, 51, 167–168
Scannell, Paddy, 4, 6, 19n1, 21n12, 131, 143–144, 155n3, 160
Scott-Baumann, Alison, 11
script-mercantilism, 172
secular, 6–9, 12–14, 17, 20n5, n6, 22n15, 23n18, 48, 50, 63, 78, 83–106, 108, 121–122, 166, 168–169, 175n14
secularism, 6–9, 13, 16–17, 21n8, n9, 22n16, 78, 83–88, 91–96, 101–102, 102n1, n3, 103n8, 117, 159, 163–164, 166, 172, 174n6
selfhood, 70, 76, 146
semiotic, 11, 16, 21n12, 57, 64, 68–69, 73, 175n12
Sengupta, Nitish, 36, 56, 58, 199
Shahani, Kumar, 82n19, 156n15
Shankar, Subramaniam, 171, 175n12
Sikhs, 92–93, 95–100, 103n4, 120, 146, 151–152, 157n19, 168, 183, 194
Silverstone, Roger, 4, 6, 19n1, 130–131, 155n2
Singh, Bhrigupati, 10, 12, 21n11
Sinha, Subir, 28–29, 35, 41, 43, 59
SITE, 35–37, 41, 44–46, 61n9, n15, 66
smrti, 172
social imaginaries, 65, 74, 98
South Asian, 2–5, 12, 15, 30–31, 40, 52, 62n21, 104n10, 106n23, 126, 154, 160–161, 171–173, 174n11, 175n15
sovereignty, 1–2, 4, 10–11, 14–19, 24–29, 31, 34–36, 42–43, 51–52, 55–59, 60n1–n3, 98, 155n3, 159, 161, 163, 172
sovereignty-discipline-governmentality, 31
spatiotemporal, 1–6, 9, 16, 18–19, 24–62, 128–129, 134–135, 154, 159
Spivak, Gayatri Chakravorty, 12–13, 22n16
Strickland, C. F., 36–38, 48
Sundaram, Ravi, 109, 174n3
Supreme Court judgment, 1, 52–53, 58

tagging, 132
telegraph, 4–5, 19n1, 20n2, n3, n4, 30–33, 39–40, 60n4
television, 1–6, 9, 14–19, 19n1, 20n5, 24, 32, 35–36, 39, 41, 43–47, 51–52, 54–58, 61n15, 62n, 63–68, 74–75, 77–78, 79n2, n4, n5, 80n6, n8, n9, 82n16, n20, 84–88, 90–93, 98, 101–102, 103n6, n8, n9, 105n15, n18, n19, 107–134, 136–154, 155n1–n4, 156n15, 157n18, n21, 159–162, 164, 166–168, 171–173, 173n1
Telugu, 133, 148, 156n16, 157
temporality, 3–4, 6, 11, 15, 19n1, 24, 64–65, 70, 73–74, 76, 84–85, 88–92, 102, 105n16, 130–132, 143, 145–146, 152
thinking across traditions, 164–166, 168–169, 172
thinking within traditions, 172
TimeSpace, 4, 192
Thorburn, David, 15, 93
Thugs of Hindostan, 175 n12
Thussu, Daya Krishna, 15, 126n6, 161
transcendental, 12–13, 16n16, 166
transnational governmentality, 26

transitional object, 130–131, 155n2
transnationalism, 171
Turkle, Sherry, 18, 130–131, 137, 155n2
Turnbull, Sue, 127–128, 140, 152, 158n21
Turner, Graeme, 160
Twitter, 133, 139–140, 156n5

Urdu, 6, 15, 20n3, 20n7, 48, 51, 62n20, 82n16, 82n17, 86, 94, 104, 116, 125n3, 133, 139, 147, 148, 150, 156n16, 157, 167, 168, 175n12

Valdes, Mario, J., 11
van Dijck, Jose, 130, 133, 154
Vanaik, Achin, 103n4
vernacular knowledge, 171, 175n12
vertical encompassment, 26, 43
village broadcasting, 16, 37–38, 41
visual regime, 107–108, 114, 123–124
vlogging, 132

Wenzlhuemer, Roland, 4–5, 31–33
Williams, Raymond, 24, 64–65, 67–68, 79n5, 80n8, 82n16, 116
Wittgenstein, Wittgensteinian, xiii, 146

yaad, 133
yaadashth, 133
Yaadein, 112
yama, 163
YouTube, 14, 18, 127–158

zahir, 165
zamindars, 37, 41
Zivin, Joselyn, 36–38

Caroline Fuseau 21/10/92

Le courage

Série Morales

dirigée par Nicole Czechowski avec un comité international de conseillers : Marc Augé, Élisabeth Badinter, Jean Baubérot, Élisabeth de Fontenay, Julia Kristeva, Emmanuel Lévinas, Alan Montefiore (Oxford), Fernando Savater (Madrid), Harald Weinrich (Munich).

« Plus d'une fois nous nous demandons où elle s'est enfuie, notre vie morale, en quoi elle consiste, et si même elle consiste en quelque chose ! Or c'est précisément dans ces instants, où elle est sur le point de s'échapper, où nous désespérons de l'attraper, qu'elle est le plus authentique : il faut alors saisir au vol l'occasion dans sa vive flagrance ! » Vladimir Jankélévitch.
Le Paradoxe de la morale.

Tél. : 47.70.12.50. Fax : 47.70.97.52. ISBN : 2-86260-353-8. ISSN : 1154-5763.
Dépôt légal : 3e trimestre 1992. Précédent dépôt : février 1992. Imprimé en France.

Le courage

En connaissance de causes

Dirigé par Pierre Michel Klein

Éditions Autrement - Série Morales n° 6

Sommaire

Préface 11
Pierre Michel Klein

1. *Idées* 17

Depuis Platon, le courage est pensé comme une vertu « cardinale », la vie morale gravitant autour de ce pivot (cardo), *comme autour des trois autres fondements de l'existence pratique : la sagesse, la tempérance et la justice. Retirer l'une de ces vertus, c'est désorienter le sens même du bien vivre et du bien agir.*
C'est le parcours de l'« idée » du courage qui se propose d'abord, l'histoire embarrassée de sa pensée.

Du mythe à la raison 18
Étienne Smoes

La vertu nommée courage n'est pas univoque. Et les difficultés rencontrées par Platon, en quête de sa définition, viennent de ce que, jusqu'au Ve siècle avant notre ère, les modèles grecs du courage subissent évolutions et variations : l'héroïsme d'Achille, enthousiaste, sûr de sa force et méprisant le danger, n'est pas le même que celui d'Ulysse, conscient de ses faiblesses, héros d'endurance et de ruse. Et la vaillance du citoyen-soldat, ferme à son poste, se distingue de la ténacité d'Archiloque ou du courage calculateur de